MW01039287

"In the spirit of Pentecost an
this book is a work of zeal ar
ecclesial breath of fresh air d
the church, the necessity of conversion, the art of faithfulness, the gift of
communal discernment, and more. All the while, this book keeps readers'
feet firmly on the ground, mindful of the most difficult ecclesial challenges
of this historical moment. Erudite throughout. Beautifully written. Laity,
priests, and bishops who love the church will discover in this book 'a pearl
of great price.'"

> —Nancy Pineda-Madrid, T. Marie Chilton Chair of Catholic Theology,
> Loyola Marymount University

"The fruit of Richard Lennan's thirty years of teaching, reflections, and
ministry, *Tilling the Church* applies to the Catholic Church the much-
needed rationale, imperative, and dynamics of tilling the earth. Responding
to Pope Francis's call for 'ecological conversion,' Lennan explores the
elements in the church that promote conversion: learning from both past
accomplishments and failures, nourishing present signs of life, and being
open to the possibilities in the unknowable future. Like a patient and
experienced farmer, Lennan teaches us where, when, and how to plant the
seeds of grace in the church-field, a task destined to remain an 'unfinished
project' until the eschaton."

> —Peter C. Phan, The Ignacio Ellacuria Chair of Catholic Thought,
> Georgetown University

"Viewing the church's mystery through the lens of the mystery of divine
grace and human freedom, Richard Lennan's *Tilling the Church* opens
up fresh perspectives on what ecclesial faithfulness to God requires.
Continuity with the living Gospel demands creativity in passing on the
faith in response to ever-new questions and challenges; the church must
be always changing in order to maintain its identity. This stimulating book
is a welcome reminder of the need for constant care in safeguarding the
church's full flourishing."

> —Ormond Rush, Australian Catholic University

"In *Tilling the Church*, Richard Lennan employs the 'homely' agricultural metaphor 'tilling' to help us recognize how God's gift of Grace works to 'till,' 'to cultivate' us as church—opens us pilgrim people not only to our past, but to a future of healing, creating, and community in history and coaxes us to care for the earth and for *all* God's human creatures—believers or not. This book encourages and lifts us in this time of anxiety and distress."

 —M. Shawn Copeland, Professor Emerita, Boston College

"Richard Lennan's *Tilling the Church* is a mature, timely, and eloquent treatment of the current Catholic ecclesial moment . . . a 'must read' for all who are concerned for the health of the church and the quality of Catholic life into the future. Born of more than thirty years of praying, thinking, teaching, writing, and pastoral service, it weaves together a lucid synthesis of the key strains in post-conciliar ecclesiology and wider theology of Catholic life with a sustained constructive invitation to become discerning participants in the way of whole-church synodality for which Pope Francis calls. It is a book for our times, written with grace and love, and will be invaluable for students, teachers, pastors, and all interested laity alike."

 —Paul D. Murray, Durham University, UK

"Richard Lennan does not shy away from the crises facing the church. These issues and others call for a new theology of the church based on the historical manifestation of God's grace in Christ and the Spirit. Lennan rises to this challenge with striking erudition and imagination. He describes the church as a Spirit-led community of faith and hope, grounded in a future-oriented past, conscious of itself as an unfinished project, and open to self-criticism in the service of the reign of God proclaimed by Jesus. He highlights the essential unity that exists between discipleship and apostolicity, change and tradition, preservation and innovation. Lennan is a creative theologian and a reliable guide in pointing to a number of different ways to address the multilayered challenges facing the church. This book is essential reading for all who care about the reform and the future of the Catholic Church in the twenty-first century."

 —Dermot A. Lane, Dublin City University

Tilling the Church

Theology for an Unfinished Project

Richard Lennan

LITURGICAL PRESS
ACADEMIC

Collegeville, Minnesota
www.litpress.org

1   2   3   4   5   6   7   8   9

Library of Congress Cataloging-in-Publication Data

Names: Lennan, Richard, author.
Title: Tilling the church : theology for an unfinished project / Richard Lennan.
Description: Collegeville, Minnesota : Liturgical Press Academic, [2022] | Includes bibliographical references and index. | Summary: "Tilling the Church explores the possibilities for a more faithful, just, and creative church, one responsive to the movement of grace. Fruitful engagement with grace requires the church's conversion, the ongoing formation of a community whose words and actions reflect the hope that grace engenders"— Provided by publisher.
Identifiers: LCCN 2021049096 (print) | LCCN 2021049097 (ebook) | ISBN 9780814667439 (paperback) | ISBN 9780814667446 (epub) | ISBN 9780814667446 (pdf)
Subjects: LCSH: Church. | Catholic Church—Doctrines. | Grace (Theology)
Classification: LCC BX1746 .L4335 2022 (print) | LCC BX1746 (ebook) | DDC 262/.02—dc23/eng/20220105
LC record available at https://lccn.loc.gov/2021049096
LC ebook record available at https://lccn.loc.gov/2021049097

For

Liz

But grace is here. It is present wherever we are.

Karl Rahner

Contents

Acknowledgments   ix

Introduction   xi

1. The Church as Project   1

2. Symbolizing Grace   39

3. The Pilgrim Community of Faith and Hope   81

4. Engaging the Graced World   123

5. The Future-Oriented Past   163

6. The Art of Faithfulness   207

Conclusion   251

Index   257

Acknowledgments

"The Church" was the first theological course I taught. That was in 1992, immediately after I completed my dissertation on Karl Rahner's ecclesiology. Since that beginning, the course on ecclesiology, under various titles and in ever-evolving formulations, has been the staple of my teaching. Likewise, "the church" has remained the focus of my research and writing—to say nothing of constant wondering.

During the last thirty years, I have had the graced opportunity to explore ecclesiology with a generation of students, beginning at the Catholic Institute of Sydney, then at Weston Jesuit School of Theology, and currently in the School of Theology and Ministry at Boston College. The students' questions, insights, and longing to be part of a church that lives what it proclaims have deepened my understanding of the Christian community and helped me to refine my teaching. I am deeply grateful for the richness of that experience.

It has also been my privilege to participate over the last three decades in a national Plenary Council (Australia, 2021–22), a diocesan synod—happily, in my home diocese of Maitland-Newcastle—and to work with pastoral planners, priests, and renewal groups in many places. Amid oft-heard frustrations with numerous aspects of the church, this involvement has confirmed for me the overwhelming desire of Catholics that their community might be more faithful, more transparent, and more generous in its service of God and humanity. My hope is that this book's analysis of the church and its mission does some justice to all that I have gained from being part of the pilgrim community of faith.

It is a pleasure to be able to acknowledge here the encouragement and support of family, friends, and colleagues, including my sisters

(Michele, Helene, and Elizabeth), and also Neil Brown, Erika and Dan Castillo, Andrew Davis, Ken Hughes, Gerard Kelly, Mark Lane, Lex Levey (RIP), Nancy Pineda-Madrid, Jacqueline Regan, and Ernesto Valiente. There are two particular sets of people whom I would like to thank: James McEvoy and Ormond Rush, who read the almost-complete version of the manuscript and whose comments aided its completion; Colleen Griffith and John Baldovin, with whom I am part of a reading-and-writing group and who have been a source of generous feedback as the book progressed. I am also most grateful to Chris Brennan for his skill and care in constructing the index for the book. Hans Christoffersen and the editorial staff at Liturgical Press have steered the manuscript to publication; I appreciate greatly their commitment and expertise.

I completed the manuscript for this book at Pentecost in 2021. Pentecost's focus on the Holy Spirit as the source of grace, and of the hope that grace engenders even in the midst of loss, seems especially fitting in the context of a world seeking to emerge from the COVID-19 pandemic. This reminder of the enduring presence of the Spirit and the transformative role of grace is always relevant for the life of the church that is, and will remain, an unfinished project.

Introduction

"Tilling," writes Pope Francis, "refers to cultivating, plowing or working."[1] In *Laudato Si'* (LS), his encyclical promoting care for the earth, humanity's "common home," the pope includes tilling among the activities that nurture the earth. The document describes the natural world as "a collective good, the patrimony of all humanity," a status that establishes the physical environment as "the responsibility of everyone" (LS 95). Tilling the earth models human behavior that reverences rather than ravages this patrimony. As with the effort to nurture a vineyard (Isa 5:1-10) or stimulate the fertility of a fruitless fig tree (Luke 13:6-9), tilling fosters the earth's potential for future bounty by supporting existing growth, attending to present needs, and redressing what neglect or misuse has wrought. Tilling, then, expands the likelihood that coming generations will receive their patrimony in a robust condition.

Against the backdrop of human-driven climate change that imperils the earth, Pope Francis supports efforts "to restore the various levels of ecological equilibrium, establishing harmony within ourselves, with others, with nature and other living creatures, and with God" (LS 210). To achieve this equilibrium, *Laudato Si'* advocates for "integral ecology." This category weaves together God, humanity, and the physical environment, underscoring that humanity's right relationship with

---

1. Pope Francis, *Laudato Si'* (LS), On Care for Our Common Home (2015), 67, http://www.vatican.va/content/francesco/en/encyclicals/documents/papa-francesco_20150524_enciclica-laudato-si.html. For analysis of *Laudato Si'* and its reception, see Michele Dillon, *Postsecular Catholicism: Relevance and Renewal* (New York: Oxford University Press, 2018), 51–65.

God is inseparable from a right relationship with all that God creates, sustains, and fulfills.[2] Integral ecology, since it seeks to reflect God's desires for the whole of creation, extends its attention to political culture and social structures, both of which affect the human as well as the physical environment. From the perspective of integral ecology, the commitment to protect air and water against pollution requires not only support for low-impact manufacturing processes, but resistance to the siting of factories close to residential areas in which vulnerable human populations live. Integral ecology, then, champions policies that serve justice and equity in housing, health, and other social programs, as well as in access to natural resources and renewable energy.[3]

Consistent with his vision for integral ecology, Pope Francis depicts the retrieval of ecological equilibrium as critical for the health of humanity's relationship with the creator God, no less than for the future of life on earth. The pope presents humanity's efforts to live harmoniously with nature and pursue social and economic justice as furthering "a spirituality of that global solidarity that flows from the mystery of the Trinity" (LS 240). *Laudato Si'* develops the spiritual dimension of ecology by arguing that the repair of environmental damage requires the conversion of human hearts and minds beyond a narrow framing of self-interest. Pragmatic decisions alone will not ensure the healthy continuation of life on earth.

Conversion is both an ongoing process and a multidimensional one. Its numerous facets include the disposition to "look at ourselves, to acknowledge our deep dissatisfaction and to embark on new paths to authentic freedom" (LS 205). These actions give shape to humanity's "God-given ability to respond to [God's] grace at work deep in our hearts" (LS 205). The pope's analysis of conversion locates it as the doorway to a more authentic human existence. This authenticity requires human participation, but, to anticipate a principal theme of this volume, it also depends on grace.

---

2. Chapter 4 of *Laudato Si'* develops the notion of "integral ecology."

3. For a fuller discussion of integral ecology, see Daniel Castillo, *An Ecological Theology of Liberation: Salvation and Political Ecology* (Maryknoll, NY: Orbis, 2019), 38–63.

Grace, God's self-bestowal, gives life to humanity and to all of God's creatures. Far from being a "thing" or even quantifiable, grace is the self-expression of the God who is other than "a static, distant, non-interactive God."[4] As God's self-bestowal, grace is relational: without suppressing the uniqueness of God's creatures, including the complexity and inconsistency of humanity, grace draws respondents into a deeper communion with God and God's creation. A corollary of the relationship with God that grace initiates is the human vocation to safeguard creation through "disinterested concern for others, and the rejection of every form of self-centeredness and self-absorption" (LS 208). Together with "keeping," which involves "caring, protecting, overseeing and preserving" (LS 67), tilling enacts humanity's role as a graced curator of God's graced creation.

The grace of God has "an incarnational tendency," which establishes grace as "not merely the principle of a merely transcendental 'interiority,'" but as what comes "right down into [humanity's] concrete, tangible daily life, where it receives its 'expression' and takes on corporality."[5] This "corporality" applies to creation, to the gift of God's self-offering in Jesus Christ, and, so this book will stress, to the presence of the Holy Spirit in the church. It is "the witness to that divine self-giving in Scripture and tradition [and] in individuals who freely accept in faith this divine offer of salvation," that is an enduring resource for the ecclesial community.[6]

A core principle for this book is that the centrality of grace does not diminish the humanity of the church. As discouraging and disappointing as policies and practices, as well individuals and communities, in the church can be, these realties are not damning evidence of a lack of relationship between grace and the ecclesial community. They are, on the other hand, sure signs of the church's need for tilling, for the conversion that advances greater transparency to grace.

4. Cynthia Rigby, "Knowing Our Limits and Laughing with Joy: Theology in Service to the Church Invisible," in *Theology in Service to the Church: Global and Ecumenical Perspectives*, ed. Alan Hugh Cole (Eugene, OR: Cascade Books, 2014), 107.

5. Karl Rahner, "Personal and Sacramental Piety," in *Theological Investigations*, vol. 2, trans. K-H. Kruger (New York: Crossroad, 1983), 119–20.

6. Ormond Rush, *The Eyes of Faith: The Sense of the Faithful and the Church's Reception of Revelation* (Washington, DC: Catholic University of America Press, 2009), 42.

This book applies to the Catholic Church the rationale, imperative, and dynamics of tilling the earth. It locates tilling as an aspect of the integral ecology that applies to the church. The church's self-understanding provides a foundation for this application. More specifically, the image of the church as "the seed and the beginning of [God's] kingdom," a metaphor that the Second Vatican Council (1962–65) employed to describe the ecclesial community, endorses the need for attention to all that might nurture or impede the well-being of the church and its mission.[7] Hence, the opening to "tilling."

In establishing that the church, like the earth, exists through God's initiative, the image of the "seed" suggests that the ecclesial community can be faithful to its origin only by continuing to grow. This book employs "tilling the church" as a shorthand formula for all that contributes to the church's authenticity and serves its growth. Faithful tilling, which can take shape as innovation, reform, or support for existing expressions of the church's life, serves the future of the ecclesial community.

Preeminent in the process of tilling are the elements that further conversion: learning from both earlier accomplishments and past failures; nourishing present signs of life; and embracing openness to the possibilities likely to emerge in the unknowable future. These actions all express a response to God's call. All are likewise integral to the discipleship that embodies the church's faithfulness in its engagement with the wider world. The elements of conversion make plain that growth for the church implies something other than gaining more members or attracting the acclaim of the wider world.

A thesis flowing through this book is that the faithfulness of the ecclesial community is a graced, free response to grace, to God's continual self-offering. Faithfulness is not an outcome programmed into the DNA of the church's members, such that "choice" and "decision" would be meaningless categories within the church. The interweaving of grace and humanity generates the depths and complexity of the church. The same interweaving both frustrates all efforts at a definitive

---

7. The Second Vatican Council, *Lumen Gentium* (LG), Dogmatic Constitution on the Church (1964), 5. Unless otherwise acknowledged, quotations from the council's texts come from Austin Flannery, ed., *Vatican Council II: Constitutions, Decrees, Declarations; The Basic Sixteen Documents* (Collegeville, MN: Liturgical Press, 2014).

appraisal of the ecclesial community and subverts every plan to achieve a specific future for the church.

To respond to grace constructively, the community of the church must accept its need for conversion. Conversion moves the ecclesial community away from those aspects of its own life that contradict the God whose call to the church is constant, unchanging, and accessible even in the ceaselessly fluid circumstances of human history. Only through the church's conversion is it possible for grace to permeate and flavor every aspect of ecclesial life, all forms of the church's relationship with God, other people, and the whole of God's creation. Until the fulfillment of God's reign, then, "tilling the church" remains a critical task, a means to unsettle complacency and break open the potential for growth.

As fruitful as the image of tilling the seed of God's kingdom might be, the appropriation to the church of language proper to an agricultural process is not without its dangers, especially if it spirals downwards into a morass of increasingly awkward metaphors related to farming. Alert to that possibility—and anxious to avoid it—this volume employs "tilling" principally as a synonym for the panoply of grace-inspired actions that further the health of the church. Nowhere in its pages, then, will the book suggest that the ecclesial community designate a specific group of its members as "tillers," nor will it nominate a class of ecclesial activities that are expressly classifiable as "tilling." Rather, the book proposes that grace, which permeates the church and the wider world, works for the health of the community's life and witness through a myriad of agents and means, including those bearing no explicitly religious label.

In a way that parallels the embrace of integral ecology by *Laudato Si'*, the book considers "health" for the church as requiring attention to more than any single feature of ecclesial life.[8] For the church to reflect the trinitarian God who sustains it, ecclesial health requires that all aspects of the church's life exhibit the *perichoresis*, the dance-like connections and interrelationships characteristic of the Trinity.

---

8. From a different perspective than this volume's, Judith Gruber also identifies ecclesiological applications for *Laudato Si'* in "Ec(o)clesiology: Ecology as Ecclesiology in *Laudato Sí*," *Theological Studies* 78 (2017): 807–24.

The church's mission in the world and the internal ordering of the ecclesial community, then, must interweave and nurture each other in vibrant and creative ways that are responsive to grace. Equally, ill health or dysfunction comes about when the various elements do not coexist harmoniously, when there is a neglect of either an individual component or the balance between them. The church's principal resources—Scripture, sacramental worship and life, the faith and lived spirituality of all the community's members, and the church's ongoing encounter with the wider world—all serve the tilling that grace inspires and reinforces.

A Graced and Human Church

Grace is the vascular system of the church. As such, grace enlivens every aspect of the ecclesial community and orients the church to the fullness of life in Christ. The members of the church can neither instigate nor cancel grace, but are free to accept its call or close themselves to its summons. The fulfilment of God's life-giving grace extends beyond human history, beyond any vulnerability to human rebellion. Within history, however, human action, including its mode as inaction, can shroud the efficacy of grace, a fact that reinforces humanity's need for conversion. The relationship between grace and humanity that is the heart of the church establishes the church as "tillable," as a project in need of actions that mirror the "cultivating, plowing or working" necessary for care for the earth.

As an aid to the church's conversion toward greater transparency to grace, tilling, as noted above, entails attention to the consequences of past failings, engagement with present challenges, and cultivation of grounds for hope in the future in light of the church's orientation toward the fulfilled reign of God. This orientation signals that the church shares in "the ultimate destiny of the universe [that] is in the fullness of God" (LS 83). The conversion of the ecclesial community embodies the graced willingness to be self-critical rather than to assume that the life of the church always aligns perfectly with the prompting of grace.[9]

9. For the importance of the self-critical stance in the life of the church, see Karl Rahner, "The Function of the Church as a Critic of Society," in *Theological Investiga-*

A self-critical stance, which is a theme that will feature throughout this book, is an antidote to complacency; it fosters the ecclesial form of the "ecological equilibrium" that Pope Francis endorses. In the arena of the church, this equilibrium is the product of a balance between reception of the past, attention to present experience, and the enduring preparedness to engage with emerging possibilities for the church's future. Efforts to accomplish ecclesial equilibrium, like their ecological equivalent, need to be continual. Equilibrium is not a once-and-for-all achievement, but a process that requires the constant rebalancing of multiple elements.

Alone, the human reality of the ecclesial community, specifically its existence in historical circumstances that are not static, would be sufficient to indicate why the balance between past, present, and future requires the ongoing attention of the community. The fact that this human reality is inseparable from grace, which is both inexhaustible and eschatological, having its fulfillment beyond history while being accessible in history, increases exponentially the need for the members of the church to understand themselves as people whose story is unfinished. All of these factors suggest that it is prudent to eschew predictions about the church's future. Consistent with such prudence, this book will resist the temptation to become a compendium of predictions, but it will address present issues likely to influence the church's future.

The case for tilling the church, for seeking its conversion, has a particular cogency. The earth's generative processes, through which grace is operative, will follow their evolutionary pathways unless some disruptive external force—too often, sadly, human beings—interferes with them. Such is not the case for the church. The ecclesial community is neither the product of a biological process nor independent of human beings and their action: the church *is* human beings. At every moment of the church's history, therefore, decisions and choices within the ecclesial community affect, for good or ill, the church's health. The thriving of the church's communal life and the community's faithfulness to its mission both depend on responses to grace rather than evolution.

When human action in the physical environment displays the "self-interested pragmatism" and "the paradigm of consumerism" (LS

---

tions, vol. 12, trans. D. Bourke (New York: Crossroad, 1974), 229–49.

xviii   *Tilling the Church*

215) that ignore the God-given beauty of nature, what results is indiscriminate plundering of the earth. Ideological divisions in the church exemplify actions whose effects on the life and mission of the ecclesial community are similarly detrimental.[10] These divisions can express the sinfulness that disdains commitment to the common good. Beyond rendering tilling more exigent, divisions in the church are reminders that grace, even though it suffuses humanity, invites rather than compels. What is true of human experience generally is no less true of ecclesial life: human freedom ensures that the efficacy of grace in specific circumstances eludes prediction.

The freedom of human beings to resist grace complicates discussion of the church as a graced reality. In fact, the well-chronicled history of the great and small events, past and present, that portray an "ungodly" church clouds all claims of a relationship between grace and the church. Omissions and commissions at every level of ecclesial life, the individual and institutional transgressions that contradict all that the church professes, argue against a role for the church in the revelation of God. This is perhaps especially so when it is members of the ordained hierarchy, with whom "the church" is often synonymous, who fail to reflect the life-giving God. Such failures are not merely theoretical, but all too real, as the clerical sexual abuse crisis that has blighted the Catholic Church during the last two decades illustrates tragically.

In light of the church's inconsistent witness to God, efforts to account theologically for the church in terms of grace are prone to the suspicion that they produce idealized portraits that are incongruent with the historical record and present landscape of the church. Clearly, such concerns are pertinent for this text, in which the role of grace in the life of the church is critically important. In its endeavor to engage the conundrum that is the graced and human church, the church that is holy and sinful, this volume devotes a great deal of space to the relationship between grace and humanity.

---

10. For the source, impact, and possible resolution of ideological divisions in the contemporary church in the United States, see Michael Peppard, "Can the Church Transcend a Polarized Culture?," in *Polarization in the US Catholic Church: Naming the Wounds, Beginning to Heal*, ed. Mary Ellen Konieczny, Charles Camosy, and Tricia Bruce (Collegeville, MN: Liturgical Press, 2016), 145–57.

In exploring that relationship, the chapters of this book bring to the fore the many ways in which the interweaving of grace and humanity amplifies the church's reality as neither complete nor failure-proof, but as tillable and in need of tilling. Grace, then, does not license presumption, smugness, or mediocrity in the Christian community. Even as the church remains a community in need of conversion, the presence of the Holy Spirit within the community of faith makes it possible for members to experience, and share, the "love, joy, peace, patience, kindness, generosity, faithfulness, gentleness, and self-control" (Gal 5:22-23) that flow from the Spirit. That both emphases can be true simultaneously points to the uniqueness of the interweaving of grace and humanity that is the church.

The incarnational proclivity of grace, which was noted above, ensures that the church is not separable from the vicissitudes endemic to human history. Even more, it ensures that the church, as a graced human community not an angelic one, will experience its own vicissitudes that will stamp it as other than a model of unimpeachable perfection or imperturbable stillness. The incarnational dynamics of grace indicate that accurate portrayals of the connection between grace and the church need exclude only one-dimensional interpretations of the church, irrespective of whether that one dimension is proper to God alone or humanity alone.

The grace at work in the church is the same grace at work in the wider world, the world that is the setting for the church. Grace does not generate an ethereal and ahistorical ecclesial community, but situates the church within the "joys and hopes, the grief and anguish of the people of our time," as Vatican II famously declared at the start of *Gaudium et Spes* (GS), its Pastoral Constitution on the Church in the Modern World. Since the graced mission of the church is to be "a sign and instrument . . . of communion with God and of the unity of the entire human race," the ecclesial community must involve itself in the world (LG 1). This immersion can be fertile if members of the church are open to learn from the civic societies to which the church belongs, and to participate in them sympathetically and with a critically constructive spirit. The preparedness to do so is an acknowledgment that grace transcends the church even as it constitutes the church.

The fact that the ecclesial community neither controls grace nor is always responsive to grace highlights further the church's need for conversion, for which the Holy Spirit is the catalyst. The profile of the Spirit as "the element of dynamic unrest if not of revolutionary upheaval" in the church makes plain that grace is far from being anemic.[11] The tilling necessary to facilitate a more faithful church will differ significantly, then, from both a genteel activity in a domestic garden and a fleeting sentiment that does not translate into action. Indeed, the tilling of the church can require the resolve to confront the "hypocrisy" of those members "not acting consistently with the truth of the gospel" (Gal 2:11-14).

Conflict in the church, even when it furthers the conversion that results in greater faithfulness to the mission of the ecclesial community rather than in division, is always a source of tension and discomfort for those it touches. As challenging as it can be to navigate conflict in helpful ways, the ripples it produces are not necessarily harbingers of schism in the church: "When we are united in faith in Christ and the Church and in mutual love, we do not need to demonstrate to the world that we are also united in everything. A lack of unity can be a symbol of real life and the way to avoid stagnation and the peace of the graveyard, it can be the way new tasks and solutions are sought and found."[12]

Paradoxically, the Spirit who can be the source of unrest also cultivates unity and the "bond of peace" (Eph 4:3) in the ecclesial community. The Spirit also stimulates both the convergences between the church's past, present, and future and the corrective influences that each period can exert on the others. Since traces of the Spirit are evident in both unrest and unity, discerning the movement of the Spirit, rather than co-opting the Spirit for one's preferred option, is clearly critical for the health of the church.

The fact that the church can undergo conversion without ceasing to exist, and can look to the future without obliterating its past and present, indicates the church's Spirit-driven potential for imagina-

11. Karl Rahner, *Nature and Grace*, trans. D. Wharton (London: Sheed and Ward, 1963), 79.

12. Karl Rahner, *Kritisches Wort: Aktuelle Probleme in Kirche und Welt* (Freiburg: Herder, 1970), 54; my translation.

tion and creativity. This text will stress that imagination and creativity are not merely permissible in the church, but are integral to all that establishes the church's specificity. As such, those qualities, too, are instruments of grace that are no less essential to tilling the ecclesial community than is the acknowledgment of failings and the commitment to learn from those failings. Both learning from the past and openness to the future, then, illustrate that the church's foundations continue to foster the life of the ecclesial community.

"Foundations" refers commonly to decisions and actions that occur at the dawn of an institution or group. It is by no means exceptional for all that emerges in the founding period to govern every aspect of the group's life, including whether the endorsement of change and new directions for the future is acceptable. Unlike the constitution of states or the charters of companies, the church's foundations are both personal and present. The church's primary foundation, and the source of all potential, is its graced relationship to God, in Jesus Christ through the Holy Spirit: "The things that maintain the Church today in its being the Church of God are precisely the same christological and pneumatological realities which gave it origin."[13] The grace that animates the church is not a relic of the past, nor a vague memory, but fuel for the imagination of the ecclesial community in every age.

The conviction that the grace of the Spirit stimulates movement in the church is at odds with the view that the ecclesial community's foundations, packaged regularly as "tradition," sanctify only what comes from the past. This perception of tradition can frame the past as sacrosanct, thereby limiting acceptance of anything new. With this tension in mind, a key task of this book is to examine the relationship between the church's foundations and the creative reception of the past in light of the influences on the present. Grace is not fickle, moving one way today and another tomorrow, nor is each generation in the church more insightful or faithful than its predecessors. Yet, the limitlessness of grace—"the newness which God himself mysteriously brings

---

13. Pedro Rodriguez, "Theological Method for Ecclesiology," in *The Gift of the Church: A Textbook on Ecclesiology*, ed. Peter Phan (Collegeville, MN: Michael Glazier, 2000), 139–40.

about and inspires, provokes, guides and accompanies in a thousand ways"[14]—and the constantly changing world in which members of the church seek to express their faith both enable and evoke creativity within the ecclesial community.

Since grace is the church's abiding foundation, construing the church's future must differ from both a comprehensive repudiation of the church's past, as cloaked as that past inevitably is with the ambiguity inseparable from humanity's response to grace, and an equally doctrinaire refusal to take up new questions. The space between those two extremes is expansive, even if not always well-delineated. This indicates that one element of ecclesial imagination, for communities no less than individuals, is the ability to recognize the movement of grace in what has come from the past, vivifies the present, and draws the church toward the future.

In relation to horticulture and agriculture, tilling requires appropriate tools for specific tasks. Less obviously, but no less essentially, it requires the ability to "read" the soil, to recognize its needs and strategize on responses likely to be effective in meeting those needs. These conditions apply equally, *mutatis mutandis*, to the tilling of the church. Thus, the Second Vatican Council emphasized that the effectiveness of the church's mission in the world was inseparable from "the responsibility of reading the signs of the times and of interpreting them in the light of the Gospel" (GS 4).

For the members of the church, this "reading" can be a synonym for discerning the presence of the Spirit, of grace. Since the church's historical context and the life of the Christian community in every age manifest unique "signs of the times," an alertness to those signs and the facility to interpret them "in the light of the Gospel" are components of the tilling that forms the church for its ongoing mission. Significantly, this facility, as a gift of grace, is proper to all the members of the ecclesial community, requiring that all references to "the church" affirm the inclusive reach of the Spirit's gifts—an emphasis that will recur through this volume.

---

14. Pope Francis, *Evangelii Gaudium*, On the Proclamation of the Gospel in Today's World (2013), 12, http://www.vatican.va/content/francesco/en/apost_exhortations /documents/papa-francesco_esortazione-ap_20131124_evangelii-gaudium.html.

A thoroughgoing theology of the church, one attentive to the vast array of "signs of the times," requires awareness of all that affects ecclesial life in the manifold settings in which the members of the Catholic community live. Contemporary ecclesiology reinforces this conviction, especially in its sensitivity to particular expressions of ecclesial faith and, its corollary, an appreciation of the role that "locality" plays in ecclesial life.[15] Both emphases are compatible with imagining a range of possibilities for the future of different communities within the one church, especially when those possibilities are consistent with the church's own resources.

Current thinking about the church is less hospitable to any approaches suggesting that the life of the church should follow a single pattern applicable everywhere. The reluctance to endorse a hegemonic model increases if that model offers little connection to the unique circumstances of different groups in the church—"After all, if [descriptions of the church] are not true of anyone in the Church, what can it mean to say they are true of the Church?"[16] The imperative to do justice to particular experiences of ecclesial life is most evident in the burgeoning expressions of "global Catholicism," which acknowledge that diversity in Catholic life is a present reality, not simply a theoretical possibility.[17]

Alert to this trend and to the diversity of the church's contexts, it is important to state that the present work has its roots principally in the issues and literature that arise in the contemporary ecclesial context of North America, Europe, and Australia. Issues prominent in those settings include not only the church's engagement with pluralistic societies, but possibilities for the ecclesial leadership of women, and for more collaborative and coresponsible forms of ecclesial life, especially in light of the revelations of clerical sexual abuse. These topics might not feature currently in the same way for every ecclesial community

15. See, for example, Pascal Bazzell, "Towards an Empirical-ideal Ecclesiology: On the Dynamic Relation between Ecclesiality and Locality," *Ecclesiology* 11 (2015): 219–35.

16. Joseph Komonchak, *Who Are the Church?* (Milwaukee, WI: Marquette University Press, 2008), 10.

17. For an example of theologies reflecting the insights of "global Catholicism," see Jane Linahan and Cyril Orji, eds., *"All the End of the Earth": Challenges and Celebration of Global Catholicism* (Maryknoll, NY: Orbis, 2020).

throughout the world, but they do have implications that transcend a single culture. It is likely, too, that ongoing discernment of these issues will be significant beyond the present moment of the church's history, contributing to shaping the church into the future.

Expressions of faith and practice that become part of "the universal church" tend to have a local source from which they spread, rather than emerging throughout the entire church at the same time or being the result of a mandate from "the center." In addition, members of the church, in every setting, share the struggles and challenges intrinsic to the building of community. Creative participation in this task requires responsiveness to the grace at work through the proclamation of the word and the church's sacramental life, and to the call to discipleship in the world. Since this challenge is common to members of the ecclesial community throughout the world, ecclesial life in one context will be relevant to its form in all contexts.

As this book develops "tilling" as its primary frame for reflecting on the ecclesial community and clarifying its mission, the relationship between grace and humanity will be its lodestar. The specifics of ecclesial life in every setting—past, present, and future—reflect the particular interweaving of grace and humanity that gives the church its unique identity. To begin the exploration of the relationship between grace and humanity in the life of the church, the first chapter will explore "the church" to establish that being tillable, being incomplete and in need of attention, is essential to all that the term encompasses.

1

The Church as Project

Henry Ford's assembly line disrupted the history of manufacturing. By enabling the high-volume, time-efficient, and cost-effective production of reliable cars, Ford launched a new era in the supply of consumer goods. The assembly line was similarly revolutionary in its impact on human labor. To ensure that his system maintained maximum efficiency, Ford limited workers to the repetition of discrete actions, making it impossible for them to exercise initiative or vary their routines. Ford envisaged personnel in his factories as components of a machine, so he would not allow them "to talk, hum, whistle, sit, lean, pause for reflection, or otherwise behave in a nonrobotic fashion while working, and [they] were given just one thirty-minute break per shift in which to go to the lavatory, have lunch, or attend to any other personal needs."[1] Ironically, then, the assembly line, a monument to humanity's technical and aesthetic imagination, achieved its goals by stifling human freedom and spontaneity.

So intent was Ford on protecting the manufacturing process against the vagaries of human behavior, he insisted that even the pedagogy of the "English School," a facility that his company provided for its employees, should serve this purpose. To satisfy the carmaker's stipulation,

---

1. Bill Bryson, *One Summer: America, 1927* (New York: Doubleday, 2013), 235.

the school readied recently arrived immigrants to the United States for absorption into Ford's factories, even as it taught them the language and culture of their new homeland. The manifesto for the school highlighted its intent to engineer a new type of worker: "As we adapt the machinery in the shop to turning out the kind of automobile we have in mind, so we have constructed our educational system with a view to producing the human product we have in mind."[2] The evolution of technology eventually liberated carmaking from any excessive reliance on "the human product." With the advent of real robots, immune to distraction and without "personal needs," Ford's assembly line found its ideal acolytes.

The Catholic Church confounds all that Henry Ford prized. The church might not be chaos writ large, but is far from echoing the hum that efficient machines emit. Accounts of "the Catholic vote" and the profiles of "devout Catholics" that portray the ecclesial community in primarily institutional terms could give the opposite impression. These accounts incline at times toward dated depictions of the church by portraying it as the archetype of a vertically integrated structure, one in which "the faithful" obey without demur all directives from the pope, bishops, and even parish priests. This snapshot bears little resemblance to the reality of contemporary ecclesial life.

Far from being a monolith, the Catholic Church is a body of diverse communities whose individual members fit no single pattern of identification with, or participation in, the ecclesial community. Nor do Catholics generally demonstrate the unquestioning obedience to authority that legend ascribes to their ilk. Indeed, suspicion rather than deference may be the hallmark of currently prevailing attitudes toward the church's officeholders. This suspicion is ascribable in part to contemporary cultural trends unsympathetic to authority and structure. More specifically, and more radically, distrust of the church's ordained ministers is a response to the clerical sexual abuse crisis that has rippled around the world since the beginning of the twenty-first century.

The abuse crisis is the most distressing example of circumstances that can emerge suddenly and with little warning, from within the

---

2. The manifesto is quoted in Jill Lepore, *These Truths: A History of the United States* (New York: Norton, 2018), 384.

church or beyond it, yet be of great moment for the life of the ecclesial community. As catalysts for turmoil and demands for change in
the church, these situations testify to the "unfinished" reality of the
church.[3] They make clear that the church is not the embodiment of
the perfection proper to God. Equally, the challenges underscore that
the church differs from an object on which neither the circumstances
of history nor the actions that span the spectrum of possible human
behavior make any impression. The lack of predictability, the need for
responsiveness to influences shaping the church's life in history, and
the imperative of conversion on which faithfulness depends, all reveal
that the church is tillable, that it is a project requiring attention. These
features of the church witness unequivocally to the church's humanity.
Central to this volume is the contention that the same features disclose,
albeit indirectly, the church's relationship to the grace of God.

Since the church "exists wherever 'the cause of Jesus' is made present
by the Spirit, taken hold of in faith, and put into practice in love, [it]
is primarily an event; it is something happening."[4] In response to the
grace of God who "is indeed the mystery past all grasp," the church
can be what God enables only if it is "an event of human beings giving
themselves to God."[5] This "event," a term applicable to an ongoing
and dynamic process rather than simply to an individual occurrence
with circumscribed boundaries, takes place in history, even as it looks
toward the fullness of life in God's ever-new future. The church's orientation, because it extends beyond history, ensures that no era in the
life of the ecclesial community marks the finality of the church, the
end of the ecclesial event.

As an initial step in the process of detailing all that "tilling the
church" might imply, this chapter considers what "the church" implies.

3. "Unfinished" as a designation for the church comes from Bernard Prusak, *The Church Unfinished: Ecclesiology Through the Centuries* (Mahwah, NJ: Paulist, 2004).

4. Walter Kasper, *An Introduction to Christian Faith*, trans. V. Green (New York: Paulist, 1980), 139; for an analysis of the application of "event" to the life of the church, specifically to the Second Vatican Council, see Joseph Komonchak, "Vatican II as 'Event,'" in *Vatican II: Did Anything Happen?*," ed. David Schultenover (New York: Continuum, 2007), 26–45.

5. Karl Rahner, "Ignatius of Loyola Speaks to a Modern Jesuit," in *Karl Rahner: Spiritual Writings*, ed. Philip Endean (Maryknoll, NY: Orbis, 2004), 41.

In so doing, it makes the case for characterizing the church as a project that is tillable and in need of tilling. Simply put, the chapter differentiates the church from both a finished product of Ford's assembly line and the invariable assembly process itself. To accomplish its goal, the chapter pursues a three-pronged approach. First, it surveys trends in present-day ecclesiology, trends reflecting the church's unfinished state. Next, the chapter examines how theological reflection on the church as a graced body in history can accentuate the church's dynamism. The final section profiles "mystery," a theological theme applicable primarily to God but derivatively to the open-ended and tillable church.

Locating "the Church"

No theory of human behavior encompasses all possible variables evident in the conduct of human subjects. Similarly, no theological analysis of the church exhausts everything relevant to the ecclesial community. The limitation of each form of inquiry reflects the unfathomable depths of its topic rather than methodological inadequacies. To repeat a claim from the introduction, the interweaving of grace and humanity that constitutes the church generates the breadth and depth that frustrate all efforts to articulate a definitive appraisal of the ecclesial community. The material in this section supports this contention by reviewing contemporary ecclesiologies that showcase the complex reality of the church as a datum of experience more than a theoretical construct.

As a graced and human reality, the church differs from "a Platonic fiction" floating above the world like an eternal "form."[6] The church's existence in history challenges the complacency evident when the church's officeholders—and perhaps even theologians—concentrate on "questions that nobody asks" rather than acknowledging the truths of the church's present situation.[7] These truths can be agents for the church's tilling, disturbing for settled practice but likely to be gateways for new possibilities in the life of the ecclesial community.

---

6. Michael Jinkins, *The Church Faces Death: Ecclesiology in a Post-Modern Context* (New York: Oxford University Press, 1999), 100.

7. Pope Francis, *Evangelii Gaudium*, 155.

Significant issues in the life of the contemporary church provide ample evidence of the impact that the flow of history has on the church. As already noted, the clerical sexual abuse crisis, to begin with the most catastrophic example, has called into question many aspects of ecclesial faith and practice. The harm that criminal actions by abusive priests inflicted on a vast number of minors and vulnerable adults continues to fuel outrage and precipitate large numbers of departures from the Catholic community. Compounding the damage, the failure of many bishops to extend justice and compassion to the survivors of abuse has deepened the scandal and ignited demands for reforms in the church, including in the exercise of episcopal authority.[8]

The fact that male clerics are the principal agents of the abuse has intensified the long-simmering theological discussion—and, more broadly, disillusionment and anger—on many matters that touch on the full and equal participation of women in the church.[9] Prominent among these matters is the prohibition against the entry of women

8. See the discussion in Massimo Faggioli, "The Catholic Sexual Abuse Crisis as a Theological Crisis: Emerging Issues," *Theological Studies* 80 (2019): 572–89; Richard Lennan, "Beyond Scandal and Shame?: Ecclesiology and the Longing for a Transformed Church," *Theological Studies* 80 (2019): 590–610; Richard Lennan, "Unlearning, Learning, and Relearning: Ecclesial Conversion in Response to the Sexual Abuse Crisis," *Josephinum Journal of Theology* 29 (2019): 93–107; and Neil Ormerod, "Sexual Abuse, a Royal Commission, and the Australian Church," *Theological Studies* 80 (2019): 963–65.

9. Representative writings on many issues regarding women in the church include Mary Doak, *A Prophetic Public Church: Witness to Hope Amid the Global Crises of the 21ˢᵗ Century* (Collegeville, MN: Liturgical Press, 2020), 75–115; Susan Ross, "Feminist Theology and the Clergy Sexual Abuse Crisis," *Theological Studies* 80 (2019): 632–52; Cristina Lledo Gomez, *The Church as Woman and Mother: Historical and Theological Foundations* (Mahwah, NJ: Paulist, 2018); Elaine Graham, "Feminist Critiques, Visions, and Models of the Church," in *The Oxford Handbook of Ecclesiology*, ed. Paul Avis (Oxford: Oxford University Press, 2018), 527–51; Tina Beattie, "Transforming Time—The Maternal Church and the Pilgrimage of Faith," *Ecclesiology* 12 (2016): 54–72; Ninna Edgardh, "(De)gendering Ecclesiology: Reflections on the Church as a Gendered Body," in *Ecclesiology in the Trenches: Theory and Method under Construction*, ed. Sune Fahlgren and Jonas Idestrom (Eugene, OR: Pickwick, 2015), 193–207; Mary Ann Hinsdale, "A Feminist Reflection on Postconciliar Catholic Ecclesiology," in *A Church with Open Doors*, ed. Richard Gaillardetz and Edward Hahnenberg (Collegeville, MN: Michael Glazier, 2015), 112–37.

into those ecclesial ministries for which ordination is a requirement. Frustration with existing policies that affect women in the church underscores in two ways the symbiosis between grace and human history. First, the realization that many groups in society have dismantled long-standing barriers to the full participation of women in roles once the exclusive preserve of men offers a model for those desiring similar changes in the Catholic Church. Second, convictions on the equality of the baptized in the ecclesial community, convictions with a basis in the New Testament (Gal 3:28), fuel the belief that pressures for changes in the church are not merely social protests, but the work of grace: "Women with deep gladness are responding to a call from the Holy Spirit of God, heard in the depths of their hearts, to take the giftedness of their 'one wild and precious life' and meet the world's deep hunger for meaning and healing, liberation and redemption."[10]

The way ahead on issues affecting the ongoing engagement of women with the church's structures and ministries may be unclear, but the fact that the questions and the demands for change persist amplifies the church's status as an unfinished project. This status likewise makes evident that theological reflection on the ecclesial community must be ongoing. In light of all that the tumultuous early decades of the twenty-first century have witnessed, it is scarcely imaginable that contemporary ecclesiology could proceed as if the church were straightforward, flawless, or static. Such was not always the case for theologies of the church.

Ecclesiology in the not-too-distant past resided in Roman Catholic, Orthodox, Anglican, and various Protestant denominational settings that collectively practiced mutual exclusion, while exhibiting little doubt that their own tradition was the apotheosis of all things ecclesial.[11] Symptomatic of the persistent divisions within the one Christian Church, each sectarian ecclesiology sought to bolster the legitimacy of its host by contrasting its own tradition with other, necessarily lesser,

---

10. Elizabeth Johnson, "'Your one wild and precious life': Women on the Road to Ministry," *Theological Studies*, 80 (2019): 203.

11. For the history and development of a range of denominational ecclesiologies, see the chapters in part 2 of *The Oxford Handbook of Ecclesiology*, ed. Paul Avis (Oxford: Oxford University Press, 2018), 183–357.

ecclesial embodiments. The tradition-specific ecclesiologies directed their attention primarily to the internal concerns of their sponsoring body, often elevating those concerns above engagement with the church's mission in the wider world.

Today—happily—most ecclesiologies, including those that concentrate on a single ecclesial tradition, as this work does in discussing the Catholic Church, recognize that the many bodies within the one Christian Church share a common pool of resources and a common mission, both of which have their source in God's self-revelation in history, from which ecclesial faith springs. It is certainly true that different communities, even now, weave these common elements into formulations of "the church" that do not necessarily promote closer relationships with other communities. Nonetheless, dialogue, a theme that will be prominent in a number of places throughout this book, has largely eliminated both the mutual anathemas and extreme vituperation that scarred previous eras of ecclesial life. Steps toward enduring reconciliation and expanded possibilities for shared mission now appear where once hostility reigned. The new age of dialogue has enabled deeper appreciation of commonalities between Christian communities. It has likewise facilitated new approaches to the contentious issues inherited from earlier periods, issues that remain obstacles to full communion between the churches.[12]

A less congenial stimulus for efforts at reconciliation between the churches has come from the marginalization of ecclesial faith in pluralist societies. Neither depth of history nor the assertion of uniqueness is enough to spare any individual church, the Catholic Church included, from the diminution that has increasingly become their shared lot. This situation makes plain that prioritizing past divisions over present opportunities and challenges endangers the church's mission in the contemporary world, whose religious landscape is no longer identical with that of the sixteenth century.[13]

12. For an overview of contemporary ecumenical theology, see Gesa Elsbeth Thiessen, ed., *Ecumenical Ecclesiology: Unity, Diversity and Otherness in a Fragmented World* (London: T. and T. Clark, 2009).

13. On this point, see Richard Lennan, "Truth, Context, and Unity: Karl Rahner's Ecumenical Theology," *Philosophy and Theology*, 27 (2015): 497–512.

The Catholic Church, especially as a result of the Second Vatican Council, has been active in helping to craft a new ecumenical landscape, one better able to reflect the realities of the twenty-first century.[14] Present-day Catholics are likely to affirm the wisdom of Christian traditions other than their own, and to accept these traditions as a gift that enhances the whole church. In this vein, current ecumenical engagement, even as it grapples with the legacy of church-dividing controversies and struggles to translate theological agreement into everyday practice, directs attention to what the churches can receive from, and offer to, each other for the sake of the fundamental unity of the one church of Jesus Christ.[15]

Just as the years since Vatican II have altered the ecumenical landscape, the same period has witnessed significant shifts in the ecclesial self-understanding of Catholics, shifts that owe much to the council's stimulus. The council's teaching on the church, with which later chapters will engage more amply, offered alternatives to a theology of the church as "perfect society," the imaginary that dominated the ecclesial worldview of Catholics between the Council of Trent (1545–63) and Vatican II, as the final section of this chapter will illustrate.

A frequent companion of the emphasis on the church as a perfect society was the stress on the church in Europe as the lynchpin of ecclesial life. The Eurocentric emphasis relegated Catholics in other parts of the world to being little more than recipients of what emanated from a centralized "export firm," which dispatched "to the whole world a European religion along with other elements of this supposedly superior civilization and culture."[16] In the era of the "export firm," Catholic communities were often more attentive to Rome than to their local social, economic, religious, and political settings. These circumstances

---

14. For a detailed analysis of Vatican II's ecumenical theology, see Ormond Rush, *The Vision of Vatican II: Its Fundamental Principles* (Collegeville, MN: Liturgical Press, 2019), 371–424.

15. See Paul Murray, "Receptive Ecumenism and Catholic Learning: Establishing the Agenda," in Paul Murray, ed., *Receptive Ecumenism and the Call to Catholic Learning: Exploring a Way for Contemporary Ecumenism* (Oxford: Oxford University Press, 2008), 5–25.

16. Karl Rahner, "Basic Theological Interpretation of the Second Vatican Council," in *Theological Investigations*, vol. 20, trans. E. Quinn (New York: Crossroad, 1986), 78.

nurtured the belief—psychologically compelling, but reflecting reality only partially, at best—that Catholic communities around the world resembled each other in every detail, as well as being able to rely unreservedly on authoritative structures that guaranteed stability.

The hegemony of a European model reflected, and buttressed, a narrow interpretation of Catholic life. This interpretation understood unity in the church as requiring communities in every place to practice an identical approach to worship, structure, and all else that expresses the church in the world. Conversely, the current challenge is to preserve a commitment to "one Lord, one faith, one baptism" (Eph 4:5) that maintains unity but does not require uniformity in all aspects of the church's life, either between the many churches that claim the title of "Christian" or within the Catholic Church itself.

The contemporary church's engagement with the tsunami that is the multi-faith, digital, and globalized world—phenomena unimaginable in previous decades—has generated challenges that Christian communities, individually or collectively, have not previously confronted.[17] The dramatic interference to "normal" life that the COVID-19 pandemic precipitated in 2020 and beyond has affected even the practice of the church's worship, and so demonstrated that no dimension of ecclesial life is exempt from the world's fluidity.[18] Consequently, attention to the church's historical and cultural setting has become a guiding principle for much contemporary ecclesiology: "If distinctively theological notions must govern any adequate ecclesiology, exclusive attention to them tends to abstract the Church out of history and out of those quite particular realizations that are the individual churches assembled

---

17. Daniella Zsupan-Jerome, *Connected toward Communion: The Church and Social Communication in the Digital Age* (Collegeville, MN: Liturgical Press, 2014) examines the impact that the evolution of digital technology has on the church; see also Anthony Godzieba, "*Quaestio Disputata*: The Magisterium in an Age of Digital Reproduction," in *When the Magisterium Intervenes: The Magisterium and Theologians in Today's Church*, ed. Richard Gaillardetz (Collegeville, MN: Liturgical Press, 2012), 140–53. For a discussion of how ecclesiology might respond to the challenges of globalization, see Vincent Miller, "Where Is the Church? Globalization and Catholicity," *Theological Studies* 69 (2008): 412–32.

18. See, for example, Kevin Irwin, *Liturgy and Sacraments in a COVID World: Renewal, Not Restoration* (Mahwah, NJ: Paulist, 2021).

locally, that is, in particular times, places, and cultures, with distinctive historical tasks to undertake."[19]

This principle highlights the identity of theology, including ecclesiology, as a "situated" activity, one that requires practitioners to take account of the circumstances in which human beings encounter God.[20] The circumstances of time and place influence the ways in which humanity experiences God, but they also have an impact on reflection on that experience. From this perspective, ecclesiology is a contextual theology: it necessarily takes place somewhere at some time. Ecclesiology, then, must be alert to the topography of those particular times and places, no less than to their effects on the people who form the ecclesial community.

Contemporary Trends in Ecclesiology

The consolidation of ecclesiology as a contextual theology has facilitated the emergence of the human and social sciences as influences on thinking about the church.[21] Building on the recognition of grace as embodied and historical, theological reflection on the church can draw fruitfully from the insights of those disciplines whose bailiwick is human behavior. These disciplines help to identify and evaluate the dynamics of the ecclesial community as a human reality. The insights of these nontheological disciplines aid, too, in the identification of deficits that either militate against the healthy practice of shared ecclesial life or impede the effectiveness of the church's mission in the world. Lessons from sociology can be sources of insight into, for example, how the church's structures function—or become dysfunctional—and how ecclesial communities might navigate change without descending into internecine conflicts.

The sociological trend in ecclesiology that has brought demography and ethnography to the fore has altered the measure of authenticity

19. Joseph Komonchak, "The Epistemology of Reception," *The Jurist* 57 (1997): 187.

20. Dan Stiver, "Theological Method," in *The Cambridge Companion to Postmodern Theology*, ed. Kevin Vanhoozer (Cambridge: Cambridge University Press, 2003), 179.

21. For discussion of the background and dynamics of the use of social scientific methodologies in ecclesiology, see Neil Ormerod, "Social Sciences and the Ideological Critiques of Ecclesiology," in *The Oxford Handbook of Ecclesiology*, ed. Paul Avis (Oxford: Oxford University Press, 2018), 535–72; see also Ormerod's "*Sensus fidei* and Sociology: How Do We Find the Normative in the Empirical?," in *Learning from* All *the Faithful: A Contemporary Theology of the* Sensus Fidei, ed. Bradford Hinze and Peter Phan (Eugene, OR: Pickwick, 2016), 89–102.

for all descriptions of the ecclesial community. Today, it is important that such descriptions locate their subject in relation to the needs, desires, and struggles characteristic of specific groups and locations, rather than as timeless, transcendent, and universally applicable.[22] Such developments have honed sensitivities around references to "the church." Absent this awareness, professions about the church might resemble "ideas disconnected from realities," the sort of ideas that "give rise to ineffectual forms of idealism and nominalism, capable at most of classifying and defining, but certainly not calling to action" (EG 232). In relation to the themes of this volume, such "disconnected" approaches to the church would be irreconcilable with the need for self-criticism, revision of priorities, and openness to new questions that "tilling" promotes and encapsulates.

   As part of ensuring that ecclesiology is not abstract, present-day ap-proaches reclaim the voice of groups, including communities of color, people living with disabilities, and the victims of unjust economic and political systems, especially refugees and migrants, long dwelling on the margins of the Christian community's attention and priorities.[23] Nota-bly, the exclusive focus on European experience as the universal norm

22. See, for example, Paul Avis, "Ecclesiology and Ethnography: An Unresolved Relationship," *Ecclesiology* 14 (2018): 322–37; Paul Lakeland, "Ecclesiology and the Use of Demography: Three Models of Apostolicity," in *A Church with Open Doors*, ed. Richard Gaillardetz and Edward Hahnenberg (Collegeville, MN: Michael Glazier, 2015), 23–42; Pete Ward, ed., *Perspectives on Ecclesiology and Ethnography* (Grand Rapids, MI: Eerdmans, 2012). *Ecclesial Practice*, a journal that began publishing in 2014, is dedicated entirely to exploring the use of ethnography in studies of the church.
   23. Illustrations of ecclesiology done from the perspective of the marginalized in-clude M. Shawn Copeland, ed., *Uncommon Witness: The Black Catholic Experience* (Maryknoll, NY: Orbis, 2009); Gemma Tulud Cruz, "A New Way of Being Christian: The Contribution of Migrants to the Church," in *Contemporary Issues of Migration and Theology*, ed. Elaine Padilla and Peter Phan (New York: Palgrave Macmillan, 2013), 95–120; Ignacio Ellacuria, "The Church of the Poor, Historical Sacrament of Liberation," *Mysterium Liberationis: Fundamental Concepts of Liberation Theology*, ed. Ignacio Ellacuria and Jon Sobrino (Maryknoll, NY: Orbis, 1993), 543–64; Mary Carlson, "Making the Invisible Visible: Inviting Persons with Disabilities into the Life of the Church," *Horizons* 45 (2018): 46–73; Natalia Imperatori-Lee, *Cuéntame: Narra-tive in the Ecclesial Present* (Maryknoll, NY: Orbis, 2018), 134–58; and Agnes Brazal, "Church as Sacrament of Yin-Yang Harmony: Toward a More Incisive Participation of Laity and Women in the Church," *Theological Studies* 80 (2018): 414–35.

for the church has receded as ecclesiological insights from around the globe have become more prominent.[24] This development, reflective of the emergence of the "world-Church" at Vatican II, has at least made it more possible to imagine the Catholic Church as a body characterized by "all its parts exercising a reciprocal influence on one another."[25] The activities representative of tilling, so this book contends, are essential for this possibility to move from imagination to realization.

Attention to diverse voices contributes to the richness of the church's life. In addition, this attention facilitates the recognition that the Holy Spirit's activity extends beyond the "middle-class, middle-aged, relatively educated, articulate, skilled, if not professional, and, in general, given to a fairly responsible level of participation in the world of business, work and social life."[26] In so doing, theological reflection on the church can echo Pope Francis's conviction that "the poor," a term he understands as "primarily a theological category rather than a cultural, sociological, political or philosophical one" (EG 198), can "evangelize" the rest of the church through the witness of lives lived in hope built on trust in God rather than possessions or personal accomplishments. This emphasis makes clear the distinction between the gospel message and societal norms for success and purpose.

The endorsement of attentiveness to the church's diversity and cultural context as a theological source is not a concession to the Zeitgeist of postmodernity or to contemporary trends in "identity politics." In fact, it reflects the New Testament, where "the church" is interchangeable with "the churches" (Acts 15:41; 1 Cor 7:17; and 1 Thess 2:14).[27]

24. Examples of ecclesiologies emerging from contexts previously overshadowed by European dominance include Agbonkhianmeghe Orobator, ed., *The Church We Want: African Catholics Look to Vatican III* (Maryknoll, NY: Orbis, 2016); Simon C. Kim, *A World Church in Our Backyard: How the Spirit Moved Church and Society* (Collegeville, MN: Liturgical, 2016).

25. Rahner, "Basic Theological Interpretation of the Second Vatican Council," 78.

26. John O'Brien, "The Authority of the Poor," in *Authority in the Roman Catholic Church: Theory and Practice*, ed. Bernard Hoose (Burlington, VT: Ashgate, 2002), 217 30.

27. For a brief overview of the New Testament's usage of "the church" and "the churches," see Michael Fahey, "Church" in *Systematic Theology: Roman Catholic Perspectives*, 2nd ed., ed. Francis Schüssler Fiorenza and John Galvin (Minneapolis:

The willingness to be attentive to the spectrum of voices in the church can be an expression of faith, an acknowledgment that "as the flesh of the church is the flesh of Christ in every age, the flesh of the church is marked (as was his flesh) by race, sex, gender, sexuality, and culture."[28] The same willingness is essential if the church is to show itself in the world as other than a body "shut up within structures which give us a false sense of security" (EG 49).

The fact that the church is not identical in every time and place differentiates the ecclesial community from the processes of an assembly line. The same fact identifies ecclesiology as "an aspirational undertaking," one that is proper to a people "trying to build that ideal community of justice and righteousness which Christians refer to as the Kingdom of God."[29] Different generations of believers, and even synchronous ecclesial communities, address this task in unique ways, ways peculiar to their own context and interpretations of their mission.

Diversity within the one ecclesial community highlights that "what Church is, unfolds in and through the drama of salvation mediated in the lives of engaged individuals and communities," rather than being "found all packaged as it were, within a doctrinal system."[30] To anticipate an aspect of a later chapter, this emphasis does not mandate the rejection of ecclesial tradition, but rather drives the effort, itself a form of tilling, to appropriate the tradition creatively in circumstances different from its origin. The circumstances might differ, but every generation in the church shares with every other one the gift of the same Holy Spirit.

The existence of the church as a community of different voices, as well as the lack of predictability in the church's own life and its

---

Fortress, 2011), 328–31; for more detailed studies of particular churches, see Raymond Brown, *The Churches the Apostles Left Behind* (Ramsey, NJ: Paulist, 1984), and Frederick Cwiekowski, *The Church: Theology in History* (Collegeville, MN: Liturgical Press, 2018).

28. M. Shawn Copeland, "Marking the Body of Jesus, the Body of Christ," in *The Strength of Her Witness: Jesus Christ in the Global Voices of Women*, ed. Elizabeth Johnson (Maryknoll, NY: Orbis, 2016), 280.

29. Gerard Mannion, "Ecclesiology and Postmodernity: A New Paradigm for the Roman Catholic Church?," *New Blackfriars* 85 (2004): 305.

30. John O'Brien, "Ecclesiology as Narrative," *Ecclesiology* 4 (2008): 151.

participation in the world, are formative factors for ecclesiology. They indicate how important it is that theological analyses of "the church" are able to hold together both the diversity and unity of the Christian community, an outcome that is at least conceivable since both qualities reflect the presence of grace. No less crucially, the same factors argue convincingly against the existence of a "blueprint" at the disposal of the church.

A blueprint would create the impression that there is a "single right way to think about the church," a way applicable to every situation in every era, regardless of the circumstances of time, place, and people.[31] Without a blueprint, theological reflection on the church must respond to the embodiments of the Christian community in its manifold contexts: "Critical theological analysis of those contexts, and the present shape and activity of the church within them, should therefore be one of the central tasks of ecclesiology."[32] To depict the reality of its subject accurately, then, a portrait of the church must do justice to the ways in which members of the church live their faith, rather than impose a theological superstructure that detaches them from any historical and social context.

Since the church does not have a blueprint guiding it through the uncertainties of history, Nicholas Healy insists that the ecclesial community must be willing to learn from the wisdom of "social psychology, organizational and network theories, phenomenology, leadership and educational theories."[33] As mentioned above, these sources of insight into human behavior can inform and expand the church's self-

31. Nicholas M. Healy, *Church, World and the Christian Life* (Cambridge: Cambridge University Press, 2000), 38. Healy develops his thesis concerning the blueprint in a number of other publications, which include "Ordinary Theology, Theological Method and Constructive Ecclesiology," in *Exploring Ordinary Theology: Everyday Christian Believing and the Church*, ed. Jeff Astley and Leslie Francis (Burlington, VT: Ashgate, 2013), 13–21, and "Ecclesiology, Ethnography, and God: An Interplay of Reality Descriptions," in *Perspectives on Ecclesiology and Ethnography*, ed. Pete Ward (Grand Rapids, MI: Eerdmans, 2012), 182–99.

32. Healy, *Church, World and the Christian Life*, 39.

33. Nicholas M. Healy, "Ecclesiology and Practical Theology," in *Keeping Faith in Practice: Aspects of Catholic Pastoral Theology*, ed. James Sweeney et al. (London: SCM, 2010), 117.

understanding, including the way it might frame and enact its mission in various contexts. If theology perceives the church as transcending history by following a design that could claim Jesus himself as its architect, it is likely to neglect the contributions that human wisdom, which is itself graced, might make to the church's realization in history.

A church that locates its identity in isolation from history leaves little room for the articulation of "rich, critically informed descriptions of church life that point to areas for improvement—better leadership, more appropriate practices, more engaged and fruitful internal social dynamics, greater openness to other churches or the surrounding society, or growth in membership."[34] A blueprint would inoculate the community against any obligation to question whether or not its self-understanding and forms of presence in the world were authentic appropriations of what the Spirit enables. Equally, a blueprint would likewise render irrelevant the ambiguities and failures of the church's own history, as well as the need for critical reflection on "the praxis of the church [and] the history of ecclesiology itself and the ways they have shaped that praxis."[35] In terms central to this book, the blueprint would obscure the unfinished state of the church, and so obviate any need for tilling.

The desire to separate reflection on the church from any hint of an ecclesial blueprint can extend to a disinclination to use metaphors in the work of ecclesiology. Here, so the critique runs, the concern is that metaphors for the church tend to reduce boundless complexity to a single, often simple image, while also being "too idealistic, disconnected from the church we actually experience, providing widely diverging views of what the church 'should' look like."[36] It is certainly true that uncritical appropriation of "you are a chosen race, a royal priesthood, a holy nation, God's own people" (1 Pet 2:9), to say nothing of "perfect society," could convey both flawlessness and completeness, qualities not easily reconcilable with a church that is to walk "by faith, not by sight" (2 Cor 5:7).

---

34. Ibid., 117.

35. Neil Ormerod, *Re-Visioning the Church: An Experiment in Systematic-Historical Ecclesiology* (Minneapolis: Fortress, 2014), 5.

36. Brian Flanagan, "The Limits of Ecclesial Metaphors in Systematic Theology," *Horizons* 35 (2008): 47.

Metaphors, on the other hand, can give a focus to particular aspects of the church. They can do so without erasing the church's complexity or status as a project, and without implying that the church is immune to the impact of history, including its own history. As ecclesial communities in multiple contexts confront their own limitations and failures; as they engage in the messy, often angst-ridden, processes of discerning, dialogue, and decision-making; and as they seek to articulate a faithful response to the Holy Spirit when new questions arise, metaphors for the church can play a positive role. Without imposing a "one-size-fits-all" approach that prevents local adaptations, metaphors can help communities to articulate their goals, while also being a stimulus for them to inquire into their own reception of the gospel, and representation of it. With the aim of indicating how metaphors can be helpful, this volume will make use of "mystery," "sacrament," and "pilgrim," all common metaphors for analysis of the church that feature in the documents of Vatican II.

If members of the church—to say nothing of theologians—did not need to grapple with how best to embody faithfulness to grace, they could dwell untroubled in "transcendental contentment," enjoying the serenity reflective of immunity to the uncertainties of history and the flux of societies.[37] From a different but no less significant standpoint, a community of believers exempt from the need for decision-making would never experience the excitement inherent in that activity. The joy that can be manifest in decision-making reflects the grace that facilitates an ongoing conversion to deeper faithfulness to Christ and the Spirit—"it has seemed good to the Holy Spirit and to us" (Acts 15:28). The same grace promotes the ongoing commitment to mission, even when missionary endeavors are "unsuccessful," at least by standards that Henry Ford would be likely to endorse.

The current approaches in ecclesiology are consistent with the identification of the church as a tillable body, an unfinished project. Both the developments in perceptions of the church and the range of cultural influences that the ecclesial community must navigate suggest that the unity of the church's faith, the vitality of its worship, and the fruitful-

---

37. Roger Haight, *Christian Community in History: Ecclesial Existence*, vol. 3 (New York: Continuum, 2008), 35.

ness of its service in the world are themselves ongoing tasks, rather than "one-and-done" activities. Since no element of the church's life and mission is set in concrete, impervious to questions, doubts, and possibilities, theological reflection on the church can do justice to its subject only by being itself an open-ended exercise.

As this review of contemporary ecclesiology concludes, it is important to acknowledge that this volume is not a study of a specific group in the church that exists in a particular social setting. Yet, as mentioned in the introduction, the book is alert to cultural context and sensitive to the danger of the divorce between ecclesiology and the flow of history. As necessary as this sensitivity is, the next section of this chapter will argue that doing justice to the uniqueness of the church requires attention not only to the contextual experiences of the human community—the "horizontal" reality of the church—but also to God's activity—the "vertical" reality of the church—and, most critically, to the interweaving of the two dimensions. The ambit and approach of theological reflection on the church must seek to be faithful to both, and to the relationship between them, a relationship that, reflecting the incarnational tendency of grace, is itself inseparable from life in the world.

Theology and the Tillable Church

The diversity of ecclesial communities within the contemporary Catholic Church and the general sociological turn in ecclesiology are forms of tilling that expose the church's humanity. These developments remind members of the church that they do not possess a blueprint providing untroubled passage through turbulent times. Such reminders reinforce the grounding of the church in history and culture. Nevertheless, the project that is the church is not one that sociological categories alone can guide, and certainly not determine. The ecclesial community's profession of faith proclaims the church to be a work of grace, of God's relationship to humanity in Jesus Christ through the Holy Spirit. Theological reflection on the church, if it is to be adequate to this dimensions of its subject, must maintain a focus on God's action, no less than human action. Most importantly, theology must maintain its alertness to the inextricable link between the two.

Yves Congar (1904–95), one of the most significant Catholic theologians of the twentieth century, argues that an exclusive concentration on the "life" of the church risks "so focusing upon the church in its human framework, according to the relativity and contingency of its historical dimensions, that its reality as a supernatural mystery might seem diminished."[38] Congar's emphasis resonates ecumenically in present-day theology, as is evident in the claim from Gary Badcock, an evangelical Protestant theologian, that an approach to the church dedicated solely to consideration of praxis and social processes misrepresents the church, which is "a creedal subject, a subject on which practical theory can undoubtedly be brought to bear, but which finally cannot be captured by it."[39] Likewise, the Lutheran scholar Vitor Westhelle argues that the church "is not of our doing. . . . What we 'do' is not our action, but only our re-*action*. The church happens as God speaks."[40]

At issue in this section of the chapter is not a particular formulation of "the church" but consideration of how theological reflection on the church might do justice to both attentiveness to the historical and social context of the ecclesial community and the existence of the church as a "creedal subject." Nicholas Healy, even as he repudiates blueprints, acknowledges that all descriptions of the church will be partial if they fail to account for what is "theo-logically necessary," for the movement of grace in and through the ecclesial community.[41]

Consistent with the interweaving of grace and humanity in the church, Healy contends that "an ecclesiology needs to show how grace is the condition for the possibility of the church, and how a doctrine of grace can be developed so as to address the full range of the church's empirical realities."[42] The primary implication of Healy's counsel is that a theology of the church as a graced and human reality, the approach

---

38. Yves Congar, *True and False Reform in the Church*, rev. ed., trans. P. Philibert (Collegeville, MN: Michael Glazier, 2011), 11.

39. Gary Badcock, *The House Where the Church Lives: Renewing the Doctrine of the Church Today* (Grand Rapids, MI: Eerdmans, 2009), 154.

40. Vitor Westhelle, *The Church Event: Call and Challenge of a Church Protestant* (Minneapolis: Fortress, 2010), 40; original emphasis.

41. Healy, "Ecclesiology and Practical Theology," 123.

42. Healy, "Ordinary Theology," 18.

that is the primary emphasis of this book, would distort its subject if it disregarded either grace or history. The concern that theological analyses might ignore or devalue the "empirical realities" of the church is certainly valid in light of certain "dogmatic" approaches to the church throughout the history of theology, approaches that the next section of this chapter will review. Fortunately, such an outcome is not inevitable.

An appreciation of the "incarnational tendency" of grace, to which the introduction referred, offers a way of proceeding that honors the role of grace in the life of the church, the experience of the community of faith, and the indissoluble bond between them. This emphasis enables theological reflection to affirm the church's unfinished reality, and so its need for tilling. This need arises as the unfolding of history presents the ecclesial community with new tasks or brings to light a lack of congruence between profession and action in the church. Each of these factors can be a means through which grace calls the church to a deeper conversion.

In taking the significance of the church's historical existence into account in its consideration of the church, theology affirms that an authentic relationship with the God of Jesus Christ can never be disembodied. Since the grace of the Holy Spirit neither negates nor neglects historical realities and the specifics of the church's engagement with the world, nor can theology disregard them.

The Spirit, who, like the wind, "blows where it chooses" (John 3:8), can give "voice" to those who name for the ecclesial community what damages the church's communal mission and life, as well as what may enhance their integrity.[43] Practices and policies in the church likely to "silence, invisibilize, and demonize" members of the ecclesial community, whether on the basis of race, gender, sexuality, social status, or any other criteria alien to the gospel, are likely to be in opposition to all that the grace of the Spirit embraces.[44] The voices of those on the margins of the ecclesial community—a location that might well be at odds with their own longings for a deeper belonging—can stir the

43. Eboni Marshall Turman, "The Holy Spirit and the Black Church Tradition: Womanist Considerations," in *The Holy Spirt and the Church: Ecumenical Reflections with a Pastoral Perspective*, ed. Thomas Hughson (New York: Routledge, 2016), 111.
44. Ibid., 107.

community of faith to move toward closer alignment with the Spirit. In advocating for greater faithfulness and justice in the church, these voices can expand the likelihood that the presence of the church in the world will symbolize God's life-giving grace.

As a community of faith in history, the church's discipleship of Jesus Christ through the Holy Spirit extends beyond private piety, and beyond the doors of the church's buildings. As chapter 4 will argue, living authentically as a follower of Jesus in the world involves "an act of ecclesial transcendence, by which the faithful move beyond the boundaries of religion alone and into the wider space (the *saeculum*), which believers share with the rest of the world and in which the incarnation took place."[45] For this reason, the fruitfulness of theological reflection on the church "is dependent on its embeddedness in the temporal and spatial context."[46] To reinforce that life in the world is the primary venue for the practice of Christian discipleship, ecclesiology must avoid limiting itself to concern with the inner, institutional life of the Christian community, as if that focus could exhaust everything significant about the church.

Reflecting the church's irreducible complexity, an outward-looking stance need not mean that a theology of the church must prescind from any attention to the "inner" aspects of the Christian community. The grace that calls the Christian community to creative engagement with the world in its proclamation of the gospel and work for justice is vital to the spiritual life and worship of believers, the determination of the community's faith, and the functioning of ecclesial institutions, all of which also affect the church's presence in the world—these are themes that chapter 6 will develop. Consequently, every element constitutive of ecclesial life is raw material for theological reflection on the authenticity of the church and its action in the world.

In asking whether each expression of the church gives substance to "the presence of the Spirit inspiring the action of the Christian community," theological reflection exemplifies the self-critical approach to

45. Paul Crowley, "Mystagogy and Mission: The Challenge of Nonbelief and the Task of Theology," *Theological Studies* 76 (2015): 26–27.

46. Lieven Boeve, *Interrupting Tradition: An Essay on Christian Faith in a Postmodern Context*, trans. B. Doyle (Louvain: Peeters, 2003), 25.

the church that the introduction mentioned.[47] Self-criticism can aid the tilling of the Christian community, including its worship, ministries, and other structures. Rather than assuming that the actions of individuals, communities, and structure within the church align exactly with the self-understanding of the church that the community's teaching proclaims, a self-critical approach tests whether words and actions "hang together," tests whether or not there is "coherence" between the two.[48] The goal in so doing is to enhance the faithfulness of the ecclesial community.

As an activity that seeks to further the faithfulness of the church, ecclesiology exemplifies "the end purpose of theology," which is "that the Reign of God be realized in this world, and the specific role of the theological logos is to illuminate, promote, and direct the formation of this Reign."[49] By giving prominence to the church's orientation to the fulfilled reign of God, a fulfillment that transcends history even as it begins in history, theology contributes still more to clarifying why the church is an unfinished project. This is not to say that theology merges with futurology or that theologians have privileged insight into possible developments in society and the church. The resources with which theologians pursue their work allow no determinations regarding "how the personal history of the individual will turn out," let alone the destiny of larger bodies such as the church.[50]

Still, the future has a place in theology because the discipline's proper subject—God's relationship to all that God creates—ranges from the beginning of God's creation to the promised fulfilment of God's kingdom, God's reign, in and through Jesus Christ (1 Cor 15:20-28; Col 1: 15-20; Rev 12:10). Even though the future is a core element of God's promises, acceptance of those promises does not eliminate for human

47. Gustavo Gutiérrez, *A Theology of Liberation*, trans. C. Inda and J. Eagleson (Maryknoll, NY: Orbis, 1988), 9.

48. Paul Murray, "Searching the Living Truth of the Church in Practice: On the Transformative Task of Systematic Ecclesiology," *Modern Theology* 30 (2014): 266.

49. Jon Sobrino, *The Principle of Mercy: Taking the Crucified People from the Cross*, ed. Robert Barr (Maryknoll, NY: Orbis, 1994), 39.

50. Karl Rahner, "The Quest for Approaches Leading to an Understanding of the Mystery of the God-Man Jesus," in *Theological Investigations*, vol. 13, trans. D. Bourke (New York: Crossroad, 1983), 200.

beings the obscurity that enfolds what is to come, be it the events of tomorrow or what "the end of time" might involve. Theology, born of faith, shares this nescience.

In exploring the relationship between God and humanity, theology operates in the space defined by God's self-revelation in human history—grace—and humanity's response to God—faith. Theology builds on the conviction that God's grace underpins and supports faith, that faith is not the accomplishment of sovereign humanity. As it reflects on faith, "the task of theology is not to prove that the truth of faith resides elsewhere than in the act, the attitude, the gesture, the confession of faith as conscious adherence to the revealed Mystery of God."[51] What theology can do, especially in its form as "fundamental theology," is to present faith as a reasonable exercise of human freedom, one conducive to the thriving of communities and individuals, and to the creative engagement of human beings with all of creation.[52] When theology fulfills this role constructively, it clarifies faith. Even more, it does so without reducing the relationship between the mystery of God and the mystery of faith to something bland and uninspiring.

In a way that parallels the ambit of fundamental theology, a specific task of ecclesiology is to elucidate the relationship of the ecclesial community to God's revelation. The next two chapters will address this theme at length, but it will be helpful to note a few points immediately. The history of revelation, which is as broad and ancient as God's creation of the physical world and God's covenants with Israel, is the church's bedrock. God's self-communication in Jesus Christ, "the way, the truth, and the life" (John 14:6), and the Holy Spirit, through whom God brings to realization "the things that are to come" (John 16:13), is the immediate source of the church, providing its orientation towards the yet-to-be-experienced fullness of God's reign.

This foundation requires ecclesiology, if it is to reflect the span of God's grace at work in the Christian community through the Holy Spirit,

51. Joseph Doré, "The Responsibility and Tasks of Theology in the Church and the World Today," *Irish Theological Quarterly* 62 (1996–97), 216.
52. For an overview of the goals and methods of fundamental theology, see Gerald O'Collins, *Rethinking Fundamental Theology: Towards a New Fundamental Theology* (Oxford: Oxford University Press, 2011).

to hold together the church's past, present, and future. It requires, too, that practitioners of theology be attentive to the world in which they live, alert to whatever may enhance or imperil the ecclesial community's representation of all that the fullness of life in Christ promises.

Even if refraining from predictions, all attempts by theologians to analyze and pronounce on the workings of grace in relation to the church could sound presumptuous. This suspicion has a legitimate basis in the history of theology, which is rife with instances of its practitioners co-opting God to be the guarantor and facilitator of their preferred frameworks for how God ought to work in the world, including in the church.

Adherence to a major tenet of the Christian worldview offers an antidote to any such potential misappropriation of God: "The reality of the living God is a mystery beyond all telling. The infinitely creating, redeeming, and indwelling Holy One is so far beyond the world and so deeply within the world as to be literally incomprehensible."[53] Such a God might seem a likely source of frustration, but the fact that God is "beatifically incomprehensible" highlights God as life-giving, as other than an exasperating puzzle, while also making clear that humanity will never be able to exert control over God or account for God exhaustively.[54] These limitations suggest that humility, which manifests itself in "patient, rational, and nonaggressive accounts of one's own theological position," as well as recognition of God's transcendence, is crucial if theology is to be true to its inspiration and purpose.[55]

The imperative that theologians not jeopardize God's transcendence exists in tension with God's willingness to be accessible to human beings, with all of their complexity, ambiguity, and sinfulness. Even when theologians pursue their craft as a response to grace, rather than a form of self-aggrandizement, theology "is always hard work, and its outcome fragmentary, tentative, and (often) quite technical in its quest

53. Elizabeth Johnson, *Quest for the Living God: Mapping Frontiers in the Theology of God* (New York: Continuum, 2008), 17.

54. Gabriel Daly, *Creation and Redemption* (Wilmington, DE: Michael Glazier, 1989), 26.

55. Sarah Coakley, "Theological Scholarship as Religious Vocation," *Christian Higher Education* 5 (2006): 66.

for appropriate imaginative and conceptual accuracy, not because God is complicated, but because we are—and so is the world in which we live. It is not possible without complexity to indicate, or point the way toward, the deep simplicity of the mystery of God."[56] This signals that theological insight into the church and its future will inevitably be partial and incomplete, features not unfitting to reflection on a community of faith that is itself unfinished.

Any expression of ecclesiology that situates the church within the graced reality that is humanity cannot ignore a truth that applies to the church no less than to any human enterprise: human freedom, while graced, can choose selfishness over generosity, narrowness over breadth of vision, and immediate gain over long-term benefit. In other words, human beings can choose against what serves their best interests. This realization cautions against "any idolatry towards unavoidably ambiguous human achievements."[57]

The freedom of humanity to respond positively to grace or to reject the conversion that grace facilitates ensures that "a point will never arise in the world's time at which the Church will achieve a total victory such as can be manifest in terms which this world can recognize."[58] This theological argument buttresses the facts of experience and the history of the church, each of which discourages the naïvely optimistic conviction that the church of the future will be flawless, universally admired in the wider world, or an invariably consistent force for good in the world. Hence, the church as project, one never beyond its need for tilling.

The shifting demands of discipleship, no less than the variety of voices in the church, and the challenges that theological reflection on the church must negotiate, all indicate that the church is tillable. In pointing to the reality of the church as not simply unfinished, but even "unfinishable," the factors that are the immediate catalysts for the church's dynamism suggest a larger truth about the church. This larger truth, one that draws on faith rather than deduction from empirical realities, is that the church exists in relationship to the mystery of God.

---

56. Nicholas Lash, *Easter in Ordinary: Reflections on Human Experience and the Knowledge of God* (Notre Dame, IN: University of Notre Dame Press, 1990), 291.

57. Gutiérrez, *Theology of Liberation*, 139.

58. Rahner, "Perspectives for the Future of the Church," 202.

The Mystery of God and the Mystery of the Church

Lumen Gentium, Vatican II's Dogmatic Constitution on the Church, the document that is the primary site for the council's ecclesiology, contends that the church, because of its relationship to God's trinitarian self-communication, is "the kingdom of Christ already present in mystery" (LG 3). The church, then, is to live in such a way that "it may reveal in the world, faithfully, although with shadows, the mystery of its Lord until, in the end, it shall be manifested in full light" (LG 8). This formula affirms the church's relationship to grace, the relationship that places the church beyond the grasp of any one-dimensional analyses, but also recognizes the "shadows" indicative of the need for tilling in the ecclesial community.

This section of the chapter considers the church from the perspective of its participation in the mystery of God. More particularly, it explores whether and how "mystery" might illuminate the church's life within history, including how the church might be in need of the conversion. Since "mystery" does not convey precise information about the church as a community in history, the section will discuss why the council chose the term, its advantages over theologies in vogue at the time, and the possibilities for the life of the church that the term enables. These elements of the analysis may alleviate fears that "mystery" is either tantamount to a blueprint or will issue in abstractions and idealized descriptions of the church that would negate any notion of the church as project.

"Mystery" pervades Vatican II's ecclesiology.[59] Not only does *Lumen Gentium* feature the term in the title of its first chapter, the concept flavors the document's presentation of the church. The text links the church to the "utterly gratuitous and mysterious design of [God's] wisdom and goodness" revealed in history (LG 2). In its portrayal of the church, *Lumen Gentium* identifies an intimate connection between the church and God's self-communication in history, which establishes the church as the recipient of the Spirit of Christ (LG 7). By prompting

---

59. For the importance of "mystery" to the council's ecclesiology, see Ormond Rush, *Vision of Vatican II*, 81–99; for a detailed study of the content of *Lumen Gentium*, see Richard Gaillardetz, *The Church in the Making: Lumen Gentium, Christus Dominus, Orientalium Ecclesiarum* (Mahwah, NJ: Paulist, 2006).

awareness that neither the past nor the present could have enacted comprehensively all that the Spirit enables for the church, "mystery" fosters an appreciation of the church's orientation to the future. This orientation both establishes and invigorates the expectation of further developments in the life of the church.

The use of mystery, since it "rules out the possibility of proceeding from clear and univocal concepts, or from definitions in the usual sense of the word," represents an opening to creativity in all aspects of ecclesial life, and so also in ecclesiology.[60] The vastness inherent in mystery is key to the church being other than an unchangeable reality. Doing justice to this vastness, and so to the council's stress on the connection between the Holy Spirit and the church, requires an ecclesiology with the capacity to depict the church in ways that accommodate graced fluidity, rather than non-negotiable boundaries.

From "Perfect Society" to "Mystery"

The fruitfulness of "mystery" as an ecclesiological theme becomes evident in the contrast that it offers to the description of the church as a "perfect society." In the centuries between the Reformation and Vatican II, representations of the church as a perfect society exerted a dominant influence on Catholic ecclesiology. This approach accentuated the divisions between Catholics and Protestants, as well as inculcating a sense that "the world" beyond the church was largely a domain empty of grace. Ironically in light of its profile and effects, "perfect society" appropriated "worldly" political philosophy, rather than having its source in explicitly theological sources.[61]

"Perfect," which functioned as a synonym for "complete" or "whole," announced that the church, through God's providence, lacked nothing that was necessary for its well-being. In the context of early modern Europe, this description was a declaration that the church was properly autonomous, competent and equipped to respond effectively to all issues that touched on its place in the world. The point of such a

60. Avery Dulles, *Models of the Church*, expanded ed. (New York: Image Books, 2002), 10.

61. For the origins of "perfect society," especially in the influential work of Robert Bellarmine (1542–1621), see Eric Jay, *The Church: Its Changing Image Through Twenty Centuries* (London: SPCK, 1997), 202–4.

declaration was to establish the church's ability to exist independently
of what political science would now refer to as "the state."[62] "Perfect,"
then, was not an assertion of superiority, but a tool for refuting the
claims of sundry emperors, kings, and other rulers who sought to
impose themselves on the church in order to reshape its priorities for
their own benefit.

"Society" located the church as an ordered body, one structured
from top to bottom. Although the notion of a variegated social order
was by no means a theme unique to the church, Catholic ecclesiology
understood that "society" applied to the church in ways distinct from
any other body. As the source of their society, Catholics identified Jesus
Christ himself, rather than the dynastic, military, or economic foundations common to the wider world. More specifically, official Catholic
teaching, as late as the first half of the twentieth century, interpreted
the society that Jesus formed as "essentially an *unequal* society, that
is, a society comprising two categories of persons, the Pastors and the
flock, . . . the one duty of the multitude is to allow themselves to be
led, and, like a docile flock, to follow the Pastors."[63] The taxonomy
of the church as an unequal society was consistent with the inspiration that European feudal structures, which divided their world into
strictly delineated groups, had provided for this interpretation of the
church's life.

Viewing their subject through the hierarchical lens, bishops and
theologians presented the church principally, often completely, from
the perspective of its organs of governance. This tendency flowered
as "hierarchology," which privileged the church's structures, especially
the authority of the pope and bishops, above all else.[64] Hierarchology diminished, to the point of near-extinction, any active role in the

62. For the implications of "perfect society," see Yves Congar, "Moving Towards a Pilgrim Church," in *Vatican II Revisited by Those Who Were There*, ed. Alberic Stacpoole
(Minneapolis: Winston Press, 1986), 131–35.

63. Pope Pius X, *Vehementer Nos*, On the French Law of Separation (1906), 8, in
The Papal Encyclicals 1903–1939, ed. Claudia Carlen (1906; repr., Wilmington, NC:
McGrath Publishing, 1981), 45–51; original emphasis.

64. Yves Congar, *Lay People in the Church*, trans. D. Attwater (Westminster, MD:
Newman Press, 1965), 45. For an illustration of "hierarchology," see the analysis of
the church by Adolphe Tanquerey in *A Manual of Dogmatic Theology*, vol. 1, trans. J.
Byrnes (original publication, in Latin, 1914; New York: Desclee, 1959), 95–140.

church's worship, ministry, and governance for the vast majority of the baptized. It served, too, to convey the impression that the church was a settled universe impervious to change.

Such was the influence of hierarchology that Catholics looked askance at the lack of authoritative structures they judged to be evident in the churches of the Reformation. This attitude reinforced for Catholics both a sense of the superiority of their community and appreciation for their ecclesial structures. Even immediately prior to Vatican II, official Catholic teaching classified the church's ordained leaders as the primary conduit for Jesus's guidance of the church: "Bishops, then, must be considered as the nobler members of the universal Church, for they are linked in an altogether special way to the divine Head of the whole Body and so are rightly called 'first among the members of the Lord.'"[65]

"Perfect society" might have enabled Catholics to feel more secure about their place in the world, but this confidence came at a cost. Representative of this cost were inclinations damaging not only to the church's engagement with history, but to possibilities for greater authenticity in the church itself. The first of these propensities was for members of the church to harbor a sense of preeminence in relation to the rest of the world.

"Perfect," as stated above, did not originally imply the church's flawlessness or superiority over other social groups, but the concept gradually acquired those connotations. This revised understanding became common among Catholics, especially because it could claim papal endorsement—"God indeed even made the Church a society far more perfect than any other. For the end for which the Church exists is much higher than the end of other societies as divine grace is above nature, as immortal blessings are above the transitory things of earth."[66] As Catholics, reflecting the accents of official teaching on the church's

---

65. Pope Pius XII, *Mystici Corporis Christi*, On the Mystical Body of Christ (1943), 42, in *The Christian Faith*, 7th rev. ed., ed. Jacques Dupuis (New York: Alba House, 2001), 326.

66. Pope Leo XIII, *Satis Cognitum*, On the Unity of the Church, 10, in *The Papal Encyclicals 1878–1903*, ed. Claudia Carlen (1896; repr., Wilmington, NC: McGrath Publishing, 1981), 387–404.

superiority, became less open to the world beyond the confines of the church, Catholic culture "became increasingly uniform, inward-looking, defensive, and protective of its members and its customs."[67] The stress on the church's perfection left the church ill-prepared and ill-equipped to respond to the emergence of modernity and its accompanying secularism, which saw no role for religious faith in society's new era of progress.[68]

Theologies defending the applicability to the church of a broad understanding of "perfect society" supported their conclusions by appealing to the specific intention of Jesus. This appeal relied heavily on deploying Jesus's commission to Peter (Matt 16:16-19) as a "proof-text" to justify the existing practice in the Catholic Church, especially in contrast to churches in the Reformed tradition.[69] The description of the church's institutions as a source of "indestructible steadfastness" characterized Catholic ecclesiology and influenced the ways of proceeding common to ecclesial authorities.[70] Self-criticism or calls for change were far less evident, especially as the repression that had followed "the modernist crisis" at the beginning of the twentieth century continued to exert a deleterious effect on the climate in which Catholic theologians worked.[71] These characteristics were prevalent even as the Catholic Church prepared for the Second Vatican Council.[72]

---

67. Gerald Arbuckle, *Catholic Identity or Identities?: Refounding Ministries in Chaotic Times* (Collegeville, MN: Liturgical Press, 2013), 37.

68. For an overview of the impact of modernity on the church, and the church's response, see James McEvoy, *Leaving Christendom for Good: Church-World Dialogue in a Secular Age* (Lanham, MD: Lexington Books, 2014), 3–49.

69. For a brief overview of the use of biblical "proof-texts" as support for the church's doctrine, see Raymond Collins, "Bible and Doctrine," in *The HarperCollins Encyclopedia of Catholicism*, ed. Richard McBrien (San Francisco: HarperCollins, 1995), 170–71.

70. Tanquerey, *Manual of Dogmatic Theology*, 133.

71. For an overview of the Modernist crisis, see Marvin O'Connell, *Critics on Trial: An Introduction to the Catholic Modernist Crisis* (Washington, DC: Catholic University of America Press, 1995).

72. For an overview of Catholic ecclesiology in the period before Vatican II, see Ormond Rush, "Roman Catholic Ecclesiology from the Council of Trent to Vatican II and Beyond," in *The Oxford Handbook of Ecclesiology*, ed. Paul Avis (Oxford: Oxford University Press, 2018), 263–92 and Michael Himes, "The Development of Ecclesiology:

Another damaging tendency related to "perfect society" was the transposition onto the church of a model of communal life in which reference to hierarchy was the default principle for determining all aspects of communal life. The prominence of hierarchology in Catholic catechesis, worldview, and ecclesial practice increased exponentially after Vatican I's definition of papal infallibility. As is evident in the excerpts from the papal documents already cited, the stress on hierarchy resulted in a thick line of demarcation within the church between ordained members and the broad body of the baptized.

Although hierarchology focused primarily on bishops, the perceived elevation of all clerics had significant implications for every level of the church's life. The prevailing prominence of clerics influenced the discipline and curriculum of seminaries, which largely sequestered candidates from the everyday life of the church in which they were to minister.[73] Seminary formation stressed priestly holiness for the sake of the church's mission to save souls in a corrupt world—"And if ever there was a century in the history of the Church that needed saintly priests, it is our twentieth. The world is crumbling at our feet."[74] Within this framework, the understanding of holiness tended to prize willpower and individual effort; the role of grace and the benefits of communal support were less evident. Holy priests could fulfil their unique role within the church's perfect society, and priestly holiness required a discipline that set priests above the rest of the baptized faithful, a discipline that obedience to seminary authorities helped to inculcate—"priestly sanctity depends in large measure on seminary formation, which in turn is exactly proportionate to the perfection with which the rule is kept."[75]

An inevitable corollary of the hierarchical and clerical emphasis was a "negative approach to describing the laity," a perception that "usually resulted in a division between the church and the world, the sacred and the profane. Spiritual things belonged to the clergy and religious while worldly

---

Modernity to the Twentieth Century," in *The Gift of the Church: A Textbook on Ecclesiology*, ed. Peter Phan (Collegeville, MN: Michael Glazier, 2000), 45–67.

73. For an overview of priestly formation in this period, see Kenan Osborne, "Priestly Formation," in *From Trent to Vatican II: Historical and Theological Investigations*, ed. Raymond Bulman and Frederick Parrella (New York: Oxford University Press, 2006), 117–35.

74. Thomas Dubay, *The Seminary Rule* (Cork, Ireland: Mercier Press, 1953), 24.

75. Ibid., 24.

or profane things pertained to the laity. The laity therefore had no role, responsibility, or power in the inner life of the church."[76] The Reformers had rejected the sacramental value of ordination, but ordination continued to influence an individual's standing in the Catholic community, even though each baptized person shared the same call to discipleship.

Just as it distanced the church from the world, contributed to the divisions of the church into active and passive members, and exacerbated the alienation of Catholics from Protestants, much of the ecclesiology characteristic of the decades prior to Vatican II generally displayed scant interest in either the church's eschatological orientation or the mission of the Holy Spirit. Indeed, Catholic ecclesiologies of the period reduced the Spirit's role in the church to little more than the maintenance of what Jesus had directly bequeathed to his followers.[77] Lacking in this perception was any acknowledgment of the Spirit as a source of innovation, as well as the link between the Spirit and eschatology.

A renewed appreciation of the Spirit's role in the church, as well as a movement away from hierarchology and the perfect society, were elements of a theological realignment that preceded—not without encountering major obstacles—Vatican II.[78] This realignment, the *ressourcement* that became central to the life of the church through the processes and documents of the council, involved Catholic engagement with Scripture, patristic theology, and theologies of liturgy that predated the disputes of the Reformation era.[79]

---

76. Aurelie Hagstrom, *The Emerging Laity: Vocation, Mission, and Spirituality* (Mahwah, NJ: Paulist, 2010), 22–23.

77. For discussion of the impoverished status of the Holy Spirit in Catholic ecclesiology before Vatican II, see Richard Gaillardetz and Catherine Clifford, *Keys to the Council: Unlocking the Teaching of Vatican II* (Collegeville, MN: Liturgical Press, 2012), 57–58; Elizabeth Johnson, *Abounding in Kindness: Writings for the People of God* (Maryknoll, NY: Orbis, 2015), 229–31; and Michael Fahey, "Church," in *Systematic Theology: Roman Catholic Perspectives*, 2nd ed., ed. Francis Schüssler Fiorenza and John Galvin (Minneapolis: Fortress, 2011), 338–39.

78. See Gabriel Flynn, "Theological Renewal in the First Half of the Twentieth Century," in *The Cambridge Companion to Vatican II*, ed. Richard Gaillardetz (Cambridge: Cambridge University Press, 2020), 19–40.

79. For a detailed review of the history, sources, figures, controversies, and contributions of *ressourcement*, see *Ressourcement: A Movement for Renewal in Twentieth-Century Catholic Theology*, ed. Gabriel Flynn and Paul Murray (Oxford: Oxford University Press, 2012).

The recovery of the richness of the church's theological and faith tradition freed Catholic theology from many of the ideological constraints and polemic emphases representative of the centuries that followed the Council of Trent. Where the manuals presented the church's faith in ways divorced from the Bible, from history, from openness to other Christians, and certainly from any questions indicative of the need for ongoing interpretation, the accents of the *ressourcement* moved in the opposite direction.[80] One critical consequence of the expanded Catholic vision for theology that emerged because of the *ressourcement* was the possibility for ecumenical convergence, particularly in relation to the status and interpretation of Scripture and tradition.[81] The retrieval of "mystery" as a category in ecclesiology was itself a consequence of the *ressourcement*.[82]

In their different ways, the theological shifts that *ressourcement* enabled for ecclesiology were subsets of a correspondingly significant shift in the theology of revelation. Where approaches to revelation had long adopted a "propositional" approach—God's revelation of truths about God—they moved toward a more "personalist" model—God's self-communication in human history.[83] The latter interpretation, as the next two chapters will detail, was conducive to highlighting the dynamism of faith, and so of the church.

The impact of the broader perspective on God's self-revelation transformed Christology before affecting ecclesiology. Until the middle years of the twentieth century, much Catholic Christology, often in reaction against Protestant approaches that appeared to threaten either or both

80. For a profile of the "manualist" approach in pre-conciliar Catholic theology, see Gerald O'Collins, "*Ressourcement* and Vatican II," in *Ressourcement: A Movement for Renewal in Twentieth-Century Catholic Theology*, ed. Gabriel Flynn and Paul Murray (Oxford: Oxford University Press, 2012), 374–77 and "Manualistic Theology," in *Dictionary of Fundamental Theology*, ed. René Latourelle and Rino Fisichella (New York: Herder and Herder, 2000), 1102–5.

81. For the ecumenical convergence on "Scripture and tradition" immediately prior to Vatican II, see Gerald O'Collins, *Tradition: Understanding Christian Tradition* (Oxford: Oxford University Press, 2018), 1–34.

82. For the influence that "mystery" had on theologies of the church leading to Vatican II, see Gaillardetz and Clifford, *Keys to the Council*, 47–52.

83. For a description of the distinction between the two theologies of revelation, see Gerald O'Collins, *Rethinking Fundamental Theology: Towards a New Fundamental Theology* (Oxford: Oxford University Press, 2011), 66.

the humanity and divinity of Jesus, regarded Jesus Christ exclusively through the lens of dogmatic beliefs. This emphasis resulted in what Maurice Blondel (1861–1949) termed "extrinsicism," the propensity to devalue history by regarding it as merely a background for the church's dogmatic convictions about God's revelation in Jesus Christ.[84]

In relation to Christology, Blondel argued that extrinsicism ignored both the life of Jesus Christ and "the tradition of devotion and adoration to Christ."[85] The forms of Christology that Blondel challenged separated the dogmatic definitions of the councils of Nicaea (325) and Chalcedon (451) from their biblical sources, from the human reality of Jesus, and from the church's liturgy and discipleship. As a result, Catholic Christology lacked, suggests Elizabeth Johnson, "a deeper appreciation of the genuine humanity of the Word made flesh, and of the dignity and value of every human being."[86] The church's creedal formulae that specified the relationship between humanity and divinity in Jesus became more identifiable as touchstones of orthodoxy, rather than as the heart of the church's spirituality and worship.

From the 1950s, Catholic theologians began to retrieve a broader perspective on Jesus Christ. This retrieval was itself a response to the renewal of biblical and historical studies, but also to the perspectives on human identity that derived from modern philosophy and psychology. From that time onward, the guiding light in the study of Jesus Christ became, Johnson stresses, "not his human nature, divine nature, and one hypostasis, but his life's story: What was he like as a real person in history? What did he stand for? How did he make such an impact? Why did the authorities consider him dangerous? Why was he crucified?"[87] This questioning was not in opposition to the teaching of the councils, but connected the church's doctrine to its bedrock: the life of Jesus, the biblical witness, and the faith, worship, and discipleship of believers.

---

84. Maurice Blondel, "History and Dogma," in *The Letter on Apologetics* and *History and Dogma*, trans. A. Dru and I. Trethowan (1904; repr., New York: Holt, Rinehart and Winston, 1964), 227–30.

85. Ibid., 246–47; on faith and worship as means to understand and appropriate the full reality of Jesus, see Francis Schüssler Fiorenza, "The Jesus of Piety and the Historical Jesus," *CTSA Proceedings* 49 (1994): 90–99.

86. Elizabeth Johnson, *Consider Jesus: Waves of Renewal in Christology* (New York: Crossroad, 1992), 49.

87. Ibid., 49.

This approach recovered the lived faith of the Christian community as a theological source, thereby ending the eclipse of this faith by the concentration on Jesus's ontological status. As Edward Schillebeeckx notes, "Without Jesus' human career the whole of Christology becomes an ideological superstructure. Without 'human meaning' in the life of Jesus, all religious meaning in his life becomes incredible. Only the human meaning of a historical process can become the material of 'supernatural' or religious meaning of revelation."[88] Access to "the human meaning" of Jesus comes through the gospels, which are central to the faith and worship of the Christian community.

The developments in biblical studies, in Christology, and in an appreciation of liturgical history that reached back beyond the Reformation, as well as the recognition of the need for an *aggiornamento*—a new awareness of culture and the church's manner of engaging with the world—constituted the theological groundwork for the transformation of ecclesiology at the Second Vatican Council.[89] Vatican II gave birth to "a new image" of the church, an outcome reflective of the fact that it was "a Council in which all the themes discussed were ecclesiological ones; which concentrated upon ecclesiology as no previous Council had ever done."[90] The influence of the council on ecclesiology supports the contention that Vatican II marks a "caesura" in the self-understanding and practice of the church, expressing a movement away from emphases that had been common not simply in the era of hierarchology and perfect society, but since the conversion of Constantine in the fourth century.[91]

Catholic ecclesiology acquired a new vitality in the wake of the council.[92] This vitality owes much to the fact that "in a certain sense,

88. Edward Schillebeeckx, *Church: The Human Story of God*, trans. J. Bowden (New York: Crossroad, 1990), 8; see also Karl Rahner, "Remarks on the Importance of the History of Jesus for Catholic Dogmatics," in *Theological Investigations*, vol. 13, trans. D. Bourke (New York: Crossroad, 1983), 201–12.

89. For the importance of *ressourcement* and *aggiornamento* to the work of the council, see Rush, *Vision of Vatican II*, 17–21.

90. Karl Rahner, "The New Image of the Church," in *Theological Investigations*, vol. 10, trans. D. Bourke (New York: Seabury, 1973), 3–4.

91. Rahner, "Basic Theological Interpretation of the Second Vatican Council," 83–84.

92. For the impact of the council on ecclesiology, see Richard Gaillardetz, *An Unfinished Council: Vatican II, Pope Francis, and the Renewal of Catholicism* (Collegeville,

the Council has made the Spirit newly 'present' in our difficult age."[93] Integral to this vitality is the understanding of the church as sharing, through Christ and the Holy Spirit, in the mystery of God, a formulation that holds out the likelihood of a more dynamic church than "perfect society" facilitated.

The priority that Vatican II attributes to the church's mystery was new in relation to the then-popular emphases of Catholic ecclesiology, but not new in absolute terms. The Letter to the Ephesians identifies the relationship of a wife and husband as a "great mystery" (Eph 5:32) comparable to the relationship between Christ and the church. Neither that text nor any other of the New Testament isolates "the mystery of the church" as a topic for discussion, but the mystery of the church is recognizable in the ecclesiologies evident in the New Testament, ecclesiologies that testify to the manifold dimensions of the ecclesial community.

It may seem, then, that the church's sharing in the mystery of God must preclude all efforts to portray the church more precisely. Far from this being so, the connection between grace and the human realities of the church suggests that metaphors and images for the church, to return to a topic discussed earlier in this chapter, are not merely helpful; they are necessary. The recourse to images is not a new phenomenon, but as old as descriptions of the church as the body of Christ (Rom 12:4-5) and the temple of God in which the Spirit dwells (1 Cor 3:16). There is certainly a need to differentiate images for the church from "blueprints," and to ensure that the images are not elitist, discriminatory, or anachronistic. Similarly, images useful for illuminating the

MN: Michael Glazier, 2015); Richard Lennan, "A Continuing Pilgrimage: Ecclesiology Since Vatican II," *Australasian Catholic Record* 91 (2014): 21–48; and Susan Wood, "Continuity and Development in Roman Catholic Ecclesiology," *Ecclesiology* 7 (2011): 147–72.

93. Pope John Paul II, *Dominum et Vivificantem*, 26. On Vatican II's understanding of the Holy Spirit, see Richard Lennan and Nancy Pineda-Madrid, "The Holy Spirit and the Pilgrimage of Faith," in Richard Lennan and Nancy Pineda-Madrid, eds., *The Holy Spirit: Setting the World on Fire* (Mahwah, NJ: Paulist, 2017), 44–49 and Walter Kasper, "The Renewal of Pneumatology in Contemporary Catholic Life and Theology: Towards a Rapprochement between East and West," in *That They May All Be One: The Call to Unity* (New York: Burns and Oates, 2004), 96–121.

church's complexity will eschew any claims to express comprehensively that complexity. These constraints, however, do not cancel the legitimacy of all images.

Since no single image for the church suffices, a multitude of images may be desirable. For this reason perhaps, the theologies of the New Testament "present the Church as a community of disciples, the re-established Israel, the Church of God, the body of Christ, the bride of Christ, the temple of God, and the pilgrim People of God."[94] The multiplicity of images and metaphors evident in the New Testament offers unambiguous evidence that no single ecclesiology "provides the complete picture of the transcendent whole."[95]

The authors of the New Testament depict the church as "an organic growth in response to practical problems and questions of principle arising, rather than an imposed plan."[96] The variety of ecclesiologies in the New Testament mirrors the range of experiences characteristic of the first Christian communities: "There were numerous ways of describing early communities and numerous experiences of developing within and alongside Judaism. What we can tell of one community is not necessarily true of all communities."[97] Even as it includes a variety of ecclesiologies, the New Testament testifies unequivocally to the fundamental, Spirit-guided unity of the church.[98]

94. Frank Matera, "Theologies of the Church in the New Testament," in *The Gift of the Church: A Textbook on Ecclesiology*, ed. Peter Phan (Collegeville, MN: Michael Glazier, 2000), 19–20; see also Loveday Alexander, "The Church in the Synoptic Gospels and the Acts of the Apostles," in *The Oxford Handbook of Ecclesiology*, ed. Paul Avis (Oxford: Oxford University Press, 2018), 55–97, and John Harrison and James Dvorak, eds., *The New Testament Church: The Challenges of Developing Ecclesiologies* (Eugene, OR: Pickwick Publications, 2012).

95. Raymond Collins, *The Many Faces of the Church: A Study in New Testament Ecclesiology* (New York: Herder and Herder, 2003), 149.

96. G. R. Evans, "The Early Christian Centuries," in *The Routledge Companion to the Christian Church*, ed. Gerard Mannion and Lewis Mudge (London: Routledge, 2008), 35.

97. Paula Gooder, "In Search of the Early 'Church,'" in *The Routledge Companion to the Christian Church*, ed. Gerard Mannion and Lewis Mudge (London: Routledge, 2008), 24.

98. For an overview of the New Testament's presentations of the Spirit, see James Coriden, *The Holy Spirit and an Evolving Church* (Maryknoll, NY: Orbis, 2017), 9–65.

In *Lumen Gentium,* the council follows the lead of the New Testament by utilizing a host of images from Scripture—"sheepfold," "flock," "cultivated field," "vineyard," "building," "the holy temple," "holy city," and "the new Jerusalem" (LG 6)—to depict the relationship between the church and the God revealed in Jesus Christ and the Holy Spirit. Beyond its collection of domestic and religious images, *Lumen Gentium* consistently utilizes "people of God" as a synonym for the church.[99] In the council's treatment, "people of God" indicates that the church is both more than its structures, as significant as those structures might be for the unity and mission of the church, and not reducible to the priorities and activities of a single group within it or the emphases evident at any one moment of the church's life.[100] What "people of God" summarizes is "the loving election by God, his mercy, his guidance and his immutable faithfulness. Yet, ultimately it remains open for a greater and more comprehensive fulfilment," features consistent with the church sharing in the mystery of God.[101]

The presence of the Holy Spirit at the heart of every community makes the church the one people of God, without reducing it to uniformity or stasis. In explicitly theological terms, diverse communities reveal the church's catholicity, its unity-in-difference. Within the framework of catholicity, a theme that will feature later in this book, the unity of the whole church is compatible with the specificity of local communities. As Congar notes, apropos of the church's catholicity, "Through the mission and gift of the Spirit, the church was born universally by being born manifold and particular."[102] The paradoxical union of "manifold and particular," where neither epithet is alone sufficient to summarize the church, but neither subordinates the other, is a further affirmation of the church's participation in the mystery of God.

"Mystery" defeats all efforts at definition. It is more in tune with the expanse of an ocean than the limits of an island in the middle of the

---

99. "People of God" is the title of chapter 2 of *Lumen Gentium.*

100. For the council's use of "people of God," see Wood, "Continuity and Development in Roman Catholic Ecclesiology," 161–63.

101. Walter Kasper, *The Catholic Church: Nature, Reality and Mission,* trans. T. Hoebel (London: Bloomsbury, 2015), 121.

102. Yves Congar, *I Believe in the Holy Spirit,* vol. 2, trans. D. Smith (New York: Seabury, 1983), 26.

ocean. This chapter has made the argument, counterintuitive though it might seem to be, that the transcendence of "mystery" contributes positively to thinking about the church's presence in history. It does so by thwarting efforts to restrict the church to a single model that determines all aspects of this presence or to a single period of ecclesiastical history, thereby neglecting the church's eschatological orientation. *Lumen Gentium*, through the manifold images that it applies to the church, gestures toward the transcendence proper to "mystery." This transcendence indicates not what is irrational, but what exceeds comprehension, what will always elude every endeavor to overcome complexity.

The sharp lines of order and authority inherent in "perfect society" left little room for questions about the church, for self-critical reflection, or for movement responsive to the presence of grace in "the world." The limitlessness of "mystery," the limitlessness that witnesses to the trinitarian God at the heart of the church, can be a catalyst for creativity in ecclesiology and in the relationships between the ecclesial community and the societies of which it is a part. It functions, too, as a pointer toward the future fulfillment of the church, rather than canonizing either the church's past or present as the ultimate triumph of grace.

At the same time, connecting the church to the mystery of God calls for elaboration on what this connection means for the life of the church, which is an initiative of grace but not itself divine. One key resource that Vatican II provides for addressing this topic is the notion of "sacrament," a term with an intimate linguistic bond to "mystery."[103] Chapter 2 will explore the church's sacramentality as part of further developing the relationship between grace and humanity in the context of the church. It is this relationship that unfailingly identifies the church as tillable, and as a project.

---

103. For the linguistic link between "mystery" and "sacrament," see Bernard Cooke, *Sacraments and Sacramentality*, rev. ed. (New London, CT: Twenty Third Publications, 2009), 7.

2

Symbolizing Grace

Freedom is essential for the flourishing of individual and communal relationships. Without freedom, the self-sacrifice that all relationships require becomes an imposition rather than a gift. The absence of freedom, then, is a reliable marker of relationships in peril. So significant is freedom, it is the choices of free citizens, rather than the weight of laws and institutions, that exert a determining influence on the welfare of societies. Laws delineate acceptable from unacceptable actions, institutions endorse and guide practices likely to serve social stability, but the efficacy of these instruments depends on the decisions of free citizens to support them through their attitudes and actions. Absent this free assent, laws and institutions may even yield their place to the coercion that is the language of regimes dedicated to self-interest rather than the common good.

Communities of free citizens rarely display the orderliness of Henry Ford's mechanized system or the illusory calm that dictatorships enforce, but this does not doom them to fragmentation into a host of competing interests. A shared commitment to self-restraint and solidarity over selfishness and individualism can build social harmony, redress historical failings, moderate the disparities between "haves" and "have-nots," and resolve tensions between communal and individual rights—"Charity, with its impulse to universality, is capable of building a new world."[1] Honesty, generosity, and compassion, all of which prosper in freedom, can fashion just and peaceful societies that further the common good. A key element of this commitment is an appreciation of the value of others.

The recognition that nobody "can fully know themselves apart from an encounter with other persons" (FT 87) can foster an acknowledgment of the uniqueness of each person, a readiness to support whatever is conducive to their well-being, and respectful engagement with the whole of creation. These stances all embody the constructive use of freedom that distinguishes healthy from dysfunctional societies. From a theological perspective, such stances are also indicative of the presence of grace, the gift of the trinitarian God. God's free self-donation to humanity flowers in life-giving and life-sustaining relationships that animate the description of humanity as being "the image of God" (Gen 1:27). Since these relationships require and reflect freedom, there is an inextricable link between grace and human freedom.

As God's free gift, grace is unconditional. It does not, then, limit the exercise of human freedom to those choices conducive to outcomes that God desires. This means that even the destructive potential of human sinfulness gives paradoxical witness to the freedom that grace bestows. Although grace does not preserve the Christian community from its own inconsistency and faithlessness, grace is the ongoing stimulus for the authenticity of the church. The ecclesial community's response to grace can be more or less thoroughgoing at each moment of its history and in every circumstance, affirming that no expression of the church's life is beyond the possibility of, and need for, conversion. In all these ways, and more besides, grace is intrinsic to the tilling of the ecclesial community.

This book's analysis of the church pivots around the relationship between grace and human freedom. This relationship, whose dynamics distinguish the church from all that is disembodied, frozen in place, divorced from history and culture, subject to immutable repetitions, or hostile to human wisdom, is central to the life of the church. The

1. Pope Francis, *Fratelli Tutti* (FT), On Fraternity and Social Friendship (2020), 183, http://www.vatican.va/content/francesco/en/encyclicals/documents/papa-francesco_20201003_enciclica-fratelli-tutti.html.

contours of the relationship between grace and human freedom indicate why no epoch in the church's history clones a predecessor, no two Catholic communities in the same era are identical, and no vision of the church's future can guarantee its own ability to forecast accurately all that lies ahead for the church—as the analysis of "tradition" and "reception" in later chapters of this book will substantiate. In fact, the concentration on grace champions openness in the church's planning to the unknowable "day and hour" (Matt 24:36) that identify the finality of the future as the province of God alone.

The identification of grace as the foundation of the church does more than simply call to mind events at the dawn of the Christian community, as the introduction emphasized. Grace, as the church's permanent and living foundation, draws the ecclesial community into an ongoing relationship with the whole of God's creation. Even more, grace, which bestows on human beings "the capacity for the eternal," orients the church to the future, whose specifics remain inscrutable.[2] The eschatological orientation and the graced freedom of all who form the ecclesial community reinforce the church's unfinished state, which, to echo the primary theme of chapter 1, highlights that the church is tillable, that it is a project.

The present chapter homes in on a further essential aspect of the relationship between grace and humanity in the context of the church: the existence of the church as symbol or sacrament of God's reign, a description that Vatican II employs in *Lumen Gentium*.[3] In so doing, the three-pronged thesis of the chapter is that the theology of sacramentality provides a mechanism that gives specificity to the church's place in God's self-revelation in grace, establishes broad parameters for the church's engagement with the world beyond its boundaries, and furnishes a motive for the church's ongoing conversion. In these ways, the sacramental emphasis, including the anthropological elements that

2. Karl Rahner, "Theology of Freedom," in *Theological Investigations*, vol. 6, trans. K-H. Kruger and B. Kruger (New York: Crossroad, 1982), 186.

3. For the council's use of the language of "sacrament" in relation to the church, see, for example, *Lumen Gentium*, Dogmatic Constitution on the Church (1964), 1, 9, and 48—the last of which refers to the church as "the universal sacrament of salvation," a description that will feature later in this book.

are a core constituent of sacramentality, elucidates multiple factors relevant to "tilling the church."

To provide a platform for its exposition of the church's sacramentality, the chapter traverses the rich and multilayered landscape of the relationship between grace and humanity. To establish the theological anthropology on which the chapter depends, the first section details the interweaving of grace and human freedom. In doing so, the section builds on a framework from the theology of Karl Rahner (1904–84), in whose writings the gift of grace is key to understanding human existence.

Grace and Graced Human Freedom

In identifying God as "the liberating freedom of our freedom," an analysis of the relationship between grace and human freedom furthers the realization that there is not—cannot be—a divine blueprint that governs every aspect of the life of the church independently of human action.[4] No less critically, detailing the relationship between grace and human freedom provides a theological underpinning for a truth of experience about the church: the church is not a work of divine micromanaging that eliminates the ecclesial community's complexity.

The well-being of the ecclesial community, including the fruitfulness of its mission, is not separable from human action, action that is itself not separable from a free response to grace. An appreciation of these elements contributes to clarifying what the affirmation of the church's sacramentality includes, but also and no less importantly, what it excludes. As part of its case for insisting that both grace and freedom are integral to the life of the church, this section will take the broadest possible perspective on the history of grace in the world: beginning with God's creative action, the record of which forms the opening chapters of the book of Genesis.

As Genesis presents it, God's "Let there be . . ." (Gen 1:3) initiates life. This imperative enables the "formless void" (Gen 1:2) to become the earth teeming with living things, all of which God regards as "very good" (Gen 1:31). Far from announcing a discrete moment unrelated

---

4. Karl Rahner, "Freedom in the Church," in *Theological Investigations*, vol. 2, trans. K-H. Kruger (New York: Crossroad, 1990), 94.

to all that follows, "In the beginning" (Gen 1:1), the initial phrase in the first account of creation, captures the start of an enduring relationship between God and God's creation. The chronicle in Genesis witnesses to the revelation of God as life-giver, while also conveying the implicit promise that God will support all that exists. In the context of the relationship with creation, God "is not merely the one who launched life, but the one who at every moment holds it in existence."[5] What God commences, God continues.

Rahner employs the philosophical category "causality" to elucidate God's relationship to creation. He describes God as the "quasi-formal cause" of creation.[6] The significance of this recondite term becomes apparent in explicating the distinction between "formal causality" and "efficient causality," the latter of which would be the type of causality more likely to feature in reference to processes of production.

In assembling the components of a car, robots are the efficient cause of the vehicle; by welding panels together and installing engines, robots make cars. Robots are essential instruments in the manufacturing process, but not creative forces who take initiative in so doing; the algorithm that programs their movement dictates their activity. The designers and engineers of the vehicles, who might never labor on the factory floor, can claim the designation of "formal cause" of all that emerges from the assembly line. It is their ingenuity that "creates" the cars. Designers and engineers imagine the appearance and perfor-mance of the vehicles, calculate the specification for the car's engine, take account of all safety and environmental considerations, plan all that the construction of the vehicle will involve, and even develop the assembly line and the robots that serve it. For these reasons, it is valid to describe the vehicles emerging from manufacturing plants as the self-expression, the "form," of their designers and engineers. The robots cannot claim this designation.

5. John R. Sachs, *The Christian Vision of Humanity: Basic Christian Anthropology* (Collegeville, MN: Michael Glazier, 1991), 14; see also Elizabeth Johnson, *Quest for the Living God: Mapping Frontiers in the Theology of God* (New York: Continuum, 2008), 188–91.

6. Karl Rahner, "Some Implications of the Scholastic Concept of Uncreated Grace," in *Theological Investigations*, vol. 1, trans. C. Ernst (New York: Crossroad, 1982), 329–33.

"Let there be . . ." brings God into focus as creator, the formal cause of all living things. In the first narrative of creation that Genesis records, the plants and animals that populate the panoply of life alongside "humankind" come into existence on different "days," but share the one source, whose imprint they bear (Gen 1:1-31). All living things, then, "the birds of the air [and] the lilies of the field" (Matt 6:26-28), not simply human beings, are God's self-expression. All creatures "are telling the glory of God" (Ps 19:1), while the differences between them reflect the boundlessness of God's life-giving initiative. For this reason, Pope Francis in *Laudato Si'* (LS) advocates for "creation" over "nature" as the more appropriate term to designate the physical universe within the understanding of faith. The pope argues that life "can be understood only as a gift from the outstretched hand of the Father of all and as a reality illuminated by the love which calls us together into universal communion."[7] Thus, creation speaks of the creator.

Rahner's use of "quasi-" to modify God's "formal causality" accentuates the uniqueness of God's creative act, especially in comparison to human actions. Human beings are able to exercise formal causality, which they do regularly in producing works of art, in shaping social structures, and even in devising systems for industrial manufacturing. Yet, composing a novel or sonata, preparing a unique dessert, or even designing a city's power grid or water system all typically involve the drawing of plans, the use of various raw materials and tools, the cooperation of others, and multiple attempts to align the finished product with its originating vision. God, however, requires only "Let there be . . .": God's desire to give life is both sufficient and efficacious in bringing about life. God's creativity transcends the instruments proper to efficient causality, whether exercised by human beings or robots.

A further aspect of God's formal causality that merits "quasi-" in comparison to human creativity is that God's relationship to creation is ongoing. A work of art embodies the genius and instinct of its author—a theme to which chapter 6 will return—but the completed work stands on its own, having no further need of the artist. Unlike the

---

7. Pope Francis, *Laudato Si'*, On Care for Our Common Home (2015), 76, http://www.vatican.va/content/francesco/en/encyclicals/documents/papa-francesco_20150524_enciclica-laudato-si.html.

composer of music, or the divine watchmaker in deist interpretations of the universe, God does not furnish creation with the wherewithal to continue on its own and then disengage from any involvement. God is forever indispensable to creation; God's creatures always draw life from God. Rahner coins "creatureliness" (*die Kreatürlichkeit*) to capture the enduring dependence of creatures on God. Creatureliness is "an ongoing and always actual process which for every existent is taking place now just as much as at an earlier point in time."[8] The tillable nature of the church, the potential of the ecclesial community to be more faithful to grace, expresses this same reality as the church never matures beyond its need for grace.

Human beings are, permanently, creatures of God, but this does not annul or restrict their freedom, even in relation to God. Paradoxically, the quality of God's relationship to humanity, Rahner stresses, makes plain that God "is not the one who kills so that [God] can live. God is not 'the truly real' which like a vampire draws to himself and so to speak sucks out the proper reality of things different from himself; God is not the *esse omnium*. The nearer one comes to God, the more real one becomes; the more God grows in and before one, the more independent one becomes oneself."[9] Rahner sets creation within God's desire for communion with all living things: "Nature, therefore, is in the real order willed from the outset for the sake of 'grace' and 'creation' for the sake of the covenant of personal love."[10]

The self-communicating God draws close to human beings in an act of self-emptying through which God "realizes our freedom in its (very) freedom."[11] Humanity's enduring dependence on God expands rather than cancels human freedom; it even gives human freedom the capacity to act in ways analogous to God's own life-giving creativity. This capacity applies within the church no less than in any other sphere

8. Karl Rahner, *Foundations of Christian Faith: An Introduction to the Idea of Christianity*, trans. W. Dych (New York: Seabury, 1978), 77.

9. Karl Rahner, "The Eternal Significance of the Humanity of Jesus for Our Relationship with God," in *Theological Investigations*, vol. 3, trans. K-H. Kruger and B. Kruger (New York: Crossroad, 1982), 40.

10. Karl Rahner, "Immanent and Transcendent Consummation of the World," in *Theological Investigations*, vol.10, trans. D. Bourke (New York: Seabury, 1973), 280–81.

11. Rahner, "Freedom in the Church," 94; parentheses in original text.

of human action. It is especially important for the church's mission to reflect God's love in the world, as chapter 4 will illustrate.

Rahner's exposition of the relationship between creatureliness and freedom has resonances in both ancient and contemporary sources in the Christian tradition. The ancient voice is that of St Augustine (354–430), who presents the nexus between the passionate love of God for creation and human freedom as a paradox: "Do not think that you are drawn against your will, for the soul too can be drawn, and that by love . . . I maintain that we are drawn not only willingly but with delight."[12] This "delight," the appreciation of what the gift of relationship with God offers humanity, is an effect of surrendering to the experience of creatureliness and to the dependence on God that characterizes it.

The contemporary voice affirming created reality as a gift of freedom is that of Pope Francis. In *Laudato Si'*, he showcases God's magnanimity in creation, highlighting it as an act of God's love, rather than as an exercise in God's pursuit of self-aggrandizement or an effort to construct a network of demeaning obligation: "The universe did not emerge as the result of arbitrary omnipotence, a show of force or a desire for self-assertion. Creation is of the order of love. God's love is the fundamental moving force in all created things" (LS 77). The God who creates in love is the source of "the immense dignity of each person" (LS 65). This dignity, no less than the freedom intrinsic to it, is yet another effect of God's quasi-formal causality: human beings, as noted above, bear God's own "image" (Gen 1:27), a phrase that offers a poetic framing of what Rahner's more philosophical formulation conveys.

Four Aspects of Humanity's Created Freedom

The interpretation of creation as God's free and loving self-expression has four major implications for an understanding of human freedom, implications that resonate in the life of the church. First, the orientation of this freedom, derived as it is from God, is to a future fulfillment in God. The present exercise of free human choices, and the behav-

---

12. St. Augustine, "On the Gospel of John," tractate 26, in *Tractates on the Gospel of John 11-27*, trans. J. Rettig (Washington, DC: Catholic University of America Press, 1988), 262.

ior that flows from them, give shape to humanity's immediate future, but finite human beings cannot finalize God's creation. As creatures, human beings live "on the border between God and the world, time and eternity."[13] The ecclesial community's faithful response to God's initiative is incompatible with the complacency, even hubris, that resists conversion. This resistance can manifest itself as an effort to absolutize the past or present, and so reject possibilities for the future. Equally, resistance to conversion can be evident in either the conviction that what emerges from today's planning for the future will be unsurpassable or forms of escapism that deny to the future any connection to the past and present.

Second, human freedom involves far more than the absence of restraint or the opportunity to choose between circumscribed options.[14] As a gift of God's creative freedom, human freedom is essentially the capacity to "dispose" of oneself, to be responsible for one's own decisions, irrespective of one's physical setting.[15] Freedom, then, "never occurs merely as an objective exercise, as a choice 'between' individual objects, but as the self-achievement of the objectively choosing human being."[16] In Rahner's determination, the ever-present reality of grace establishes for human freedom the capacity for self-transcendence. This freedom is infinitely more significant for human life than the type of freedom that is simply the absence of restraints on the ability to indulge all of one's desires.

This suggests that it is not only ideal conditions or popularity in civic society that facilitates the faithfulness of the church—a consideration that is especially significant for the analysis of "hope" in the next chapter. Membership of the church is a particular form of the self-disposal, of the "self-expropriation" inherent in being part of a

13. Karl Rahner, "Reflections on the Experience of Grace," in *Theological Investigations*, vol. 3, trans. K-H. Kruger and B. Kruger (New York: Crossroad, 1982), 88–89.

14. Rahner, "Theology of Freedom," 179.

15. Karl Rahner, "The Dignity and Freedom of Man," in *Theological Investigations*, vol. 2, trans. K-H. Kruger (New York: Crossroad, 1990), 246; see also Rahner, "Theology of Freedom," 184.

16. Karl Rahner, "Guilt—Responsibility—Punishment within the View of Catholic Theology," in *Theological Investigations*, vol. 6, trans. K-H. Kruger and B. Kruger (New York: Crossroad, 1982), 203.

voluntary community.[17] As such, ecclesial faith can be genuine only if it, too, is a free choice, a response to grace. Chapter 4 will stress that maximizing access to this freedom is part of the church's mission in the world. This mission differs from an exclusive focus on increasing membership of the ecclesial community as an end in itself.

Through grace, the church is a body of faith seeking to live by its profession that "neither death, nor life, nor angels, nor rulers, nor things present, nor things to come, nor powers, nor height, nor depth, nor anything else in all creation will separate us from the love of God in Christ Jesus our Lord" (Rom 8:38-39). This unequivocal profession does not categorize the church as a community that seeks its own persecution or that celebrates perversely the triumph of oppression. It is rather a proclamation of the invincible power of God to give life, a power on which the ecclesial community depends.

At every moment of its history, each instantiation of the church must discern the extent of its faithfulness to God's presence, a process that chapter 6 will explore. Even the possibility of this discernment exists because each member and every group in the church receives the invitation to trust in the constancy of grace. When acceptance of this invitation pervades the Christian community, making it a community that lives by trust in God, the church can then "rejoice with those who rejoice [and] weep with those who weep" (Rom 12:15). As it does so, the community of faith knows that neither present happiness nor present distress, as real as both are, completes the story of God's relationship to creation, including within the church itself.

Third, the creativity proper to free human beings is not in competition with God's creativity, but flows from God's quasi-formal causality. The God who encourages humanity to "be fruitful and multiply" (Gen 1:28) "is not diminished by our becoming greater."[18] This realization justifies human beings in never shrinking from claiming their freedom for fear that doing so might evoke divine envy or, worse, divine retribution. The gift of freedom can embrace planning for the future, even if no human plan can be definitive or all-encompassing. Tilling the church

---

17. Avery Dulles, "The Ecclesial Dimension of Faith," *Communio* 22 (1995): 420.

18. Karl Rahner, "Nature and Grace," in *Theological Investigations*, vol. 4, trans. K. Smyth (New York: Crossroad 1982), 177.

for the sake of its future fruitfulness embodies this same freedom. Proclaiming grace as its foundation, then, does not oblige the ecclesial community to refrain from planning, reform, and innovation in favor of waiting for God's action or explicit divine permission for members of the church to act. In fact, grace prompts the opposite set of responses.

Fourth, humanity's freedom includes the freedom to resist and reject God (Gen 3:1-8). "Sin" connects this freedom to the concrete realities of human existence since, as Rahner emphasizes, "Sin takes place in sins. Sin does not take place in a merely transcendental interiority of a noumenal subject but in the works of the flesh which are obvious and tangible."[19] Paradoxically once again, it is God, as the origin and fulfillment of human freedom, who grants human beings the possibility of a negative response to the very grace that gives them life. It is precisely this possibility that reveals the radical nature of God's gift of freedom. This same possibility dooms all efforts to failure-proof the church or to enact systems in the church that are beyond any likelihood that they could miss the mark.

The choice of individuals in the church to resist the conversion that grace stimulates, as well as the fact that the church's structures often support inequities, are—yet another paradox—indicators of the church's foundations in God's freedom. This is not to say that members of the church can do no other than resign themselves to the church's, including their own, ineradicable imperfections. The very notion of "tilling the church" is the opposite of passivity in the face of sinfulness. It also underlines the distinction between the church and the fulfilled kingdom of God. This distinction is especially important in considering the church's sacramentality, which affirms both the church's existence as symbol of grace and the fact that grace extends beyond the life of the church, as the final section of this chapter will show.

The Impact of Sinfulness on Human Freedom

Obstacles to the realization of individual and communal freedom have their source in human beings. Under the umbrella of "sinfulness," barriers to human flourishing derive, at least in part, from an individualism that ignores or rejects that "implanted deep within us is the call to transcend ourselves through an encounter with others" (FT 111). Rahner

---

19. Rahner, "Guilt—Responsibility—Punishment," 211.

broadens the implications of flawed individualism by presenting it as "self-closure before God."[20] This self-closure substitutes a limited life for the boundless freedom that comes from God. As part of this substitution, self-closure spurns God's call into the future in favor of asserting control of the present, irrespective of the illusory nature of such control.

In the contemporary world, some of the most significant barriers to the universal exercise of human freedom emanate not solely from the choices of individuals, but from the systems and structures that are intrinsic to the social existence of human beings. Systemic barriers arising from race, sex and gender, physical abilities, and wealth and social status affect possibilities for freedom no less than do the choices of individuals.[21] Just as an individual can fail to respect the consequences of relationships, a lack of respect that results in negative outcomes for others, so social and economic structures can be agents of "a readiness to discard others" (FT 20), inhibiting opportunities for those who do not have access to certain privileges. In this vein, the attitudes and actions of particular groups can convey the false impression of their own superiority or seek to escape from the shared reality of creatureliness by restricting the freedom of those they perceive as a threat or as unworthy of respect. These circumstances apply in the church no less than beyond it. This point is critical for consideration of the church's tilling, so chapter 4 will address it more fully.

The struggle to overcome individual and systemic injustices must be a constant one if humanity is to realize more of what God enables. The movement of grace in individuals and communities aligns with this end since it, too, is constant, constant in promoting the conversion of humanity, "this conditioned reality [that] is loved unconditionally by the Unconditioned."[22] God's creative power, which reveals "a

20. Rahner, "Guilt—Responsibility—Punishment," 210.

21. For examples of theological anthropologies that highlight these issues, see Mary Doak, "Sex, Race, and Culture: Constructing Theological Anthropology for the Twenty-First Century," *Theological Studies* 80 (2019): 508–29; Michele Saracino, *Christian Anthropology: An Introduction to the Human Person* (Mahwah, NJ: Paulist, 2015); and Susan Ross, *Anthropology: Seeking Light and Beauty* (Collegeville, MN: Michael Glazier, 2012).

22. Rahner, "Eternal Significance of the Humanity of Jesus," 40.

divine capacity for loving self-limitation" rather than "the power to do anything at all, regardless of the consequences," prompts human beings to enact continually this same self-limiting at the heart of their freedom in order to enhance the freedom of all people and the health of the whole of creation.[23] The basis for such responses resides not simply in the original act of creation, but in the gift of grace that God continues to bestow on creation. For human beings, grace is God's unconditional and persistent invitation to draw closer to God. This invitation encompasses other people and the whole of creation, as "integral ecology" indicates.

The invitation of grace addresses human freedom in the world of the everyday, including the everyday life of the church. By keeping humanity's social and historical existence at the forefront of its attention, discussion of grace avoids any abstraction that would separate the church from the world. Theological anthropology can help to forestall such a danger by accounting for how it is that human beings experience grace. This accounting must be mindful that the radical differences between God and God's creatures could cast doubt on whether "grace" and "humanity" can coexist in the same sentence. To further such an accounting, the next section of this chapter will develop a theology of revelation, of God's self-communication in history, which is a prerequisite for the theology of symbol that elucidates the church's sacramentality, both its value and limits. This theology, then, reinforces the ecclesial community's need for tilling even as it acknowledges the church as graced reality.

Revelation as Grace in History

Revelation "is not primarily a matter of revealing truths (plural) about God or even the truth (singular) about God," but "God disclosing the Truth or Reality that is God."[24] Through this lens of God's self-disclosure, revelation is "an historical dialogue between God and

23. Denis Edwards, *Breath of Life: A Theology of the Creator Spirit* (Maryknoll, NY: Orbis, 2004), 107.

24. Gerald O'Collins, *Revelation: Towards a Christian Interpretation of God's Self-Revelation in Jesus Christ* (Oxford: Oxford University Press, 2016), 6–7.

humanity in which something *happens* and in which the communication is related to the continuous 'happening' and enterprise of God."[25] In all of its manifestations, the "happening" that is God's revelation takes place through grace, which is "God himself, the communication in which he gives himself to [humanity] as the divinizing favor which he is himself."[26] As the creative self-giving of God that brings about, nurtures, and fosters the continuity of all that exists, grace is not a "thing," not a quantifiable substance. Nor is grace random or rare, such that efforts to provide a profile of grace would be as futile as an attempt to harness the wind.

Interpreted as God's creative self-communication, grace is interchangeable with God's quasi-formal causality. For this reason, Rahner argues that grace is "primordial," the enduring and irreplaceable source of life for human beings within creation.[27] Grace is neither an addition to something already existing nor merely a single element of life that takes its place alongside other important elements. Rather, grace is what makes all life possible.

The omnipresence of grace points to "general" revelation, to the encounters with God that occur in the everyday, usually without any explicit reference to God. This form of God's presence, which is the focus of this section of the chapter, underpins all life. Yet, theologies of revelation must also account for "special" or historical revelations that are the basis for explicit responses to God. In the Christian context, the latter category encompasses God's covenants with Israel, and, paradigmatically, the life, death, and resurrection of Jesus, and the abiding presence of the Holy Spirit that together constitute the church.[28] A deeper appreciation of God's historical revelation, then, can increase understanding of the church itself; it can also provide insight into what can enhance or detract from the church's authenticity. The next two

---

25. Karl Rahner, "The Development of Dogma," in *Theological Investigations*, vol. 1, trans. C. Ernst (New York: Crossroad, 1982), 48; original emphasis.

26. Rahner, "Nature and Grace," 177.

27. Karl Rahner, "The Concept of Mystery in Catholic Theology," in *Theological Investigations*, vol. 4, trans. K. Smyth (New York: Crossroad, 1982), 41.

28. For the distinction, and relationship, between "general" and "special" revelation, see Gerald O'Collins, *Rethinking Fundamental Theology: Towards a New Fundamental Theology* (Oxford: Oxford University Press, 2011), 56–95.

sections of the chapter, which will concentrate on "symbol" and "sacrament," respectively, will propose a theology attuned to the dynamics of God's historical revelation.

An appreciation of the breadth and depth of God's self-communication begins with the recognition that revelation is never simply an activity of "God" in an undifferentiated sense. Revelation, in fact, is the self-expression of God as three-in-one and one-in-three, of God as Trinity. In presenting revelation in terms of the Trinity, Gerald O'Collins claims that the whole of Scripture witnesses to the triune God, who "has spoken and acted in the history of Israel and of Jesus Christ, or—to put this more fully—that, in the history of the Old and New Testament, the Father, Son, and Holy Spirit are disclosed as the God who cares for all human beings with an infinitely merciful love."[29] Doing justice to this truth means that the fullest expression of every reference to "God" in religious history requires an appreciation of God's indivisible trinitarian life—"The church, after all, does not believe in God *somehow or other*. It believes in God the Father, the Almighty, the one who created us, and in Jesus Christ, the Son, who redeemed us, and in the Holy Spirit, who sustains the life of the church."[30] Even though it is possible to account for forms of revelatory action specific to each member of the Trinity, the triune God is other than a loose amalgamation of independent agents.

Scripture itself testifies to God's creative activity in particular as the activity of the Father, through whom all people are "children of God" (1 John 3:1), of Christ as "the firstborn of all creation" (Col 1:15-16), and of the Holy Spirit, "the Spirit of the living God" (2 Cor 3:3) who enables creation "to bring to birth a future beyond human imagination."[31] As the achievement of the triune God, "in and because of his love," God's creation "is *one*, ineluctably, because it has only one foundation and origin, as it has also only one end."[32] The oneness of

---

29. Ibid., 65.

30. Gerhard Lohfink, *Prayer Takes Us Home: The Theology and Practice of Christian Prayer*, trans. L. Maloney (Collegeville, MN: Liturgical Press, 2020), 5; original emphasis.

31. Edwards, *Breath of Life*, 112.

32. Wolfgang Beinert, "Catholicity as a Property of the Church," *The Jurist* 52 (1992): 468; original emphasis.

creation is both an effect of the oneness of God and—to anticipate slightly the emphasis of the next section—a symbol of this oneness.

Rahner likewise contends that God's revelation in history reflects God's trinitarian life. He argues that although the Bible, especially the New Testament, uses "God" in a way that applies primarily to the "Father," that usage, too, implies the other members of the Trinity.[33] Thus, the second person of the Trinity, the "word" uttered by the Father within the Trinity, is the Word who becomes flesh in Jesus Christ when uttered by the Father outside the Trinity. For this reason, "a revelation of the Father without the Logos and his incarnation would be the same as a wordless utterance."[34] Similarly, the indissoluble bond between the Holy Spirit and "participation in the victorious death of Jesus" means that "the chalice of the Holy Spirit is identical with the chalice of Christ" for all followers of Christ.[35] This link between Christ and the Spirit is especially important for the church, as chapter 3 will illustrate.

Grace as Uncreated and Created

As a way to do justice to, and integrate, the multiple elements constitutive of revelation, Rahner develops his theology of "uncreated" and "created" grace, both of which link to his theology of symbol. In so doing, his theology casts light on encounters with God that take place in and through the concrete world that is home to human beings. These encounters have a tangibility, reinforcing that God's self-revelation in grace attunes to humanity's reality.

"Uncreated grace" summarizes for Rahner the immediate and abiding life-giving presence of God to all that exists.[36] In its mode as "uncre-

---

33. For Rahner's detailed argument on the identity of God in Scripture, see his "*THEOS* in the New Testament," in *Theological Investigations*, vol. 1, trans. C. Ernst (New York: Crossroad, 1982), 79–148.

34. Karl Rahner, "Remarks on the Dogmatic Treatise *De Trinitate*," in *Theological Investigations*, vol. 4, trans. K. Smyth (New York: Crossroad, 1982), 91; see also Karl Rahner, *The Trinity*, trans J. Donceel (New York: Crossroad, 1997), 22–36.

35. Rahner, "Experience of the Holy Spirit," in *Theological Investigations*, vol. 18, trans. E. Quinn (New York: Crossroad, 1983), 206.

36. Rahner, "Scholastic Concept of Uncreated Grace," 329–33; see also Karl Rahner, "The Doctrine of the 'Spiritual Senses' in the Middle Ages," in *Theological Investigations*, vol. 16, trans. D. Morland (New York: Crossroad, 1983), 104–34.

ated," grace "remains anonymous, implicit, unthematic, like the widely and diffusely spread light of a sun which we do not directly see."[37] Just as human beings breathe in the air around them without needing to maintain constant alertness to the presence of oxygen or understand anything about its chemistry, so uncreated grace provides the unseen, but radically dependable, atmosphere for life. Grace sustains life while being undetectable and without requiring acknowledgment from its beneficiaries. By transcending any single expression, uncreated grace reinforces the distinction between God and God's creation while also indicating the universality of God's presence.

The all-pervasive presence of uncreated grace differentiates it from "Australia." Rahner invokes Australia as the archetype of those exotic realities that most people will know only through secondhand reports, the accuracy of which they may never have the opportunity or wherewithal to determine for themselves.[38] Unlike Australia, the uncreated grace of God suffuses the "everyday" of all people: it is simply, inescapably present for everyone.[39] It is impossible for people to travel to and experience Australia without knowing they are doing so; it is possible, even usual, for human beings to experience grace without ever alluding to the presence of God.

The omnipresence of grace places God at the center of every creature; this, of course, includes human beings. Far from being solely an option for those who might wish to engage with it—like making a trip to Australia—the grace of God defines humanity: "The capacity for the God of self-bestowing personal love is the central and abiding existential of human beings as we really are."[40] Since human beings

37. Rahner, "Experience of the Holy Spirit," 199.

38. For two examples of Rahner's numerous comparisons between Australia and grace, see "Christianity and the Non-Christian Religions," in *Theological Investigations*, vol. 5, trans. K-H. Kruger (New York: Crossroad, 1983), 131, and "The Foundation of Belief Today," in *Theological Investigations*, vol. 16, trans. D. Morland (New York: Crossroad, 1983), 11.

39. For Rahner's stress on the "everyday," see his *Everyday Faith*, trans. W. J. O'Hara (New York: Herder and Herder, 1968); see also Harvey Egan, *Karl Rahner: Mystic of Everyday Life* (New York: Crossroad, 1998).

40. Karl Rahner, "Concerning the Relation between Nature and Grace," in *Theological Investigations*, vol. 1, trans. C. Ernst (New York: Crossroad, 1982), 312.

exist in and through grace, Rahner concludes that they possess, without exception, an "obediential potency," a God-given capacity to hear and respond to God.[41] As discussed above in relation to freedom, human beings can choose whether or not to remain open to this potential, but the potential itself exists always as God's irrevocable gift.

Building on his theology of uncreated grace, Rahner contends that for human beings "the original and ultimate experience of *God* constitutes the enabling condition of, and an intrinsic element in, the experience of self in such a way that without this experience of God no experience of self is possible."[42] Consistent with this claim, Rahner posits that talking about humanity must begin "only by talking about something else: about God. . . . It is impossible to engage in anthropology without having first engaged in theology, since [humanity] is pure reference to God."[43] The inextricable interweaving of grace and humanity mandates a similar interweaving of "anthropocentricity" and "theocentricity" within theology.[44]

The creative self-giving of God constitutes every human being as "a reality absolutely opened upwards."[45] This disposition orients human beings toward their future fulfillment in God: "The seemingly unfamiliar unfathomability of our existence as we feel it is the unfathomability of God, imparting himself to us, the advent of his infinity that is pathless and appears to us as nothingness, precisely because it is infinity."[46] God's self-revelation in grace "is given as an incitement and a way to the closest immediacy of communion with him, it is all the more an opening into the immeasurable, a beginning of the illimitable."[47] Individuals and even entire communities might never develop an explicit

41. Karl Rahner, *Hearer of the Word: Laying the Foundation for a Philosophy of Religion*, trans. J. Donceel (1st ed., 1941; New York: Continuum, 1994), 16.

42. Karl Rahner, "Experience of Self and Experience of God," in *Theological Investigations*, vol. 13, trans. D. Bourke (New York: Seabury, 1975), 125; original emphasis.

43. Karl Rahner, "Thoughts on the Theology of Christmas," in *Theological Investigations*, vol. 3, trans. K-H. Kruger and B. Kruger, (New York: Crossroad, 1982), 31.

44. Karl Rahner, "Theology and Anthropology," in *Theological Investigations*, vol. 9, trans. G. Harrison (New York: Seabury, 1972), 28.

45. Karl Rahner, "Current Problems in Christology," in *Theological Investigations*, vol.1, trans. C. Ernst (New York: Crossroad, 1982), 183.

46. Rahner, "Experience of the Holy Spirit," 204.

47. Rahner, "Current Problems in Christology," 149.

relationship with God, and certainly not join the church in any of its forms, but nothing less than God can satisfy and complete human beings. This conclusion can help members of the church to grasp their own identity, while also refining their mission in the world.

The possibilities for communion with God integral to revelation do not eliminate for human beings God's "hiddenness," which neither the human intellect nor will can conquer. Even as God communicates God-self, God remains "the dark fire of love" who is knowable only through surrender to the relationship that God initiates.[48] Rahner summarizes his analysis of the paradox at the heart of God's self-communication by connecting it to God's "mystery," a topic that the previous chapter introduced and that will color discussion of the church's sacramentality. Humanity's encounter with the mystery of God confirms that finite objects will not ultimately satisfy human beings. Every encounter that human beings have with God's grace, then, has an orientation to the future, looking toward knowing God more fully (1 Cor 13:12).

The mystery of God, the fact that God exceeds humanity's grasp, is not a problem that demands a solution before human beings can know God. As Rahner portrays it, God's mystery is a constant of humanity's relationship with God; it is not a technological challenge susceptible ultimately to the reach of human ingenuity.[49] Although human beings could feel humiliated by their incapacity to understand revelation exhaustively, Rahner stresses that "this incomprehensibility is not to be taken as the limit of fulfillment but rather signifies its limitlessness which is loved and experienced as such."[50] This means that human beings, through God's self-giving in grace, can enter into relationship with the God who remains utterly "other."

To reinforce this point, Rahner emphasizes that God's "incomprehensibility" will continue for humanity even in heaven, where it will not be an obstacle to eternal happiness, but "the very object of our blissful love."[51] Since human beings experience God as mystery, grace "does not imply the promise and the beginning of the elimination of

48. Rahner, "Doctrine of the 'Spiritual Senses' in the Middle Ages," 125.

49. Rahner, "Concept of Mystery in Catholic Theology," 38–41.

50. Karl Rahner, "The Hiddenness of God," in *Theological Investigations*, vol. 16, trans. D. Morland (New York: Crossroad, 1983), 239.

51. Rahner, "Concept of Mystery in Catholic Theology," 41.

the mystery, but the radical possibility of the absolute proximity of the mystery, which is not eliminated by its proximity, but really presented as mystery."[52] The possibility that the church might be a means of encounter with the mystery of God, even as the church itself, in its members and structures, is less than fully transparent to grace, is central to the affirmation of the church's sacramentality that the final part of this chapter will consider.

The focus on the ineradicable mystery of God refines the interpretation of revelation. Since revelation is an invitation to relationship with the transcendent God, not a step toward the complete mapping of God, "the concept 'God' is not a grasp of God by which a person masters the mystery, but it is letting oneself be grasped by the mystery that is present and yet ever distant."[53] Humanity's encounter with God's mystery, Rahner asserts, "forces knowledge to surpass itself and both preserve and transform itself in a more comprehensive act"; that act is love.[54] God's mystery presents humanity with a choice between dwelling resolutely on "the little island of our so-called knowledge" or plunging into "the ocean of the infinite mystery."[55] A manifestation of the willingness to undertake this plunge is love of neighbor.

To make clear that it is concrete action, rather than disembodied spirituality, that most fully expresses humanity's response to God, Rahner accents the unity of the love of God and neighbor, an accent that converges with his theology of symbol. Love of neighbor, in Rahner's presentation, is more than "preparation, effect, fruit and touchstone of the love of God," it is itself an act of love for God.[56] As the analysis of symbols in the next section of this chapter will indicate, symbols communicate the symbolizer, so love of neighbor is an act "within that total believing and hoping surrender of [a person] to God which

52. Ibid., 55.

53. Rahner, *Foundations of Christian Faith*, 54.

54. Rahner, "Concept of Mystery in Catholic Theology," 43.

55. Ibid., 57–58.

56. Karl Rahner, "Reflections on the Unity of the Love of Neighbor and the Love of God," in *Theological Investigations*, vol. 6, trans. K-H. Kruger and B. Kruger (New York: Crossroad, 1982), 236; see also his *The Love of Jesus and the Love of Neighbor*, trans. R. Barr (New York: Crossroad, 1983).

we call love and which alone justifies [a person]."[57] Love of neighbor symbolizes both the response to God of the person performing the act and God's love for its recipients. This twofold reality further indicates what the church's sacramentality implies and the purpose of the church's mission in the world.

Rahner is unfailingly positive that the ongoing surrender to the mystery of God has a generative impact on human life. This positive emphasis notwithstanding, he acknowledges that a measure of all genuine encounters with God is that they "must always necessarily be a breaking-up of the roundedness in which the world seeks to rest in itself."[58] This is so as the transcendent God does not fit without remainder into the world that human beings construct, a point with ramifications for both love of neighbor and participation in the ecclesial community, neither of which result in a world beyond the need for ongoing conversion.

Since humanity's version of how life ought to be is unable to encompass God completely, God can seem distant, even absent, but Rahner insists that this perceived absence is, yet again paradoxically, a function of God's unbounded presence: "God's remoteness is the incomprehensibility of his all-pervading nearness."[59] To do justice to this God, "one must look at the invisible and let the silent speak in stillness," two activities that point to the importance of human receptivity over human dominance.[60] These receptive practices, Rahner asserts, make it possible to experience God's "silent immensity . . . as a protecting nearness and a tender love which does not make any reservations" but reveals itself in ways that human beings could not anticipate, as in the birth of Jesus.[61]

As counterintuitive as it seems, human beings can make their own the grace of the life-giving God only if they are willing to embrace "the personal, free, grasping-of-[their]-own-accord of their necessary

---

57. Rahner, "Reflections on the Unity," 236.

58. Karl Rahner, "The Ignatian Mysticism of Joy in the World," in *Theological Investigations*, vol. 3, trans. K-H. Kruger and B. Kruger (New York: Crossroad, 1982), 286.

59. Rahner, "Thoughts on the Theology of Christmas," 28.

60. Ibid., 26.

61. Ibid., 33.

being-unto-death."[62] This claim with its ascription of the necessity of death would be shocking, perhaps repugnant, without its grounding in Rahner's larger portrait of grace, which accentuates constantly the God who exceeds the limits of human existence in history, including even biological life itself. As it is, the reference to death locates Rahner's discussion within the mainstream of the Christian tradition and the spiritual heritage of the church, central to both of which is the life, death, and resurrection of Jesus, to which the next chapter will return in its focus on faith and hope.

It is notable that the dynamics that Rahner associates with the transcendence and mystery of God are also familiar to the larger history of religions. As Nicholas Lash observes, "Each of the great religious traditions has had its own procedures for protecting us from the illusion that the Holy One can be thus pinned down, classified, given a proper name."[63] More generally, Johann Baptist Metz claims that, as a consequence of God remaining beyond our grasp, "God simply cannot be thought of without this idea irritating and disrupting the immediate interests of the one who is trying to think it."[64]

The notion of God's "disruption" also features in David Tracy's understanding of grace, which he describes as "a power interrupting our constant temptations to delude ourselves at a level more fundamental than any conscious error; a power gradually but really transforming old habits."[65] George Schner, likewise, suggests that "experience" is what "enters as a moment of discontinuity into a larger, already established context."[66] Interruptive experience "invites consideration, discussion, revision, change" in relation to established understandings and practices.[67] In the context of humanity's relationship to God, the invitation to undertake each of those tasks is a reminder that all theologies and

---

62. Karl Rahner, "The Passion and Asceticism," in *Theological Investigations*, vol. 3, trans. K-H. Kruger and B. Kruger (New York: Crossroad, 1982), 73.

63. Nicholas Lash, *Holiness, Speech and Silence: Reflections on the Question of God* (Burlington, VT: Ashgate, 2004), 14.

64. Johann Baptist Metz, *Faith in History and Society: Towards a Practical Fundamental Theology*, rev. trans. M. Ashley (New York: Crossroad, 2007), 62.

65. David Tracy, *Plurality and Ambiguity: Hermeneutics, Religion, Hope* (London: SCM, 1987), 73.

66. George Schner, "The Appeal to Experience," *Theological Studies* 53 (1992): 54.

67. Ibid.

all structures centered on God are less than definitive in their renderings of God.

Since the mystery of God denies to humanity the capacity to determine that history has reached its end, human beings, including the community of faith that is the church, cannot legitimately claim that their projects are beyond any possibility of refinement or reform. If human beings are to forgo the option of usurping what belongs properly to God, they must develop their trust that God's grace will lead them to fulfillment, rather than annihilation. The basis for this trust is not simply an individual's personal experience, but the history of God's engagement with humanity, especially through Jesus Christ and the Holy Spirit, the foundations of the church.

One core aspect of human identity, "in the ultimate, most radical and absolute sense," is that human beings are bodily creatures, a status with implications for their experience and knowledge of God.[68] God is not corporeal, so human beings are unable to see and touch God. Nevertheless, faith in God, if it is to be authentically human, cannot bypass "our experience of the material."[69] To establish how there might be a meeting between the grace of the transcendent God and the materiality of human beings, how it is that God communicates to human beings as they are, Rahner articulates his theology of "symbol." This category, which is essential to Rahner's theology as a whole, is applicable to both "general" revelation and the specificity of God's self-communication in Jesus and in the Holy Spirit, and so, too, to ecclesiology.

God's Symbolic Self-Communication

Rahner's theology of symbol simultaneously develops and concretizes his depiction of God's presence in the world. The theology enables Rahner to shift his focus from the all-pervasiveness of uncreated grace to the specificity of "created grace." The latter is characteristic of those

68. Karl Rahner, "The Body in the Order of Salvation," in *Theological Investigations*, vol. 17, trans. M. Kohl (New York: Crossroad, 1981), 75.

69. Karl Rahner, "The Unity of Spirit and Matter in the Christian Understanding of Faith," in *Theological Investigations*, vol. 6, trans. K-H. Kruger and B. Kruger (New York: Crossroad, 1982), 154; see also Karl Rahner, "The 'Spiritual Senses' According to Origen," in *Theological Investigations*, vol. 16, trans. D. Morland (New York: Crossroad, 1983), 81–103.

encounters with God that take place through people, words, and even objects. These encounters include those that come under the heading "special" revelation, especially God's incarnation in Jesus Christ.

Symbolic encounters make God accessible in time and space without God becoming a finite object in the world. Creation itself is the symbol of God, even though no single aspect of creation is God. Rahner's theology of symbol begins with his conviction that all beings, a category inclusive of God, "necessarily 'express' themselves in order to attain their own nature."[70] This self-expression, as discussed earlier, is the formal cause of what it produces. In Rahner's construction, symbols, unlike signs, do not simply point to something beyond themselves, but make present for others the one who forms them as a symbol: "the symbol is the reality in which *another* attains knowledge of a being."[71] Symbols, in short, symbolize the symbolizer for those who encounter the symbol.

Symbols convey a reality that is not accessible more directly. As a result, their surface meaning does not disclose their whole truth. Unlike discursive statements, symbols communicate by working "on the imagination, emotions, and will, and through them upon the intelligence, the symbol changes the point of view, the perspectives, the outlook of the addressee."[72] By relying on something other than explicit discourse, symbols reinforce the capacity of human beings for transcendence, for appreciating simultaneously more than a single dimension of reality.

Notably, symbols are not a class of things that exist as such independently of their use as symbols. Words, objects, and actions function as symbols within a context, without losing the "normal" meaning they have beyond that environment. This context can be very local, existing within the boundaries of the relationship between the one who expresses herself through a symbol and the one who experiences and interprets it. This happens regularly when two people communicate their love for each other: the words and actions by which they convey

---

70. Karl Rahner, "The Theology of the Symbol," in *Theological Investigations*, vol. 4, trans. K. Smyth (New York: Crossroad, 1982), 224.

71. Ibid., 230; original emphasis.

72. Avery Dulles, *A Church to Believe In: Discipleship and the Dynamics of Freedom* (New York: Crossroad, 1982), 47; see also Johnson, *Quest for the Living God*, 20.

their love may be profoundly moving for the protagonists, but fail to connect in any compelling way with outside observers.

Since symbols are revelatory within a relationship, the impact of a symbol does not depend on its intrinsic commercial, practical, aesthetic, cognitive, or emotional values.[73] The effect of the symbol depends, rather, on the openness of the receiver to accept something more than the surface meaning of words, actions, or objects. In her novel *Adam Bede*, for example, the nineteenth-century writer George Eliot, when addressing her readers on the topic of "love," captures strikingly both the irreducible ambiguity of symbols and their profound power:

> It is almost certain that you, too, have been in love. If so, you will no more think the slight words, the timid looks, the tremulous touches, by which two human souls approach each other gradually, like two quivering rain-streams, before they mingle into one—you will no more think these things trivial than you will think the first-detected signs of coming spring trivial. . . . Those slight words and looks and touches are part of the soul's language, and the finest language, I believe, is chiefly made up of unimposing words, such as "light," "sound," "stars," "music," words really not worth looking at, or hearing in themselves, any more than "chips" or "sawdust:" it is only that they happen to be the signs of something unspeakably great and beautiful.[74]

Parents who treasure the splotchy finger-painting that their child produces confirm Eliot's insight when they "recognize" the painting as an embodiment of the child's love for them. This perception can be entirely accurate, even though those outside of the family would perhaps consider the child's art as simply the messy product typical of three-year-olds. In the explicitly religious context, Christians venerate the cross on which Jesus died as the most profound symbol of God's unconditional love for humanity and the whole of creation; the cross has this value for believing Christians even while retaining its primary meaning as an instrument of torture.

---

73. Louis-Marie Chauvet, *The Sacraments: The Word of God at the Mercy of the Body*, trans. M. Beaumont (Collegeville, MN: Pueblo, 2001), 84–85.

74. George Eliot, *Adam Bede* (1859; repr., Oxford: Oxford University Press, 2008), 441.

The role of symbols in God's self-communication generates an understanding of revelation that differs strikingly from the popular notion of spectacular and compelling divine interventions from above. The theological reading of symbols clarifies how it is that all people can encounter God beyond explicitly religious settings, but it also establishes how it is that Jesus, whose contemporaries knew him simply as "the carpenter" (Mark 6:3), could be far more than a nondescript artisan.

Rahner's theology of symbol provides a platform for acknowledging human beings themselves as symbols of grace. To amplify his conviction of the importance of human beings' bodily reality mentioned above, Rahner interprets this bodily reality symbolically, stressing that it "is the condition that makes spiritual and personal self-discovery possible, not an obstacle in its way."[75] Humanity's obediential potential, also referred to earlier, likewise requires attention to the manifold elements of embodied human life, to the social and cultural world in which all human beings live. This attention is to attune itself to "the perhaps possible possibility of a revelation" through the people and events intrinsic to the "everyday," a context in which God's presence can be anything but boisterously evident, as the life of Jesus suggests.[76]

Dei Verbum (DV), the Second Vatican Council's Dogmatic Constitution on Divine Revelation (1965), highlights the intimacy between God and humanity that God's self-revelation establishes. Through revelation, the document states, God "addresses men and women as his friends, and lives among them, in order to invite and receive them into his own company" (DV 2). This description of God's purpose is especially apt in relation to Jesus Christ, but has its roots in God's desire for intimacy with humanity that is evident in the covenants that God makes with Israel.[77]

The covenants structure Israel's relationship to God. They give the people a privileged identity: they are God's people. Foundational to the covenants with Israel is God's singular promise: "I will walk among

75. Rahner, "Body in the Order of Salvation," 84.
76. Karl Rahner, "Ignatian Mysticism of Joy in the World," 284; see also Rahner, *Hearer of the Word*, 9.
77. Articles 2 and 3 of *Dei Verbum* outline the history of God's revelation before Christ.

you, and will be your God, and you shall be my people" (Lev 26:12).[78] Since the covenants are the product of God's initiative, God assumes responsibility for maintaining them in good order.[79] The biblical authors depict God as laboring ceaselessly throughout the history of Israel to protect, teach, challenge, admonish, and comfort the people. Consequently, the space between the inauguration and promised fulfillment of the covenants is a space replete with divine activity, activity that highlights the connection between the future and the present: "I am God, and there is no one like me, declaring the end from the beginning and from ancient times things not yet done" (Isa 46:9-10).

The covenants provide Israel's most significant points of reference to the future, a future built on God's promises. The promises confirm that God's life-giving extends beyond "the beginning." They indicate, too, that every encounter with God contains the seeds of the future, which will witness the fullness of God's life-giving promises: "The LORD will fulfill his purpose for me; your steadfast love, O LORD, endures forever" (Ps 138:8). Although oriented to a future fulfillment—a theme that chapter 3 will develop—the covenants color the present reality of God's relationship with Israel. This relationship invites a response from the people, one that often requires "movement," sometimes literal as well as figurative: "We are setting out for the place of which the LORD said, 'I will give it to you' . . . for the LORD has promised good to Israel" (Num 10:29). God bridges the present and future by being accessible to Israel in the everyday world through a raft of symbols— fire, clouds, land, law, temple, judges, prophets, and kings, and still more—that give shape to God's presence. The myriad symbols through which God accompanies Israel do not reduce God's mystery, but assure the people of God's faithfulness and constancy.

God remains faithful to the people through the many social and political upheavals that flow from Israel's inconsistent faithfulness to the God of the covenants (Lam 1:1-22). God continues to reach out to

---

78. For other instances of God's promise to be with God's people, see also Exod 6:7, Jer 30:22, and Ezek 36:28; the theme of God's everlasting commitment also appears at the end of the New Testament, see Rev 21:3.

79. See the establishment of covenants in Gen 6:18; 9:9; 15:18; 17:2. For an overview of the biblical covenants, see Andrew Davis, "A Biblical View of Covenants Old and New," *Theological Studies* 81 (2020): 631–48.

the people with mercy, which does not ignore human sinfulness but denies to it the right to claim the final word in history (Isa 54:7-8). In the long story of the relationship between God and Israel, the people often grew restless with the God of mystery, preferring a divinity whom human beings could control or, at least, manipulate. This tendency, summarized as "idolatry," finds its archetypal expression, although not its only instance, in Israel's worship of "an image of a calf" (Exod 32:1-6). In light of their restlessness and lapses into idolatry, the people must relearn repeatedly to live within the paradox that the God who eludes humanity's grasp, and who alone is lord of all creation and history, seeks their liberation, not their servitude.

The Revelation of God in Jesus

Christian faith identifies the incarnation of Jesus Christ as a unique moment in the story of God's liberation of God's people and the fulfillment of God's ancient promises. The ecclesial community professes Jesus to be the primordial expression of God's self-revelation, the "mediator and sum total" (DV 2) of God's self-communicating love, and so the fullness of the relationship between grace and humanity's bodily existence. The Christian tradition insists that Jesus Christ does more than point toward God, or even represent or speak for God in a way analogous to the prophets. Jesus is "the 'word' of the Father, his perfect 'image,' his radiance, his self-expression."[80]

Since Jesus reveals God in a personal way, in the setting of human history and culture, an encounter with Jesus, like an encounter with any person, calls for a human response. To facilitate this response, Christology clarifies the identity of Jesus, expounds what it means to encounter him, and also details the impact of Jesus and the implications of coming to believe in him as the revelation of God and of coming to be his disciple. Christology has often divided these tasks into two foci: "the person" and "the work" of Jesus.[81] This twofold approach

---

80. Rahner, "Theology of the Symbol," 236.

81. For methods in Christology, see John Galvin, "Jesus Christ," in *Systematic Theology: Roman Catholic Perspectives*, 2nd ed., ed. Francis Schüssler Fiorenza and John Galvin (Minneapolis: Fortress, 2011), 256–58.

can be useful in highlighting different aspects of God's revelation in Christ, but the subdivisions are facets of the one irreducible reality: Jesus Christ as the unique presence of God in human history.

The Jesus of the gospels, like every human being is a multidimensional character. While his relationship to God is the center of Jesus's life, his "imaginative parables, compassionate healings, startling exorcisms, and festive meals" challenge, and even overturn, the prevailing expectations of how God was expected to act.[82] As an example of Jesus's challenge to dominant paradigms, Elizabeth Johnson notes that Jesus, in the context of male-female relationships, offers "new possibilities of relationships patterned according to the mutual service of friendship rather than domination-subordination."[83] Even in relation to religious norms, where it might have been anticipated that Jesus would conform to, perhaps buttress, existing standards, Jesus clashes often with religious authorities (Matt 16:1-12; Luke 11:37-53).

Indeed, Jesus seems at times to elevate his authority beyond the received religious tradition—"You have heard that it was said . . . But I say to you" (Matt 5:21-22)—even as he acknowledges the law of the covenants as the gift of God—"Do not think that I have come to abolish the law or the prophets; I have come not to abolish but to fulfill" (Matt 5:17). Such apparently contradictory statements illustrate that the Jesus of the gospels is an angular character, one whose behavior is rich in nuance: "From fellowship with the impure, [Jesus] critiques purity; from companionship with women, he unmasks patriarchy; from empathy with Samaritans, he interpellates orthodoxy and rejects racism; from compassion for sinners, he demystifies righteousness; from the perspective of a preferential solidarity with the poor, he points to the only truly inclusive solidarity there can be."[84]

Dei Verbum teaches that Jesus is the means by which God "completed and perfected revelation and confirmed it with divine guarantees" (DV 4). In Jesus, God becomes a part of human history: "as we are, yet without sin" (Heb 4:15). In Jesus, God makes present the depths of

---

82. Elizabeth Johnson, *She Who Is: The Mystery of God in Feminist Theological Discourse* (New York: Crossroad, 1993), 157.

83. Ibid., 157–58.

84. John O'Brien, "The Authority of the Poor," in *Authority in the Roman Catholic Church: Theory and Practice*, ed. Bernard Hoose (Burlington, VT: Ashgate, 2002), 220.

divine love "so that everyone who believes in him may not perish but may have eternal life" (John 3:16). In Jesus, the Word of God enters into human history underscoring humanity's capacity to receive God and reinforcing the identification of God as the source of humanity's fulfillment, the promise at the heart of God's covenants with Israel.

What Jesus reveals is that God is "personal, free, loving, merciful, just, patient, and powerful," as well as that humanity and the world are "objects of God's powerful mercies and as destined by God for redemption and glory."[85] What is implicit in creation, and communicated through the law and the prophets, becomes fully human in Jesus: "the presence of God's Word, God's freedom to love and to communicate, so permeates that piece of the human world which is Jesus of Nazareth that the fullest possible meanings of God are communicated there and the very freedom of God is acted out in that life to make us free."[86]

This profession underpins Rahner's description of Jesus as the one perfect symbol in whom, uniquely, there is no gap between the symbol and what it symbolizes:

> The incarnate word is the absolute symbol of God in the world, filled as nothing else can be with what is symbolized. He is not merely the presence and revelation of what God is in himself. He is also the expressive presence of what—or rather who—God wished to be, in free grace, to the world, in such a way that this divine attribute, once so expressed, can never be reversed, but is and remains final and unsurpassable.[87]

Jesus, simply, is the presence of God in human history.

Rahner's approach to Jesus as symbol of grace is consistent with his overarching theology of God's symbolic revelation, but this does not mean that Rahner is doing no more than adding Jesus to a list of revelatory symbols. Nor is it even the case that Rahner's interpretation of God's self-revelation in Jesus radicalizes his approach to symbols.

85. Avery Dulles, "Faith and Revelation," in *Systematic Theology: Roman Catholic Perspectives*, 2nd ed., ed. Francis Schüssler Fiorenza and John Galvin (Minneapolis: Fortress, 2011), 85.

86. Rowan Williams, *Holy Living: The Christian Tradition for Today* (London: Bloomsbury, 2017), 16.

87. Rahner, "Theology of the Symbol," 237.

More dramatically still, the symbolic reality of Jesus is the source and measure of Rahner's theology of symbol.

As a result of the incarnation, Rahner asserts, it becomes clear that humanity is "that which ensues when God's self-utterance, God's Word, is given out lovingly into the void of god-less nothing. . . . If God wills to become non-God, humanity comes to be."[88] The sequence of Rahner's argument is crucial to understanding his emphasis on the centrality of Jesus for humanity's relationship with God. The incarnation, as Rahner presents it, is not a subsequent addition to creation, and certainly not merely the correction of a damaged creation whose decline dates from the first exercise of human freedom. The incarnation is "the prior setting and condition for the supreme possibility of [God] imparting [God] 'to the outside world.'"[89] In other words, the incarnation is the reason for the whole of creation, not a supplement to it. God's desire to express Godself fully outside of God, the desire that takes flesh in Jesus, brings about creation, especially humanity that can enter explicitly into relationship with God.

The basis for Rahner's claim is his conviction that God's self-communication proceeds "by creating what is capable of receiving him."[90] Uniquely, this is humanity: God is the quasi-formal cause of all that exists, but God becomes incarnate only in humanity. Since Jesus alone is the fullness of "God's self-divestment in creation," God's self-communication in Jesus "must be the most powerful and most alive, the most original center of what is alive and of what is master of itself in the world, precisely because (and not, although) it is God himself."[91]

The humanity of Jesus, then, "is not the form in which God appears, in the sense of a vaporous and empty apparition which has no validity of its own in comparison with and in contrast to what is manifested," but is God's presence in time and space.[92] As the incarnation of God,

88. Karl Rahner, "On the Theology of the Incarnation," in *Theological Investigations*, vol. 4, trans. K. Smyth (New York: Crossroad, 1982), 116.

89. Karl Rahner, "Christology in the Setting of Modern Man's Understanding of Himself and of His World," in *Theological Investigations*, vol. 11, trans. D. Bourke (New York: Crossroad, 1982), 220.

90. Rahner, "Thoughts on the Theology of Christmas," 32.

91. Ibid., 33.

92. Rahner, "On the Theology of the Incarnation," 117; see also his "'I Believe in Jesus Christ.' Interpreting an Article of Faith," in *Theological Investigations*, vol. 9,

Jesus is profoundly other than an avatar of God or the dispenser of information about God: Jesus communicates God by embodying grace in a fully human way. The final section of this chapter will return to this point as it discusses the analogy that Vatican II draws between the uniqueness of Jesus's humanity and divinity and the presence of the Holy Spirit in the church.

Rahner's Christology gives color and texture to the conviction at the heart of his theology of symbol: symbols reveal God without collapsing God into the world of objects, and so without reducing God to something less than God. This means, however, that symbols are irreducibly ambiguous. By their very ambiguity, symbols can enable an encounter with God's immanence without imperiling the transcendence of God.

The ambiguity of symbols is clearly applicable to the church. The church, in myriad ways, can be a means of encounter with the boundless grace and mercy of God, but the church can be also—again in myriad ways—an obstacle to those seeking such an encounter. If the church, in all of its manifestations, is to narrow this ambiguity, and so increase the likelihood that it might better symbolize the hope that comes through relationship with Christ and the Spirit, the members of the church cannot settle for a mediocre church that refuses to be self-critical and so resists conversion by remaining blind to its need for tilling. An understanding of the church's sacramentality can contribute to the formation of a spirituality that challenges such complacency in all members of the church and in the church's structures.

The Sacramentality of the Church

Every sacrament "tips the everyday over into another sphere where the impossible claims to be possible. It is the excess which protests against the barriers imposed by flatness and immanence, which makes a rift in the greyness of everyday life and refuses the absolute of violence."[93] In

---

trans. G. Harrison (New York: Seabury, 1972), 165–68, and "Jesus Christ—The Meaning of Life," in *Theological Investigations*, vol. 21, trans. H. Riley (New York: Crossroad, 1988), 208–19.

93. Christian Duquoc, *Provisional Churches: An Essay in Ecumenical Ecclesiology*, trans. J. Bowden (London: SCM, 1986), 97.

this definition, "sacrament" is an omnibus term for all symbols of grace, the concrete, bounded realities that are accessible in the "everyday" of human history while being simultaneously a means of encounter with the transcendent God. Through these encounters, God invites humanity into communion with God and all creation, while also drawing all creatures to the fulfillment that history cannot contain. Through the Holy Spirit, even what seems unlikely to overcome "the absolute of violence" can be a source of possibility, encouragement, and hope in the face of all that threatens to undermine life.

As symbols of God's self-communication, the efficacy of sacraments is not at the mercy of circumstances that seem ill-suited to an encounter with God. Even when the sacraments themselves are less than obvious revelations of God, and, more radically, even when the realities that carry the designation "sacrament" seem to obscure any connection to God, the grace of the Spirit remains available. These considerations are especially relevant when viewing the church through the lens of sacramentality.

As sacrament, the church is "an undreamed of possibility for love," the inspiring yet daunting metaphor of Juan Luis Segundo.[94] The love that is to flow through all the members, worship, structures, and activities of the church is not exclusively, nor even principally, a human emotion or accomplishment, but the love that God has revealed in Jesus Christ through the Holy Spirit. At the same time, the church's sacramentality is also inseparable from its existence as a human community, with all the ambivalences characteristic of humanity. Inasmuch as the church can make present God's healing and reconciling love, it can also mask it, as the sexual abuse crisis makes painfully evident. The church can similarly fail to enact God's love when and where the need for it is greatest, as is apparent in the silence of many officeholders and other members of the church on, for example, issues of racial justice and gender equity. This complexity calls for an exposition of what it means to identify the church as a sacrament. This exposition can draw profitably from Vatican II's presentation of the theme.

---

94. Juan Luis Segundo, *The Community Called Church*, trans. J. Drury (Maryknoll, NY: Orbis, 1973) 82–83.

Lumen Gentium begins its account of the mystery of the church by acknowledging that the church "is like a sacrament (*veluti sacramentum*)—a sign and instrument, that is, of communion with God and of the unity of the entire human race" (LG 1).[95] While the prominence of the church's sacramentality in *Lumen Gentium* might suggest that sacramental ecclesiology was already a staple of Catholic thinking, such was not the case. Indeed, at the time of the council, it is likely that most Catholics, including the bishops who participated in Vatican II, would have been largely unfamiliar with the notion.[96] "Body of Christ" and "perfect society" were more commonly heard as metaphors for the church before the council than was "sacrament." Even more significantly, any reference to "sacrament" would have pointed not to "the church," but directly to the seven ecclesial sacraments at the heart of both the church's worship and its many expressions of individual and communal piety.

In Herbert Vorgrimler's assessment, sacramental theology in the centuries after the Reformation period "fell under the sway of canon law, and gradually ceased to be a theology at all."[97] As a result, canonical regulation of the sacraments, especially the conditions required for valid and licit sacramental liturgies, displaced broader considerations of sacramentality from the general consciousness of the Catholic community. In such an environment, there was little likelihood of viewing the church through the lens of sacramentality.

Catholic theology prior to Vatican II certainly defined sacraments in terms of the relationship of grace to physical realities—"A sacrament is an outward sign instituted by Christ to give grace"[98]—but did so from a narrow perspective on created grace. Such presentations of sacraments

---

95. This translation alters the Flannery text to reflect more accurately the Latin in the original document; for the Latin text, see Norman Tanner, ed., *Decrees of the Ecumenical Councils*, vol. 2 (Washington, DC: Georgetown University Press, 1990), 849.

96. For a perspective on sacramental ecclesiology prior to the council, and its influence at the council, see Dennis Doyle, "Otto Semmelroth, SJ, and the Ecclesiology of the 'Church as Sacrament' at Vatican II," in *The Legacy of Vatican II*, ed. Massimo Faggioli and Andrea Vicini (Mahwah, NJ: Paulist Press, 2015), 203–25.

97. Herbert Vorgrimler, *Sacramental Theology*, trans. L. Maloney (Collegeville, MN: Liturgical Press, 1992), 62.

98. *A Catechism of Christian Doctrine* (Paterson, NJ: St Anthony Guild Press, 1941), 60.

depicted them as mechanisms that would dispense certain amounts of grace, if all canonical conditions for valid administration were met and if the recipient approached the sacraments with a proper disposition.[99] In this mode, Catholic sacramental theology associated "the church" principally with "the ordained," who held the responsibility for the administration of the seven ecclesial sacraments. Since this grace would not exist without the sacraments, the church's responsibility was to ensure the proper governance of sacramental liturgy and the "dispensing" of sacraments through the ordained. The sacramentality of the church itself was scarcely conceivable in this framework.

The alternative view, for which the theology of Karl Rahner will serve here as the prime illustration, connects the created grace of the sacraments to the larger field of God's uncreated grace. Rahner contends that sacraments, far from being merely the efficient cause of grace in specific liturgical actions, are themselves grace manifest symbolically: "This sacramental sign of grace is an effective sign not inasmuch as it would call forth a resolve of God to bestow grace which would not exist without it, but inasmuch as through it precisely this will of God to bestow grace manifests itself at the historical level, and thereby renders itself historically irreversible."[100]

Most notably for this discussion, Rahner stresses that the seven ecclesial sacraments are expressions of the church as itself the product of grace: "What the sacraments signify first and foremost is not what they bring forth, but that which brings them forth and which they are enabled to signify because they are brought forth by it, that is, by the church."[101] In Rahner's presentation, the church is the foundation and source (*das Grundsakrament*), "the well-spring of the sacraments in the strict sense," of the liturgical sacraments.[102] The church can be such since it is the sacramental expression of Jesus Christ, the primordial sacrament (*das Ursakrament*). In this way, Rahner brings together his theology of grace, revelation, and ecclesiology.

---

99. Vorgrimler, *Sacramental Theology*, 57–62.

100. Karl Rahner, "What Is a Sacrament?," in *Theological Investigations*, vol. 14, trans. D. Bourke (New York: Crossroad, 1976), 144.

101. Karl Rahner, "Understanding the Priestly Office," in *Theological Investigations*, vol. 22, trans. J. Donceel (New York: Crossroad, 1991), 210–11.

102. Karl Rahner, *The Church and the Sacraments*, trans. W. J. O'Hara (London: Burns and Oates, 1974), 18.

The church, then, is not simply the overseer of sacraments but is itself "the social accessibility of the historico-sacramental permanent presence of the salvation reality of Christ."[103] Since the church is the overarching symbol of the grace that the sacraments make present, sacraments are irreducibly ecclesial. The seven ecclesial sacraments make present in particular circumstances, for communities and the individuals who form them, the grace of God revealed in Jesus through the Holy Spirit, the grace constitutive of the church. This means that the sacraments are other than freestanding sources of grace brought into being by priestly actions: they are never less than expressions of the church. It is the church that exists as "the abiding presence of that primordial sacramental word of definitive grace, which Christ is in the world, effecting what is uttered by uttering it in sign."[104] Hence, the church as *Grundsakrament*.

The analysis of the church in terms of grace encapsulates the degree to which the theology underpinning sacramental ecclesiology diverges from that constitutive of "perfect society." Where the pre-conciliar theological manuals attributed various aspects of the church to specific words and actions of Jesus Christ prior to his crucifixion, sacramental ecclesiology locates the church within a broader understanding of Jesus as the source of grace. This fuller portrait is no less attentive to the life of Jesus, but encompasses the whole of his life, including death, resurrection, and ascension. It establishes the church, in the formulation of Joseph Komonchak, as something other than what simply follows after Jesus: "It is not enough to say that the church arose and arises out of the event of Jesus Christ: the emergence of the church, both historically and theologically, is a dimension of the event of Jesus Christ."[105] This broader vision is crucial, especially because it creates an opening to elaborate the connection between the Holy Spirit and the church, a connection crucial to the central themes of this volume.

103. Karl Rahner, "Priestly Existence," in *Theological Investigations*, vol. 3, trans. K-H. Kruger and B. Kruger (New York: Crossroad, 1982), 248.

104. Ibid. For exposition and analysis of Rahner's sacramental ecclesiology, see Richard Lennan, "'Narcissistic Aestheticism'?: An Assessment of Karl Rahner's Sacramental Ecclesiology," *Philosophy and Theology*, 25 (2013): 249–70.

105. Joseph Komonchak, "The Future of Theology in the Church," in *New Horizons in Theology*, ed. Terrence Tilley (Maryknoll, NY: Orbis, 2005), 30.

The Holy Spirit and the Church's Sacramentality

The emphasis on the Spirit is not an alternative to the central role of Christ in God's self-communication that grounds the mystery of the church. What this emphasis does generate is an ecclesiology that takes into account "the entire action of God in Jesus Christ, from his birth, his ministry and the calling of the disciples, through to his death and resurrection and the sending of the Spirit to the witnesses of his resurrection."[106] As Ormond Rush argues, the grounding of the church in both Christ and the Spirit is a proper representation of the church's link to the trinitarian dynamics of God's self-communication: "The Spirit from the Father, with whom Jesus the *Christos* was anointed, is the same Spirit whom the Father sends upon, and whom the Risen One shares with, the community of Christ's disciples at Pentecost. . . . The church is the place where the mission of the Word and the mission of the Spirit find their clearest point of conjuncture in human history."[107]

The focus on the Spirit endows sacramental ecclesiology with depth and breadth. To substantiate that claim, it is necessary to consider the Spirit's *modus operandi*. Unlike the self-communication of the second person of the Trinity who enters into humanity in Jesus Christ, the Spirit does not become incarnate in human history, but remains "spirit." If that were all that could be said about the activity of the Spirit, then the church, its sacramental theology, and even the claim that there is a Holy Spirit would be problematic because the Spirit, as spirit, would be unknowable to bodily human beings.

Christian faith addresses this dilemma by linking the Spirit to the church: "The Church is, in a phrase used by the Fathers, the place 'where the Spirit flourishes.'"[108] As sacrament, the church is the primary

106. Hans Küng, *The Church*, trans. R. Ockenden and R. Ockenden (New York: Image Books, 1976), 110. See also, Adelbert Denaux, "Did Jesus Found the Church?," *Louvain Studies* 21 (1996): 25–45, and Daniel Harrington, *The Church According to the New Testament: What the Wisdom and Witness of Early Christianity Teach Us Today* (Franklin, WI: Sheed and Ward, 2001), 20–21.

107. Ormond Rush, *The Eyes of Faith: The Sense of the Faithful and the Church's Reception of Revelation* (Washington, DC: Catholic University of America Press, 2009), 37–38.

108. *Catechism of the Catholic Church*, 2nd ed. (United States Catholic Conference—Libreria Editrice Vaticana, 1997), 749.

means by which the Spirit makes the risen Christ present in history and by which humanity comes to know the Spirit: "The true image of the Holy Spirit is the church, the Christian community with its assemblies. An assembled congregation seeking the will of God, with one mind, attentive to every individual and making something of the love of God visible: that is the most beautiful reflection of the Holy Spirit."[109] The Spirit's relationship to the church identifies the Christian community as integral to God's self-revelation, as a theological reality that is more than a voluntary association of believers or a sociological phenomenon, while being also—as ever, paradoxically—a voluntary association of believers and a sociological phenomenon. As the "universal sacrament of salvation" (LG 48), the church is the guarantee that the Spirit of Christ offers God's reconciling love to the whole of creation.

Consequently, *Lumen Gentium* recognizes that there is "no mean analogy" (*non mediocrem analogiam*) between the role that the "social structure of the Church" plays in relation to the Spirit and the role that the human nature of Jesus plays in relation to his divine nature (LG 8).[110] This symbolic or sacramental perspective on the church's "social structure" is likely to arouse anxiety as it could sound as if the church, represented by its authorities, is asserting equality with God or commandeering grace in an imperialistic manner. Although such fears and dangers require attention, the council's teaching is a reminder of "the scandal of particularity" that accompanies God's revelation in Israel and, especially, in Jesus Christ. In other words, the identification of the church as a sacrament, the claim that a flawed church is the primary symbol of God's Spirit, is consistent with the history of revelation, especially with the paradox central to the theology of revelation: that the transcendent God, whose mystery will forever exceed our grasp, chooses to enter into human history, to engage with human beings in a human way.

The implications of the church's sacramentality emerge vividly in the work of Louis-Marie Chauvet. As part of his analysis of ecclesiology, Chauvet maintains that the church, as a sacrament constituted by the Spirit, is the only venue that lays claim explicitly to being a guaranteed means of access to Jesus Christ as crucified and risen. Chauvet's principal contention is that the church, through its proclamation of

109. Lohfink, *Prayer Takes Us Home*, 18.
110. For the Latin text, see Tanner, *Decrees of the Ecumenical Councils*, 854.

the Word, celebration of the sacraments in liturgy, and ethical action, all of which are Spirit-driven, is a source of encounter with Christ, whom the Spirit makes present.[111] As Chauvet acknowledges, this principle presents a challenge to those seeking an unmediated or private relationship to Christ: "the faith requires a *renunciation of a direct line*, one could say a Gnostic line, to Jesus Christ."[112] In stark terms, Chauvet asserts that to seek the risen Jesus without reference to the church is to seek a "corpse," since Christ lives now, through the Spirit, only in his body that is the church.[113] Rahner makes a similar point, emphasizing that the church offers a unique and necessary link to those separated in time from the historical events of God's revelation in Jesus Christ: "Christianity is a historical religion bound up with the one Jesus Christ. I heard of him only through the Church and not otherwise. . . . Attachment to the Church is the price I pay for this historical origin"—this is a claim that will also be important in chapter 5 in the context of discussing apostolicity.[114]

Neither Chauvet nor Rahner suggests that the church controls access to God's grace or can dictate the movement of God's self-communicating Spirit. Nonetheless, both theologians do insist on the centrality of the church to God's trinitarian self-communication. Were such claims to be resistant to nuance, or tantamount to an assertion of the church's perfection, they would be at odds with the facts of experience that testify to a less-than-perfect church. In that form, they would also reduce to meaninglessness this book's focus on "tilling," on seeking a more authentic and effective church.

The danger that the application of "sacrament" to the church could suggest a community beyond the need for conversion brings to the fore the possibility that this theology could be a form of blueprint ecclesiology. It is possible to frame this critique as a question: How can the church be always and everywhere a sacrament of grace if the actions of individuals and communities contradict God's life-giving grace?

---

111. Louis-Marie Chauvet, *Symbol and Sacrament: A Sacramental Reinterpretation of Christian Existence*, trans. P. Madigan and M. Beaumont (Collegeville, MN: Pueblo, 1995), 163–64.

112. Ibid., 172; original emphasis.

113. Ibid., 173.

114. Karl Rahner, "Courage for an Ecclesial Christianity," in *Theological Investigations*, vol. 20, trans. E. Quinn (New York: Crossroad, 1986), 9.

Along these lines, Paul Lakeland contends that "the Church as sacrament is only as efficacious as its individual members are faith-filled and loving witnesses to the Gospel."[115] Consequently, only what arises from the actual lives of "the people of God" in specific circumstances serves a more effective presence of the church in the world. Lakeland argues that this "inductive" way of proceeding, which involves naming where the Spirit is actually at work in the church, is in sharp contrast to the approach of those in authority in the Roman Catholic Church, which he regards as a "deductive" method that is prescriptive—at times, even proscriptive—elitist, universal, and theoretical.[116] In Lakeland's presentation, all theological descriptions of the church and its presence in the world must reflect the lived reality of the church, which he names "ecclesiality," rather than be the outcome of second-order reflection, which is "ecclesiology."[117] In other words, there ought not to be even the slightest possibility of employing blueprints when discussing the church.

Lakeland contends that if the church is to be a saving presence in the world, that presence "is to be found in the Church as the community of believers and in the lives and witness of individual believers, not in the Church as Church."[118] The excesses of the church's history—the Crusades, the medieval papacy, the Inquisition, the defense of slavery, and more—reveal the absence of the Spirit from the church: "In error, it was not in the Spirit. The Spirit returned to it in and through the prayer and faithful struggles of Catholics, who were often persecuted by the very church they sought to reclaim."[119] At the heart of Lakeland's approach is the conviction that "the faithful sociality of the whole believing community," rather than an ecclesiological theory or ecclesiastical authorities, is key to authenticity in the church.[120]

---

115. Paul Lakeland, "The U.S. Church, the Secular World and the Temptation to 'Integrism,'" *Horizons* 38 (2011): 14.

116. Paul Lakeland, "Maturity and the Lay Vocation: From Ecclesiology to Ecclesiality," in *Catholic Identity and the Laity*, ed. Tim Muldoon (Maryknoll, NY: Orbis, 2009), 247–48.

117. Ibid., 246.

118. Lakeland, "U.S. Church," 17.

119. Paul Lakeland, *Catholicism at the Crossroads: How the Laity Can Save the Church* (New York: Continuum, 2007), 4.

120. Lakeland, "Maturity and the Lay Vocation," 246.

Similarly to Lakeland, Nicholas Healy questions whether it is valid to associate the Holy Spirit with the church in an unqualified way: "Faced with the confused and sinful practices and intentions and construals of our congregations, we need to know how the Holy Spirit, rather than being 'bound' to the church and its practices, can *overcome* the effects of the churches upon their membership, and the membership upon the churches, so that in spite of the church as well as by its help we may be sanctified and brought closer to Christ."[121] In illuminating the church's limits, the sinfulness of the ecclesial community confirms that only conversion to the Holy Spirit can ensure virtue in the church: "We rightly expect the Spirit to be working freely and sometimes in unsettling ways within the church and its members as the Spirit imparts charity and other gifts, strengthens us by the sacraments and refocuses us upon our goal through the church's proclamation of the word."[122]

What, then, of "sacrament"? Is it simply a blueprint that divorces theological reflection on the church from the realities of the history and practice that leave no room for doubting the church's need for significant tilling? One way to proceed in responding to these questions is to draw from Vatican II's understanding of the church's holiness, a theme that has much to do with grace, sacramentality, and the church's humanity.

The fact that *Lumen Gentium* characterizes the church as "unfailingly holy" (LG 39) might not seem too promising a start to the endeavor to "redeem" the description of the church as sacrament from bearing the scarlet letter assigned to blueprint ecclesiologies. Yet, the council ascribes the source of the church's holiness to what has formed the backbone of this present chapter: the constancy of God's grace. The church, then, is "at once holy and always in need of purification" (LG 8). The abiding holiness is solely the product of God's self-communication that establishes the church as symbol; the need for purification reflects the humanity inseparable from this symbol.

The church's sacramentality is no less ambiguous than is true of all other symbols. Far from being a license for complacency or hubris,

---

121. Nicholas Healy, "Practices and the New Ecclesiology: Misplaced Concreteness?," *International Journal of Systematic Theology* 5 (2003): 303; original emphasis.
122. Ibid., 307.

this truth is a stimulus to tilling, to conversion that seeks to align the humanity of the church with its deepest reality—grace. Rahner confirms this claim directly when he argues that the classification of the church as "sacrament" identifies the ecclesial community as "both the proclaiming bearer of the revealing word of God as his utterance of salvation to the world, *and at the same time* [the] subject hearkening and believing, to whom that word of salvation of God in Christ is addressed.[123] From this perspective, the church's sacramentality is not simply compatible with its conversion, but requires conversion if the church is to be faithful to grace.

Lakeland and Healy make a crucial point in challenging self-satisfaction and self-righteousness in the church, but it is also true that even communities hungry for authenticity, for witnessing to grace in the world, are not failure-proof. Nor will any theology, including—sadly—the one that this book is developing, eliminate the possibility of the sinfulness that scars the church's life and witness.

The designation of the church as sacrament need not be a source of self-congratulatory pride or arrogant blindness to failures. It can stimulate the tilling that expresses conversion, the willingness to be more faithful. As God's initiative, the church's sacramentality points toward the eschatological fulfillment of the Christian community, even as the grace of that fulfillment prompts the conversion of all expressions of the church's life. At the same time, the unadulterated gift of grace manifests itself already in the church through Scripture, the ecclesial sacraments, and the example of Christian service evident in the "saints," past and present, as well as acknowledged and anonymous. In both aspects, "sacrament" leaves no doubt that the church is to be a community living by faith and hope. These two qualities serve the tilling of the church and are consistent with the existence of the church as a pilgrim, as chapter 3 will demonstrate.

---

123. Rahner, "What Is a Sacrament?," 143; original emphasis.

3

The Pilgrim Community
of Faith and Hope

Archdeacon Theophilus Grantly has a mission. Dr. Grantly, an imperious figure in the novels that begin Anthony Trollope's *Barchester* series, sets himself "to guard the citadel of the church from the most rampant of its enemies . . . and secure, if possible, the comforts of his creed for coming generations of ecclesiastical dignitaries."[1] Consistent with this resolve, the archdeacon is implacably hostile to new ideas and to even the faintest prospect of innovation in any aspect of the church's life. Equally, he opposes all social movements seeking to "improve" society, preferring that the church, from its secure place above the madding crowd, offer benign guidance to the general population. Dr. Grantly's principal interest is actually the maintenance of all that serves his personal comfort, but he styles himself a noble custodian of the church and society as God would have them, as stable, tranquil, and unadventurous.

Dr. Grantly is a caricature, a version of nineteenth-century Anglicanism that Trollope parodied to great effect. His attitudes to the church and the world might be overstated, but they are more than the stuff

1. Anthony Trollope, *The Warden* (1855; repr., Mineola, NY: Dover, 1998), 32.

of satire. The longing for the church to be a refuge in the midst of society's upheavals is certainly evident beyond the rarefied precincts of
Barchester cathedral. Among present-day Catholics, experiencing still
the wake of the clerical sexual abuse crisis, there would probably be
little enthusiasm for the clerical consolations beloved of the archdeacon, but perhaps some sympathy for Dr. Grantly's antagonism toward
the breadth and rapidity of social changes, especially when they have
an impact on the church. There might even be a sense that such resistance accords with divine desires.

God, of course, is foundational to consideration of the church, but
doing justice to the link between the church and God requires light and
shade absent from the archdeacon's worldview. When such nuance is
missing, a romanticized, even inaccurate, portrait of the church results.
Such a portrait, which might depict its subject as equivalent to the
unalloyed goodness of God, can generate a self-satisfied church, one
blind to its own shortcomings and resistant to critique. Pride in that
same divine favor can diminish the openness of the church's members
to engage with, and learn from, the restless energy of the world that
grace pervades. Any reluctance to recognize grace at work beyond the
church's boundaries turns the church inward and fuels the church's separation from the wider community. In so doing, it vitiates the church's
commitment to mission. When this occurs, there is little incentive for
addressing the limits and failures of the church's past and present in the
hope of shaping a future more in tune with grace. Enthusiasm for all
that "tilling the church" captures would then be hard to find.

The present chapter depicts the relationship between the grace of
the trinitarian God and the ecclesial community in ways that diverge
sharply from the preferred options of Archdeacon Grantly. The emphasis here will be on grace as the motive for "movement" in the church, for
conversion and the embrace of all that deepens the faithfulness of the
church. The sections of the chapter will stress that God's relationship
to the church is the catalyst for the ecclesial community's open-ended
pilgrimage toward God's ever-new future, rather than justification for
inertia, and certainly not for self-satisfaction. These emphases prepare
the way for chapter 4, which will consider how the church might engage
constructively with the wider world.

The bedrock of this chapter is its presentation of the church as a
community of faith and hope. This community is unimaginable out-

side of its explicit, even unique, relationship to the grace of God. It is grace that guides the church on its pilgrimage through the multiple complexities of time, place, and human behavior to the fulfillment of life in Jesus Christ. Grace provides the impetus for faith as well as its nourishment. The more that receptivity to grace characterizes the life of the church, then, the more the church develops as a community of faith. Equally, receptivity to grace can form the church into a symbol of hope for people searching for models of fruitful participation in twenty-first-century society. Through this same receptivity, the church can become more fully a community that spreads God's love beyond itself.

Grace and the Community of Faith

The abuse crisis in the Catholic Church has brought into relief the deleterious effects of a fixation on the church's divine favor. As the result of "a preoccupation with protecting the institution's 'good name' and reputation," many bishops failed to act decisively against abusive priests but also ignored, rebuffed, or even discredited survivors of abuse.[2] Various inquiries into abuse have documented that such responses were widespread, even though they exacerbated the suffering of survivors and contradicted the core responsibilities of the church's authorities.

The abuse crisis has aggravated the proliferation of "nones," those rejecting traditional religious belonging, not least belonging to the Catholic Church. Subsets of this phenomenon include "disaffiliation" and "deconversion," terms conveying an explicit choice to sever connection to a community of faith, rather than a casual drifting away or "lapsing" from religious practice.[3] The decision to disaffiliate can give

---

2. The quote is from the judicial inquiry that investigated abuse in the Catholic Church in Australia; see *Report of the Royal Commission into Institutional Responses to Child Sexual Abuse* (December 2017), vol. 16, book 1, 28, https://www.childabuse royalcommission.gov.au/religious-institutions.

3. For discussion of the key terms, see J. Patrick Hornbeck, "Deconversion: What, Who, Why, How?," in Tom Beaudoin, J. Patrick Hornbeck, and William Portier, "Deconversion and Disaffiliation in Contemporary US Roman Catholicism," *Horizons* 40 (2013): 267; see also Tom Beaudoin and J. Patrick Hornbeck, "Deconversion and Ordinary Theology: A Catholic Study," in *Exploring Ordinary Theology: Everyday Christian Believing and the Church*, ed. Jeff Astley and Leslie Francis (Burlington, VT: Ashgate, 2013), 33–44.

expression to the conviction that traditional ecclesial communities are either an obstacle to spiritual development or do not foster it sufficiently.[4] The reasons why people sever their ties to the church are usually multifaceted rather than one-dimensional, but may well include a sense of distrust or feeling unwelcome in the ecclesial community.[5] In the context of issues that touch on gender and sexuality, alienation from the church is especially evident. In relation to these issues, the divergence between contemporary social values and the church's official stances is unmistakable, and often has significant implications both for participation in the ecclesial community and for employment in parishes, schools, and other settings under the sponsorship of the Catholic Church.[6]

The abuse crisis and the trend away from ecclesial belonging challenge complacency in the church. They challenge especially any tendency to inflate the extent to which policies and practices within the church automatically and unerringly reflect the life-giving God. This challenge is highly significant for the future of the church. Hope for the church's future does not require membership of the church to be surging exponentially or that every element of the church's life receives popular acclaim. Still, it is difficult to reconcile faith in the connection between the church and God's life-giving Holy Spirit if self-protection, while being mired in scandal, is a dominant concern for leaders of the ecclesial community.

Similarly, a church that acts in the world as "an impregnable fortress with small arrow-slits in the walls from which the defenders shoot at their enemies" is unlikely to be a church that manifests all that the

4. For the challenge of ecclesial faith in a time of "spiritual dislocation," see Paul Crowley, *The Unmoored God: Believing in a Time of Dislocation* (Maryknoll, NY: Orbis, 2017), 10–13.

5. For analysis of reasons for disaffiliation, see Robert McArty and John Vitek, *Going, Going, Gone: The Dynamics of Disaffiliation in Young Catholics* (Winona, MN: St Mary's, 2017), and James Michael Nagle, "The Thinker and the Guide: A Conversation Concerning Religious Disaffiliation from the Catholic Church," *Journal of Ecumenical Studies* 54 (2019): 328–51.

6. For an overview of these issues among Catholic "nones," see Kaya Oakes, *The Nones Are Alright: A New Generation of Believers, Seekers, and Those in Between* (Maryknoll, NY: Orbis, 2015).

Holy Spirit enables.[7] In light of these considerations, a key task for ecclesiology must be to promote the appropriation of all that would enable the ecclesial community to be life-giving for a diverse membership, and so be a hope-filled body that fosters hope in others.

Just as the theology of symbol in chapter 2 argued that the efficacy of grace does not require symbols to be rare, precious, or irresistible—in a word, "perfect"—so grace operates in and through the church's complexity, rather than despite this complexity. Nonetheless, as this book has insisted from the beginning, grace neither eliminates the possibility of individual and communal sin nor inoculates the church against all experiences of failure and inconsistency.

The dynamics of the Holy Spirit's presence by grace in the life of the community of faith reflect the mystery of God's relationship to humanity: grace is not a vaccine against any possibility of mediocrity and smugness, but nor does it conform to "human standards" by choosing the powerful, wise, and strong (1 Cor 1:26-29). As the unwavering constant of the church's life, the Spirit stimulates the discipleship of the church, its faithfulness to the call of Christ. Authentic faithfulness includes the commitment to narrowing the gap between what God enables and what the Christian community and its individual members actually do. When members of the church embrace and enact this commitment, their actions contribute to the tilling of the church.

A major task of ecclesiology is to explore what it means for the church to live as a body that grace constitutes, a body that is the sacramental expression of grace yet remains human rather than assuming an angelic aura. The specifics of responses to grace belong to the circumstances of particular communities, as chapter 1 detailed. Nonetheless, overarching reflection on the elements common to ecclesial faith can help to inform those responses.

With this purpose in mind, this section will focus on the place of the church in what the Christian tradition refers to as the act of faith, rather than on individual beliefs.[8] The concentration here will be on

---

7. Karl Rahner, "The Christian in His World," in *Theological Investigations*, vol. 7, trans. D. Bourke (New York: Crossroad, 1977), 96.

8. The Christian tradition distinguishes, without separating, the "act of faith" (*fides qua*) and the "content of faith" (*fides quae*); see Wolfgang Beinert, "Faith," in *Handbook*

three interrelated elements of faith: its role in defining the purpose of human life; its communal dimension, which has implications for the interweaving of faith and history; and its orientation to the future, the orientation that frames the church's pilgrimage as the meeting point of faith and hope. This threefold analysis will underscore that ecclesial faith is a lifelong process of conversion, rather than a once-for-all action that is exempt from stages, gradations, or even the possibility of regression.[9]

The Dynamics of Faith

The Christian tradition portrays faith as a graced response to God's free act of self-revelation.[10] As a relationship with God, rather than with a lesser reality, faith moves human beings from the center of their own lives. Faith surrenders that centrality to God. Consistent with the disruptive nature of encounters with God that the previous chapter discussed, faith is an acknowledgment that human beings are not self-sufficient, that they are neither their own source nor their own fulfillment. As confronting as such an analysis could be, the Christian tradition is unequivocal in its insistence that this displacement enables the full flowering of humanity, including of the human intellect: "Illumined by faith, reason is set free from the fragility and limitations deriving from the disobedience of sin and finds the strength required to rise to the knowledge of the Triune God."[11]

The grace of the Spirit sets all people on the path to "the radical re-ordering of [our] transcendent nature in knowledge and freedom towards the immediate reality of God through God's self-communication in grace."[12] Faith embraces this "re-ordering." Humanity's acceptance of

---

of Catholic Theology, ed. Wolfgang Beinert and Francis Schüssler Fiorenza (New York: Crossroad Publishing, 1995), 249–53.

9. For an overview of the elements proper to a theology of faith, see Joseph Doré, "Theology's Responsibility and Tasks in Today's Church and World," *Theological Studies* 65 (2004): 699–713.

10. See, for example, the exposition of revelation and faith under the heading "The Profession of Faith," in the *Catechism of the Catholic Church*, 26–184.

11. Pope John Paul II, *Fides et Ratio*, Faith and Reason (Boston: Pauline Books, 1998), 43.

12. Karl Rahner, "Experience of the Spirit and Existential Commitment," in *Theological Investigations*, vol. 16, trans. D. Morland (New York: Crossroad, 1983), 27–28.

a relationship with God expresses, Pope Francis contends in *Lumen Fidei* (LF), openness to a "primordial gift" (LF 19) that is inseparable from the invitation to surrender to what human calculation and control cannot determine.[13] From within the context of humanity's graced existence, to recall the centerpiece of chapter 2, it is possible to interpret what may appear to be the demanding nature of faith as something other than an imposition by the powerful partner—God—on the lesser party—human beings. Still, it remains true that God will never fit neatly into humanity's schemes for managing or enriching life. As both a gift and a path to freedom, faith plants the seed for the growth of hope. Hope will feature later in the chapter, but it is immediately relevant to note that hope is incompatible with the assertion of self-sufficiency by finite human beings.

In an effort to convey the challenge and possibility of faith, John Henry Newman (1801–90) approaches it as an expression of love, which he contrasts with reason. Newman is not suggesting that faith is irrational, but that reasons for belief, consisting more of "presumptions and ventures after the truth than of accurate and complete proofs," do not fully ground the commitment of faith.[14] Ultimately, Newman stresses, it is the willingness to risk oneself to the love of God, rather than reasoned assessments—"but calculation never made a hero"—that issues in faith.[15]

From a different angle, but toward the same conclusion, Karl Rahner depicts faith as an act of love, rather than of knowledge: knowledge implies control over the object known, while faith, like love, relinquishes the campaign to control what is other. The encounter with the God of mystery, claims Rahner, "forces knowledge to surpass itself and both preserve and transform itself into a more comprehensive act, that of love."[16] Faith in God, then, parallels the loving commitment

---

13. Pope Francis, *Lumen Fidei*, The Light of Faith, http://www.vatican.va/content/francesco/en/encyclicals/documents/papa-francesco_20130629_enciclica-lumen-fidei.html.

14. John Henry Newman, *An Essay on the Development of Doctrine*, 3rd ed. (1878; New York: Cosimo, 2007), 327.

15. Ibid., 328.

16. Karl Rahner, "The Concept of Mystery in Catholic Theology," in *Theological Investigations*, vol. 4, trans. K. Smyth (New York: Crossroad, 1982), 58.

between human beings, since both require a degree of self-emptying and risk-taking:

> The act of self-commitment to the other has a radical, absolute, unconditional quality by no means adequately founded or based on the antecedent grounds for that act. In this self-abandonment, once all antecedent considerations, verifications, and demands of reasonableness and legitimation are posited—one ventures more, and *must* venture more than these grounds seems to justify.[17]

Debates about the rationality of faith dominate much contemporary discussion of the topic, but, as Newman and Rahner demonstrate, the human dynamics of faith extend beyond that single concern.[18] In his analysis of faith, Pope Francis likewise focuses not on the intertwining of faith and reason, but on faith as a form of "listening," more specifically as listening to God. As Pope Francis formulates it, God speaks to human beings not with the voice of a stranger but as one who can reach all people, since God is "a faithful God who enters into a relationship of love with [humanity] and speaks his word to [humanity]" (LF 29). As a response to the invitation of the transcendent God, faith is not one activity among the many in which human beings engage. Properly understood, faith is the activity that colors all others: "Faith is not a landscape to be seen, but eyes for seeing. It is not a world, but a gaze upon the world. It is not a book to be read, but a grammar for reading—for reading all books."[19] Faith, then, is not something a person possesses, but an activity that involves the whole person and every dimension of life, all of which God's self-giving in grace encompasses. This means that the concerns of faith do not belong solely within the ambit of "religion," but stretch toward all that God's grace enlivens.

---

17. Karl Rahner, *The Love of Jesus and the Love of Neighbor*, trans. R. Barr (New York: Crossroad, 1983), 17; original emphasis.

18. For a helpful overview of contemporary challenges to faith, especially in light of "the new atheism," see Neil Brown, *Believing in God: Challenges of the Twenty-First Century* (Strathfield, NSW: St Pauls, 2016).

19. Clodovis Boff, *Theology and Praxis*, trans. R. Barr (Maryknoll, NY: Orbis, 1987), 123.

This conclusion illuminates further how the "integral ecology" that *Laudato Si'* promotes is radically compatible with faith.

The decentering proper to humanity's relationship with God has an echo in faith's communal dimension, the second of the facets of faith that this section is detailing. Faith's communal dimension is consistent with the fact that human beings are social beings rather than monads.[20] Humanity's social existence does not mean that large numbers of individuals simply exist in the same time and place, something they could do while remaining isolated from each other. Rather, human beings develop relationships as they share ideas, feelings, and experiences, and as they unite to pursue joint projects, affirm shared values, or resist collective threats. There can be, as Newman phrases it, "a principle of sympathy and a bond of intercourse between those whose minds had been thus variously wrought into a common assent."[21] These connections reflect more than intellectual agreement with abstract principles ordering life.

As bodily creatures, human beings can construct personal bonds of warmth and friendship, illustrating that "the finite, spiritual essence of [humanity] only comes to self-expression in relationship to what is other, and in the ultimate analysis this other must be personal."[22] Yet, "personal experience" does not exist in a vacuum or bear the hallmarks proper only to "uniqueness, irreducibility, or exemption from critique."[23] What is personal is not necessarily "private," such that it includes only the individual at the heart of the experience. The communal identity of human beings is not hostile to individuality, nor need it result in a featureless collectivism. What the emphasis on the communal dimension of human life does highlight is that even individuality is not independent of the "social, mediated, and linguistic character of consciousness."[24] Even individuals are not islands.

---

20. For an analysis of humanity's social existence as one aspect of a series of "anthropological constants," see Edward Schillebeeckx, *Christ: The Experience of Jesus as Lord*, trans. J. Bowden (New York: Seabury, 1980), 731–43.

21. John Henry Newman, *An Essay in Aid of a Grammar of Assent* (1870; repr., Notre Dame, IN: University of Notre Dame Press, 1979), 85.

22. Rahner, "Experience of the Spirit and Existential Commitment," 28.

23. George Schner, "The Appeal to Experience," *Theological Studies* 53 (1992): 48.

24. Ibid., 47.

The human experience of God is also personal without being private. It is particular to each person, such that no surrogate can substitute for the unique profile of any other person, but this does not suggest that each person has her own God or that an encounter with the trinitarian God who is the source of all life has no effects on a person's social existence. Since community "provides the overall horizon of understanding within which human experience begins to make sense," the human experience of God is comprehensible only within a community.[25]

The communal nature of the response to God depends in part on the irreducibly communal aspect of human life, but it depends, too, on the dynamics of God's grace, which is the self-communication of the trinitarian God. As such, the dynamics of grace engender the recognition that being human "is not to be finally from, or for, or with oneself alone," but to be "ecstatic," directed beyond oneself.[26] For this reason, fully developed responses to God are irreconcilable with solipsism and all forms of social apartheid.

Faith, like every relationship, "involves not only believing in the other to whom one is related, but doing for and receiving from the other."[27] In the context of faith in God, "receiving from the other" draws believers into relationship with the whole of God's creation—again, the guiding insight of integral ecology. To reflect the life-giving God who is their source, human relationships require a commitment to justice (Isa 58:6-7) and to generosity (Mark 12:31). Even when they are not a product of explicitly religious faith and do not lead to a specific relationship with God, selfless ways of living can be an "anonymous" form of faith.[28] Dedication to the well-being of others and generous

---

25. Dermot Lane, *The Experience of God: An Invitation to do Theology*, rev. ed. (Mahwah, NJ: Paulist, 2003), 21.

26. Tony Kelly, *An Expanding Theology: Faith in a World of Connections* (Newtown, NSW: E. J. Dwyer, 1993), 118.

27. Terrence Tilley, *Faith: What It Is and What It Isn't* (Maryknoll, NY: Orbis, 2010), 95.

28. Karl Rahner develops a theology of "the anonymous Christian" around the possibility of loving actions undertaken in response to grace by those without explicitly Christian faith, and even without any exposure to that faith; see, for example, "The Christian among Unbelieving Relations," in *Theological Investigations*, vol. 3, trans. K-H. Kruger and B. Kruger (New York: Crossroad, 1982), 355–72, and "Observations

self-giving to them, rather than accruing everything for oneself and separating oneself from others, is a further expression of the decentering of the self that is a response to grace, a response at the heart of faith.

The social nature of humanity is central to the biblical presentation of the covenants between God and Israel. Just as Genesis depicts the creator God as envisaging humanity in relationship with the rest of creation (Gen 2:18-25), so God forms a covenant with a people, a people that is constituted by being brought together in the relationship with God (Exod 19:3-6). The covenants leave no room for doubt that "the revelation of God is directed towards the convocation and renewal of the people of God."[29] Jesus, too, addresses himself to the people of Israel, especially the "lost sheep" among them (Matt 10:6), but also acknowledges that God's life-giving reach extends to all people "from east and west" (Matt 8:5-13). Most dramatically of all, the Holy Spirit at Pentecost binds disparate nationalities together in the one community of faith that is the church (Acts 2:1-36), a community whose members share the one mission, the theme on which chapter 4 will elaborate.

As a body that exists through Jesus and the Holy Spirit, the church attests to the communal reality of Christian faith. Pope Francis emphasizes that faith "is not simply an individual decision which takes place in the depths of the believer's heart, nor a completely private relationship between the 'I' of the believer and the divine 'Thou,' between an autonomous subject and God. By its very nature, faith is open to the 'We' of the Church; it always takes place within her communion" (LF 39). The Christian tradition includes the church as part of the content of faith—"I believe in one, holy, catholic and apostolic church"[30]—thereby asserting that the church is integral to the relationship between God and humanity. The church is where the act of faith and the content of faith meet.[31] In other words, the church is more than an optional venue

---

on the Problem of the 'Anonymous Christian,'" in *Theological Investigations*, vol. 14, trans. D. Bourke (New York: Seabury, 1976), 280–94.

29. International Theological Commission, "Theology Today: Perspectives, Principles and Criteria," *Origins* 41 (2012): 646.

30. See *Catechism of the Catholic Church*, 751-57.

31. See Avery Dulles, "The Ecclesial Dimension of Faith," *Communio* 22 (1995): 418–32, and Jean-Marie Tillard, "Faith, the Believer, and the Church," *One in Christ* 30 (1994): 216–28

for the exercise of the communal dimension of faith, more than "the bearer of the message of Christ which it delivers to individuals (and which then disappears again like a postman)."[32]

Accepting the church as a core constituent of Christian faith can be a particularly confronting exercise. The challenge has manifold aspects, but two principal elements: the association between the church and God can lead to an exaltation of the church that holds the potential for distortions, as the clerical sexual abuse crisis highlights; engagement with the church's structures, and with the range of people who form the church, can decrease the appeal of ecclesial faith, as the earlier discussion of "disaffiliation" noted. The magnitude of these obstacles supports the claim that the willingness of people "to be gathered and interweave their lives with those of others . . . even though in reality each of us wants to be his or her own master and although we would prefer to shut ourselves up within our own four walls—that is the real miracle of the church."[33] The next two sections of the chapter, those exploring "pilgrimage" and "hope," respectively, may help to clarify how it is that this "miracle" need not be rare and spectacular.

Before moving to the future orientation of faith—the third facet of the topic that this section is exploring—it is important to consider that the social dimension of human experience situates human beings in a specific historical and cultural context: "Experience always belongs to someone who exists as a subject at a particular time in a particular place with a particular value system."[34] The experience of God, since it, too, is a genuinely human one, has its location within the setting of a particular history and culture. As God's revelation to Israel and the incarnation of Jesus indicate, there can be "no transhistorical kernel" to the experience of God, but "God's revelatory engagement through history is the thing itself in all its husk-i-ness that is God's self-disclosure."[35] As

---

32. Karl Rahner, "'I Believe in the Church,'" in *Theological Investigations*, vol. 5, trans. K-H. Kruger (New York: Crossroad, 1983), 109–10.

33. Gerhard Lohfink, *No Irrelevant Jesus: On Jesus and the Church Today*, trans. L. Maloney (Collegeville, MN: Liturgical Press, 2014), 158.

34. Lane, *Experience of God*, 33; see also, Stephen Bullivant, *Faith and Unbelief* (Mahwah, NJ: Paulist, 2013), 27.

35. Michael Jinkins, *The Church Faces Death: Ecclesiology in a Post-Modern Context* (New York: Oxford University Press, 1999), 100.

a result, to underline a prevailing emphasis of this volume, the effort to understand how God might be drawing humanity more deeply into communion with God and with the whole created world must engage with the living reality of particular human communities, rather than assuming that individual and communal appropriations of grace follow an invariable pattern.

Particular communities, "alive in creaturely ambiguity and in the creative and redemptive purposes of the God to whom history is the site of salvation," are never frozen in time.[36] These communities, *pace* Dr. Grantly, change. Change comes about as communities engage with the manifold influences at work in their unique social context and among their own members. The reality of the changing world in which every expression of ecclesial life takes place underscores that it is illusory to propose a "golden age" in the history of the church. Such a notion would suggest, falsely, that a certain epoch was the apogee of all possible faithful responses to grace, and offers a pattern applicable to all subsequent periods.

The fact that faith is both shared and to be lived in specific contexts indicates the need for discernment about what constitutes appropriate expressions of faith in particular circumstances. To be faithful to the breadth and depth of the ecclesial community's faith, authentic discernment—a principal theme of chapter 6—requires a commitment to maintain a common faith in the present. It requires the same commitment to maintain continuity with those who have professed faith in Christ over the long history of the church, as well as openness to the transcendent mystery of God that moves humanity toward the future. In *Gaudium et Spes* (GS), its Pastoral Constitution on the Church in the Modern World, Vatican II emphasized that the goal of the Christian community's discernment was to identify "the true signs of God's presence and purpose in the events, the needs and desires which it shares with the rest of humanity today" (GS 11). The argument of this book is that "God's presence and purpose" unites the past, present, and future.

To enrich its discernment, the community of faith draws on the distilled wisdom that "tradition" summarizes. As chapters 5 and 6 will detail, appropriating the richness of tradition requires the creativity

---

36. Ibid.

and faithfulness of the community and its members in their particular circumstances—"Being Christian engages imagination and emotion, energy and passion, not as 'extra' to belief but as integral, central to it. . . . For if these dimensions of our lives are not engaged, can we effectively and seriously believe in any case?"[37] Receiving the church's tradition, which embodies grace not in a fossilized form but as a present reality, requires, then, the creativity of the community that is itself an expression of the Spirit's presence.

The recognition of grace at work through the fluidity of history can act as a bridge to the third feature of faith: its orientation to God's future. This orientation reinforces that faith is not a possession for the present, but a graced willingness to trust that neither the past nor present of human history has exhausted what the trinitarian God can accomplish: "Faith's home is in heaven. She retires from the comfortable, sleeps lightly, eyes heavy with wanderlust. *Your* world is not *the* world, she whispers, which insists on being more, yet again more, and different, sometimes intensely and mysteriously more foreign than you can grasp or tolerate at once. Though it frightens, it draws you still; it has precisely what you didn't know you needed."[38] Vibrant faith does not claim full possession of its object, but remains open to the transcendence of God, which cannot be an artifact from the past or even an object in the present.

Throughout the tumultuous experience of Israel, God calls the people to entrust their future to the faithfulness that God has displayed throughout their history (Deut 32:4-14). This trust, which Pope Francis classifies paradoxically as "remembrance of the future" (LF 9), is what draws Israel into the future, even when external conditions suggest that evil will triumph over God. The history of Israel, especially the promise of a savior at the heart of it, reinforces the idea that trust in God's promises concerning the future, the future that God alone can bring about, is integral to faith.

---

37. Ann Loades, "Word and Sacrament: Recovering Integrity," in *Faith in the Public Forum*, ed. Neil Brown and Robert Gascoigne (Adelaide, SA: Australian Theological Forum, 1999), 30.

38. Michael Heher, "Why We Still Need Theologians," in *The Convergence of Theology: A Festschrift Honoring Gerald O'Collins SJ*, ed. Daniel Kendall and Stephen Davis (Mahwah, NJ: Paulist, 2001), 68; original emphasis.

The biblical prophets illustrate richly the ways in which understanding God as the future of Israel serves as a means to interpret the present of God's people. As God's agents promoting attentiveness to the covenants, the prophets mentor and censure the people of Israel, according to the people's actions in various situations. Although popular usage associates prophets with predictions, the biblical books depict the group principally as God's authentic messengers, rather than as seers: "While it is true that foretelling is an important ingredient and may serve as a sign of the prophet's authority, his essential task is to declare the word of God to the here and now; to disclose the future in order to illumine what is involved in the present."[39] An aspect of prophetic authenticity is the prophet's insistence that God alone is lord of the future, no less than of the present and past.

The prophets dramatize God's unique efficacy in relation to the future by associating the promises of God with current circumstances that are highly inauspicious, circumstances that offer little encouragement for those longing for liberation from suffering and alienation. As a result, God's promises come into relief with dramatic force, standing in contrast to a present blighted either by personal and social sin—"though your sins are like scarlet, they shall be like snow" (Isa 1:18)—or by exile and oppression—"there is hope for your future, says the LORD: your children shall come back to their own country" (Jer 31:17). The prophets not only locate God at the center of the future, they derive that emphasis from the fact that God is the center of the past and present.

God's mercy promises Israel a future fulfillment (Jer 7:23; Ezek 11:20) whose sole source is God, a fulfillment that will come about through God's Anointed One who brings good news (Isa 61:1-4). God's promise and the history of God's faithfulness presage, to repeat Walter Kasper's description that chapter 1 noted, "a greater and more comprehensive fulfillment" than Israel could imagine.[40] Those possibilities, all of which derive from God's self-giving, promote trust in the God who offers assurance that sinfulness will not have the final word in the individual and communal history of human beings. This trust is likewise conducive to engagement with the unknown future, an engagement

---

39. Abraham Joshua Heschel, *The Prophets* (Peabody, MA: Hendrickson, 2010), 12.

40. Walter Kasper, *The Catholic Church: Nature, Reality and Mission*, trans. T. Hoebel (London: Bloomsbury, 2015), 121.

that expresses confidence that God's life-giving power encompasses the future.

The Christian tradition takes up the notion of "salvation" as the category under which to gather the ongoing possibilities and promise that the relationship with God opens for humanity and the whole of creation.[41] Expressions of the longing for all that God can accomplish span the entirety of the Bible, from Genesis (Gen 49:18) to Revelation (Rev 19:1). The God who is interwoven with the promise of an ever-new future for God's people is also the God of Jesus Christ, in whom "everything has become new" (2 Cor 5:17). The particularity of Christian faith lies in naming Jesus Christ as the center of the future, as the one through whom all life will come to its fulfillment.

In the Christian context, faith involves a response to the God whom Jesus makes known, the God who continues to be present through the Holy Spirit. Emblematic of Christian faith is the willingness to trust that "the one who began a good work among you will bring it to completion by the day of Jesus Christ" (Phil 1:6). Faith, then, bears an intrinsic orientation toward God as what Rahner names "the absolute future," which transcends all that human beings might imagine as the limits of possibility.[42] This orientation locates humanity in relation to the "more" that God alone can enable.

This "more" of God requires of those open to receive it the willingness to move, either through a change of attitudes, which gives birth to new ways of acting, or through a physical change of place. In his analysis of faith, for example, Pope Francis associates listening and responding to God with the nature of faith as a "journey," one proper to human beings as "wayfarers," terms that evoke humanity's orientation toward God as the source of the future (LF 29–35). The existence of

41. For an overview of the biblical and theological history of "salvation," see Gerhard Ludwig Müller, "Salvation," in *Handbook of Catholic Theology*, ed. Wolfgang Beinert and Francis Schüssler Fiorenza (New York: Crossroad, 2000), 639–42.

42. Rahner's description of God as "the absolute future" pervades his theology; see, for example, "Marxist Utopia and the Christian Future of Man," in *Theological Investigations*, vol. 6, trans. K-H. Kruger and B. Kruger (New York: Crossroad, 1982), 59–68, and "A Fragmentary Aspect of a Theological Evaluation of the Concept of the Future," in *Theological Investigations*, vol. 10, trans. D. Bourke (New York: Crossroad, 1977), 235–41.

the church as "the people of God," a term that expresses "the being-on-the-way in history of God's people and, at the same time, God's being with us and among us on this way," amplifies the connection between faith, specifically ecclesial faith, and the church's orientation to the future.[43] As part of the process of being on the way, believers, as Pope Francis stresses, "must be ready to let themselves be led, to come out of themselves and to find the God of perpetual surprises" (LF 35).

The principal features of graced faith in God—that it "decenters" believers, that it is communal and embodied in a tradition able to respond to the circumstances of the present, and that it moves toward the fullness of God's life—all indicate faith's dynamism. The image of the church as a pilgrim accords well with these dynamics. As the next section of the chapter will argue, the church's relationship to God's unknowable future, to the fullness of God's reign, can prompt the tilling that challenges complacency in the ecclesial community and deepens the awareness that encounters with grace in the present moment of history call for movement in the church.

The Spirit-Led Pilgrim Church

The use of "pilgrim" in relation to the church can locate its ancestry in the long history of God's promise of salvation. The journey from Egypt to the "land that I swore to their ancestors to give them" (Josh 1:6) is the archetype of the movement that the people of Israel undertake as part of their relationship with God. Many other forms of journey connect conversion to God with the willingness to move. This movement can apply to attitudes, to the process of attuning to the God who defies neat categories: "For my thoughts are not your thoughts, nor are your ways my ways, says the LORD" (Isa 55:8-9). The endeavor to embrace individual and social attitudes that reflect God necessitates particular external forms: the development of right relationships with others (Deut 10:17-19), especially through the practice of justice. Justice is the alternative to all-consuming self-absorption, which witnesses to a lack of trust in God and fails to express authentic faith—"Such fasting

---

43. Kasper, *Catholic Church*, 122. *Lumen Gentium* uses "The People of God" as the title for its second chapter.

as you do today will not make your voice heard on high. . . . Is not this the fast that I choose: to loose the bonds of injustice, to undo the thongs of the yoke, to let the oppressed go free, and to break every yoke?" (Isa 58:3-6).

When Israel's relationship to God involves journeying physically into unfamiliar territory, journeys undertaken in response to God's beckoning, the journey become the instrument for encounter with God. During those journeys, Israel experiences that "God reveals himself as the God who guides and leads in a history that cannot be tied down beforehand, a history in which he will always be present in a nondeducible, sovereign, and—yet again—unexpected way and who is again and again the ever-new future of his people. He is not a god of a particular place, but rather displays his power in every place his people encounter along their way."[44] Through such experiences the people of Israel learn, and relearn, that the final word in their history is still to come. They learn and relearn, too, that there is an intimate association between God and that final word. Attention to God in the present anticipates the future, which is inseparable from God.

Abraham, a model of faith for both Judaism and Christianity, exemplifies the journey of faith. Abraham leaves his country in response to God's promises (Gen 12:1-3), but he is also prepared, remarkably, to trust God's call even when it seems, as in the summons to sacrifice Isaac, that faithfulness to God will render impossible the fulfillment of God's primary promise: that Abraham will be the father of nations (Gen 22:1-14). No less astonishingly, and most significantly for the unfolding of God's self-communication in the incarnation, Mary consents to God's invitation to accept the gift of a child, an acceptance that comes at an unforeseeable cost (Luke 1:26-55). Mary and Abraham trust that, on the basis of what God has done in the past, God will remain faithful and effective in fulfilling the promises to which they have responded. In this spirit, they commit to their unique pilgrimages.

Much of the life of Jesus is life on "the road" (Luke 9:51-62). "The road," with its inevitable fluctuations in literal and metaphorical contours, is where his companions learn, for example, about what being

---

44. Walter Kasper, *Mercy: The Essence of the Gospel and the Key to Christian Life*, trans. W. Madges (Mahwah, NJ: Paulist, 2014), 47.

"first" is to mean for disciples of Jesus (Matt 20:17-28). It is also where they learn what it means to be a herald of "the good news" (Luke 9:1-6) in the world. As Jesus moves from place to place—"Let us go on to the neighboring towns, so that I may proclaim the message there also; for that is what I came out to do" (Mark 1:38)—he makes clear that the call to "follow" him (Mark 1:17) involves movement. At times, that call can occasion a crisis in its recipients—as it did for the wealthy man (Mark 10:17-22)—but it is not one on which Jesus ever compromises.

Beginning with the revelation of the Holy Spirit at Pentecost (Acts 2:1-13), the Christian community has recognized that the grace of the Holy Spirit directs disciples of Jesus outward, sustaining its engagement with history, a theme that will be a principal motif in chapter 4. The Spirit is "the power bonding humans together in the eschatological community that is the final destiny of human life; it is the prophetic power already working in history to achieve that relating of humans to one another in justice and peace that is the 'reign of God.'"[45] The grace of the Spirit works through the complex human beings who compose the ecclesial community, each of whom is "carried and supported by the 'we' of faith, by the Church as the one people of God embracing synchronically and diachronically all time and space."[46] The Spirit's role neither renders superfluous human activity in the church nor grants to this activity the last word in the story of the church.

The history of the church, a history of grace accepted and grace rejected, is a continuing story as the Holy Spirit draws the church beyond the present. The outcomes of the engagement between grace and human freedom defy prediction, but the engagement itself establishes the church as a dynamic rather than a static reality, one whose present and future are no less significant than its past. Consistent with its dependence on the Spirit, the Christian community must remain attentive to "what the Spirit is saying to the churches" (Rev 2:7, 11, 17, 29; 3:6, 13, 22). This attention has its full flowering when the church not only listens, but responds to the Spirit. Integral to this response is

45. Bernard Cooke, with Bruce Morrill, *The Essential Writings of Bernard Cooke: A Narrative Theology of Church, Sacrament, and Ministry* (Mahwah, NJ: Paulist, 2016), 104.

46. Kasper, *Catholic Church*, 126.

the church's willingness to move in accord with the call of the Spirit, a call that may be toward greater justice within the church or action for justice in the world.[47] In listening and moving, the church identifies itself as a pilgrim.

Pilgrimage and the Life of Faith

In its description of the Christian community as a pilgrim, the Second Vatican Council encapsulates both the Spirit's guidance of the church and the church's call to movement into the future.[48] The movement is toward the future fullness of life in Christ; the Spirit initiates and accompanies this movement, but the specifics of the future are unknowable to pilgrims in advance. The eschatological fulfillment of the relationship between grace and history further reinforces that no period of the church's past or present is unsurpassable in its witness to the gospel. Through its eschatological orientation, the church is permanently a body "in faith and in the praise of God on the way to the heavenly Jerusalem," rather than one with a less ultimate end point.[49]

The current popularity of the *Camino de Santiago* has breathed new life into the experience of pilgrimage, an experience with a long history in Christian spirituality and practice.[50] An array of books and films on the *Camino* testify to both an exponential increase in participants in that storied walk and a noteworthy diversity of motives and interests among pilgrims. Where Chaucer and other medieval commentators understood pilgrimage as the activity of saints or sinners, modern pilgrims may not define themselves in relation to either holiness or repentance. Instead, undertaking the *Camino*, or other forms of pilgrimage, may express a search for an alternative to consumerism, a "fast" from technology and social media, or a wistful longing for a

47. Eboni Marshall Turman, "The Holy Spirit and the Black Church Tradition: Womanist Considerations," in *The Holy Spirt and the Church: Ecumenical Reflections with a Pastoral Perspective*, ed. Thomas Hughson (New York: Routledge, 2016), 111.

48. *Lumen Gentium* uses "The Pilgrim Church" as the title for its seventh chapter.

49. Kasper, *Catholic Church*, 126.

50. For a brief overview of the tradition of pilgrimage in Christian history, see Gerald O'Collins, *Tradition: Understanding Christian Tradition* (Oxford: Oxford University Press, 2018), 93–95.

simpler life.[51] Although the nontraditional backgrounds and intentions
of today's pilgrims could indicate that pilgrimage has become merely
another manifestation of postmodern restlessness or the narcissistic
pursuit of "experience," it may also signify that pilgrimage transcends
what is explicitly religious, that it engages a primal urge, one that involves a quest for fulfillment in what is not yet possessed: "The desire
to go a-pilgriming, it seems, is part of our human condition."[52] The
link between pilgrimage and non-possession resonates well with the
Second Vatican Council's ecclesiology of pilgrimage.

Vatican II's *Lumen Gentium* (LG), The Dogmatic Constitution on
the Church, relies on "pilgrim" to clarify the implications of both the
church's relationship to God and its existence in history:

> until the arrival of the new heavens and the new earth in which
> justice dwells . . . , the pilgrim church, in its sacraments and insti-
> tutions, which belong to this present age, carries the mark of this
> world which will pass, and it takes its place among the creatures
> which groan and until now suffer the pains of childbirth and await
> the revelation of the children of God. (LG 48)

"Pilgrim" makes plain that the church is not yet complete, that it is
inseparable from God's grace in history, and that the Spirit of Christ
draws the ecclesial community toward the realization of all that God
promises. Reinforcing the dynamism inherent in "pilgrim," Vatican II
makes explicit the association between the church's pilgrimage and the
Holy Spirit's presence in the church: "Animated and drawn together in
his Spirit we press onwards on our journey towards the consummation

51. For an analysis of contemporary forms of pilgrimage, see Ellen Badone, "Conventional and Unconventional Pilgrimages: Conceptualizing Sacred Travel in the
Twenty-First Century," in *Redefining Pilgrimage: New Perspectives on Historical and
Contemporary Pilgrimages*, ed. Antón Pazos (Burlington, VT: Ashgate, 2014), 7–31;
for a detailed anthropological analysis of the relationship between pilgrimage and
Christian faith, see Victor Turner and Edith Turner, *Image and Pilgrimage in Christian Culture: Anthropological Perspectives* (New York: Columbia University Press,
1978), especially 1–39.

52. Tony Kevin, *Walking the Camino: A Modern Pilgrimage to Santiago* (Melbourne,
Vic: Scribe Publications, 2008), 32.

of history which fully corresponds to the plan of his love: 'to unite all things in him, things in heaven and things on earth' (Eph 1:10)" (GS 45).

Since Vatican II, papal teaching from Pope John Paul II—"The Church's entire life . . . means going to meet the invisible God, the hidden God: a meeting with the Spirit 'who gives life'"[53]—to Pope Francis—"Once the seed has been sown in one place, Jesus does not stay behind to explain things or to perform more signs; the Spirit moves him to go forth to other towns"[54]—has continued to associate the Spirit's presence in the church with movement.

The Holy Spirit "abides" (John 14:17) with the people of God, but the Spirit is not a disinterested fellow-traveler as the church follows Christ on the road. *Lumen Gentium* teaches that the Spirit "guides the church in the way of all truth . . . and, uniting it in fellowship and ministry, bestows upon it different hierarchic and charismatic gifts, and in this way directs it and adorns it with his fruits" (LG 4). The "hierarchic and charismatic gifts" will receive attention later in this book, but the council's statement is significant for the current discussion because it brings to the fore the Spirit's role in the church's reception of the grace, in what directs the ecclesial community to the fullness of life in God.

Ormond Rush identifies the Spirit as "the principle of reception in the human appropriation of salvific revelation coming through God's Word, Jesus Christ."[55] Rush maintains that this activity in the church parallels what occurs in the Trinity, where the Spirit is "the *receptio* in the mutual exchange between Father and Son."[56] As the principle of unity in the Trinity, the Spirit is no less active in promoting unity in the church, in shaping the church as a "community of reception," formed by "the divine trinitarian life that transforms human lives."[57] Central to this Spirit-driven transformation for members of the ecclesial community is liberation from "all that impedes them from being lured into the

53. Pope John Paul II, *Dominum et Vivificantem*, 54.

54. Pope Francis, *Evangelii Gaudium*, 21.

55. Ormond Rush, *The Eyes of Faith: The Sense of the Faithful and the Church's Reception of Revelation* (Washington, DC: Catholic University of America Press, 2009), 26.

56. Ibid., 26.

57. Ibid., 29–30.

inner life of God, that is, all that impedes the reign of God."[58] Chapter 6 will consider "reception" from multiple angles, but it is important to note here that authentic reception of the Spirit's impulses flowers in the tilling of all aspects of the church's life that may have become oxidized, and so resistant to the movement and pilgrimage that grace impels.

As an ecclesiological term, "pilgrim" applies to every aspect of the church's life. This means, for example, that the church's sacramental worship, its ministry, and its work for justice and peace in the world must all remain open to fulfillment in Christ. More concretely, the dynamism proper to "pilgrim" serves as a reminder that the specificity of the church is not independent of times and places, to say nothing of the unexpected and the changeable. A pilgrim church does not know in advance its response to every exigency, nor even what exigencies may arise. The church, rather, must discern in the circumstances of each time and place how best to respond to the Spirit.

These responses need to balance, or at least hold in tension, both the church's orientation to the fullness of God's reign and the church's place in history. Toward the maintenance of that tension, Vatican II acknowledges, for example, that while Christians "are to seek and value the things that are above," they are also to demonstrate "not less, but greater commitment to working with everyone for the establishment of a more human world" (GS 57). This suggests both that the church of the present will not resemble the past or future in every detail and that there may even be distinctions between the church in different places at the same period.

Since a pilgrimage is radically other than a tightly choreographed military parade, the pilgrim church can be a community of imagination and creativity, qualities mentioned above as proper to faith. Creativity in decision-making demonstrates that faith, as a fully human reality, "has inevitably the character of a bold venture, of uncertainty, of walking into the dark," features that reinforce that a pilgrimage defies all efforts to anticipate its every detail.[59] "Walking into the dark" is scarcely an attractive notion, but it is not alien to Christian faith,

58. Ibid., 30.
59. Karl Rahner, "The Dignity and Freedom of Man," in *Theological Investigations*, vol. 2, trans. K-H. Kruger (New York: Crossroad, 1990), 254.

which is home to the paradox that acknowledges darkness, including the darkness of death, as a possible path to the light. This aspect of the church's pilgrimage highlights the link between faith and hope, a link that the next section of this chapter will develop.

The uncertainty inherent in the experience of being a pilgrim can tempt the ecclesial community, like Israel during the Exodus (Num 11:1-23), to consider turning back, out of frustration that it is unable to proceed purposefully and deliberately on a well-signposted and secure route. As a result, the church that has responded to voices other than that of the Spirit will need often to regain its bearings by realigning itself on what is more in tune with the reign of God. This need for the tilling that is conversion applies to individuals, but also to groups and structures within the church.

To appreciate what the dynamics of pilgrimage might ask of the church as it journeys toward the fullness of God's reign, familiarity with five elements common to any pilgrimage can be helpful.[60] First, pilgrims share a goal that unites them, but does not eliminate their individuality. As pilgrims support and encourage each other by sharing their food, drink, and information, the communal nature of pilgrimage emerges and the pilgrims become a body in which what binds the members together is more significant than any distinction between them. Second, pilgrims as they travel must be willing to respond to the unexpected, since they can neither mandate who will be their fellow pilgrims nor determine in advance what will occur on their journey. Third, the unpredictable incidents that transpire during a pilgrimage, some of which may be discouraging, make urgent the need to clarify, and appropriate ever anew the reason for undertaking the pilgrimage. The motivation of pilgrims must be sufficient not only to initiate movement, but to sustain hope and nurture energy in the face of the weariness, physical discomfort, and tedium that are inevitable during the journey. Fourth, since pilgrimage involves a journey not merely a destination, the participants in a fruitful pilgrimage will engage with the world around them, convinced that encounters along the way contribute to both how and whether they will reach their goal. Fifth, and perhaps most importantly, pilgrimage brings about changes in participants, changes that are intimately connected to

---

60. For a contemporary account of the dynamics of pilgrimage see Kevin, *Walking the Camino*, 18–32.

the four previous points. Pilgrims, then, must be open to change if they are to access the full richness of pilgrimage. Taken as a single, yet multidimensional process, pilgrimage exposes its participants to what they could not have anticipated at the beginning of their time on the road.

The church's pilgrimage has elements specific to its existence as a community that the Spirit forms to manifest faith, hope, and love, but it shares, too, in features common to all pilgrimages. These features represent forms of tilling, forms of witnessing to the church's unfinished reality. As all pilgrims need to appropriate repeatedly their guiding purpose, especially in the midst of difficulties, so, too, does the church. As a pilgrim, the church faces discouragement, including the discouragement that arises from the ecclesial community's own failures to remain united and to respond faithfully to the urgings of the Spirit and the challenges of discipleship. Along its journey, then, the church must continue to renew, especially via its engagement with the Spirit of Christ present in word and sacrament, its appreciation of what it means to be a pilgrim people.

The resources that the Spirit makes available for the renewal of the church on its pilgrimage include the diversity within the church itself. "The church" on pilgrimage expresses the collective identity of the disciples of Christ, an identity that is properly "catholic" since it enhances rather than eliminates the characteristics of each disciple and every group of disciples. "Blueprint," to return to the critique of images in ecclesiology, is not applicable to "pilgrim" since no two pilgrimages resemble each other in every way. The catholic dimension of pilgrimage ensures that the church is a community of difference, rather than a monochromatic or uniform community.

Diversity could suggest individualism, but the ecclesial community on pilgrimage has access to shared resources that serve differentiated communion rather than prompting division. Together, the community celebrates its life, especially in the liturgy, where "the power of the Holy Spirit acts on us through sacramental signs" (LG 50). These signs include, most notably, the meal-setting of the Eucharist, in which "the Lord draws the faithful and sets them aflame with Christ's compelling love."[61] In addition, as Vatican II emphasized, each community consists

---

61. The Second Vatican Council, *Sacrosanctum Concilium* (1963), The Constitution on the Liturgy, 10.

of more than those who are living in the present moment: it embraces the "cloud of witnesses" (Heb 12:1) that includes Mary and the saints, in whose lives "God shows, vividly, to humanity his presence and his face. He speaks to us in them and offers us a sign of his kingdom. . . . Exactly as Christian communion among pilgrims brings us closer to Christ, so our communion with the saints joins us to Christ, from whom as its fountain and head flow all grace and life of the people of God itself" (LG 50).[62]

The enduring accompaniment of the saints, the shared nourishment of the Eucharist, and the abiding gift of the Spirit do not reduce the church to a mechanism that functions independently of human desires and activity, or one that is separable from time and place. Consequently, as the history of the church demonstrates unambiguously, the unity of the body of Christ is always a project to be negotiated, one that requires conscious choices and commitments, as well as sustained attention. The diversity of gifts among the baptized, the unfolding of history, with its endless array of new questions, and the ever-present temptation for members of the church to confuse personal preferences with responsiveness to the Spirit, a temptation that exempts neither individuals nor groups, all reinforce that the pilgrim church is a project that requires tilling. Those same components expose the potential for division in the church, even over the celebration of the liturgy, as debates about the post–Vatican II "reform of the reform" make painfully clear.[63] This potential highlights the importance of conversion in the ecclesial community, an emphasis that is itself inseparable from the dynamics of pilgrimage.

The need for conversion amplifies the truth that grace does not eliminate human complexity from the life of the church. As Yves Congar stresses, the church is not a community of perfect, or even perfectible, human beings, but is "the result of the synergy of a gratuitous divine gift that is pure in itself and a human activity that is characterized by human freedom, limitations, and natural fallibility."[64] Since the mem-

62. On the role of the communion of saints in the history of pilgrimage, see Turner and Turner, *Image and Pilgrimage*, 15–16.
63. For discussion of the debates over liturgy, see John Baldovin, *Reforming the Liturgy: A Response to the Critics* (Collegeville, MN: Pueblo, 2009).
64. Yves Congar, *True and False Reform in the Church*, trans. P. Philibert, rev. ed. (Collegeville, MN: Michael Glazier, 2011), 90.

bers of the church, and the structures and offices they operate, are not flawless, they do not ever transcend their capacity for sinful rejection of God and damage to others. If the expressions of the church's life are to manifest the grace at work in the ecclesial community, the ongoing conversion of all members of the church remains necessary.

The need for conversion, for returning to God, is not an obligation imposed on the church from without, but is a consequence of the centrality of grace to the life of the church. It is a reminder to the church that God alone is the source of salvation and that the primary act of faith is in God, not the church.[65] Acknowledgment of both the centrality of grace and need of the Christian community for repentance is at the heart of the Eucharist, in which the church recognizes "its incompleteness, fracture and hope for a new time. It can do this precisely because the Eucharist bears witness to and embodies the true and abiding life of the ecclesia, which is Christ the Lord in the midst. . . . The fullness of its true life lies ahead or in what is coming from the future."[66] In prompting the church to respond wholeheartedly to the present, the Spirit is simultaneously summoning the church toward the fullness of life in the God of Jesus Christ.

In being alert for the unanticipated indicators of God's presence, the church is being faithful to its foundations, and being responsive to grace. Just as Jesus's companions experienced him as overturning their expectations of God's way of proceeding (Luke 4:22-30), so the contemporary expressions of God's presence can similarly defy conventional certainties, occurring as they do in "the human vicissitudes of our human existence, ever new, ever unanticipated and incalculable as these are."[67] This possibility is yet another indicator that the church's pilgrimage involves a commitment to "walk by faith, not by sight" (2 Cor 5:7).

---

65. For an analysis of the relationship between faith in God and faith in the church, see Karl Rahner, "Dogmatic Notes on 'Ecclesiological Piety,'" in *Theological Investigations*, vol. 5, trans. K-H. Kruger (New York: Crossroad, 1983), 341–46.

66. Stephen Pickard, *Seeking the Church: An Introduction to Ecclesiology* (London: SCM, 2012), 228–29.

67. Karl Rahner, "Being Open to God as Ever Greater: On the Significance of the Aphorism 'Ad Majorem Dei Gloriam,'" in *Theological Investigations*, vol. 7, trans. D. Bourke (New York: Crossroad, 1977), 36.

The acknowledgment of its status as a pilgrim encourages the community of faith to avoid settling for less than God, even as it endures the uncertainties of its moment in history. Every aspect of "pilgrim" confirms the dynamism of the church, as Isabelle Graesslé contends: "It would indeed be wrong to think of the church in passage as a concession to the post-modern age, a sacrifice on the altar of generalized relativity and of the evolution of Western culture. . . . The church needs to change simply because it is itself movement, taking to the road, journey."[68] This reminder has implications for reform of the church's inner life, the church's pursuit of its mission in its different contexts, and for efforts to overcome the divisions between the churches, all of which requirements remain urgent "until [the one church] shall happily arrive at the fullness of eternal glory in the heavenly Jerusalem."[69]

As a pilgrim, the church is a body with a direction, rather than one wandering aimlessly. In orienting the church to God's ever-new future, through Christ and the Spirit, "pilgrim" clarifies the church's identity and mission, which provide the basis for continuity in the church without proscribing openness to change. The Spirit who stimulates the church's movement is also central to the church's enduring identity, inspiring the community to safeguard the tradition of faith that has nurtured it. The Spirit neither begins the church anew in every age nor conforms the church exclusively to the priorities of a single time or place. That the one Spirit is the source of both tradition and innovation attests to the radical challenge that the Christian community faces in its endeavor to be faithful to what God enables.

Clearly, the Spirit who guides and accompanies the church is at home with paradox. As a pilgrim, the church is linked inextricably with the paradoxical world of the Spirit. The church cannot outgrow either its need for openness to new learning from manifold sources through which the Spirit can be at work or the need for ongoing reception of its tradition, through which the Spirit binds the church to all that comes from Christ and finds its fulfillment in Christ. When the Christian

---

68. Isabelle Graesslé, "From Impasse to Passage: Reflections on the Church," *The Ecumenical Review* 53 (2001): 26.

69. The Second Vatican Council, *Unitatis Redintegratio*, The Decree on Ecumenism (1964), 3.

community, at every level, commits to "seeking the will of God and making something of the love of Christ visible," it becomes "the true image of the Holy Spirit," that differs from "a gathering of Christians who are stiff and unfree, or disunited and in conflict."[70]

The dependence of the church's pilgrimage on the graced decisions of the pilgrims means that ecclesiology has a particular interest in "the dynamics of choice and performance" within the church.[71] The creative engagement with culture, tradition, and history, all of which can be indicators of the "new life" (Rom 7:6) associated with the Spirit, is essential for the ecclesial community in each local manifestation, no less than in its larger configurations. These dynamics shape the church as "this" body, rather than "that" one; they identify the ecclesial community as being always a work in progress, one dependent on responses to grace even as its members, individually and communally, retain the freedom to reject that grace.

In the light of these dynamics, Joseph Komonchak categorizes ecclesiology as "a heuristics of the self-realization of the Church."[72] Ecclesiology, in other words, accompanies the ongoing efforts of Christians to "make sense" of their individual and communal experience of God and to embody their understanding in the forms of worship, belief, and action that constitute the life of the church in the world.[73] Since each of those elements must remain open to the eschatological dimension of grace, ecclesiology, like the church itself, is an activity that continues as members of the church open themselves to conversion and respond to the grace that draws them more fully into the mystery of God. Ecclesiology is an activity for pilgrims who are seeking to embody the hope that reflects the grace at work in the community of faith. No less than the church itself, ecclesiology remains unfinished, and unfinishable, this side of the eschaton.

---

70. Gerhard Lohfink, *Prayer Takes Us Home: The Theology and Practice of Christian Prayer*, trans. L. Maloney (Collegeville, MN: Liturgical Press, 2020), 18.

71. Bernard Prusak, *The Church Unfinished: Ecclesiology Through the Centuries* (Mahwah, NJ: Paulist, 2004), 8.

72. Joseph Komonchak, *Who Are the Church?* (Milwaukee, WI: Marquette University Press, 2008), 56.

73. Rush, *Eyes of Faith*, 67.

Hope and the Life of the Church

Hope manifests grace. The connection between the church and hope, then, is not in competition with the relationship between faith and the church, but adds color and texture to that relationship. As part of its effort to make a case for the contribution of hope to ecclesiology, and especially to all that furthers the tilling of the church, this section will begin in a counterintuitive way: by addressing several reasons why linking hope to ecclesiology may arouse some misgivings.

First, if the invocation of hope looks exclusively to the future, as is often the case, it could seem to absolve the church from attending to past failings and present exigencies. Second, perceptions of hope as either a "soft" virtue or an option of last resort might call into question the capacity of a theology of hope to address contemporary ecclesial challenges that require imagination, difficult decisions, and tenacity. Third, there might be a fear that the focus on hope will "spiritualize" discussion of the church, abstracting it from the messy reality of the human story that is no less integral to the church than to all human projects. The interplay between the church's foundations and the present influences on the ecclesial community, a pivotal connection for this volume, offers a way to allay these concerns.

In the Christian tradition, hope is inseparable from faith in God. More specifically, hope is inseparable from the conviction that God, the source and sustainer of life, guarantees that life will not end with the dissolution of meaning and goodness: "For surely I know the plans I have for you, says the LORD, plans for your welfare and not for harm, to give you a future with hope" (Jer 29:11). Hope "has God as its primary object, and in particular our right relationship with God and eternal life. It looks forward to the full coming of God's kingdom. And it has as its basis God's person and promises."[74] The creator God, as the origin of life, is also the origin of hope, which embodies the conviction that darkness is not all-powerful, even when reasons for despair abound. The relationship to God confers a boldness on hope, which looks beyond mere survival to "things that fill our heart and lift our spirits

---

74. Daniel Harrington, *What Are We Hoping For? New Testament Images* (Collegeville, MN: Liturgical Press, 2006), vii.

to lofty realities like truth, goodness and beauty, justice and love."[75] In these ways, hope makes life more fully human, which means human decisions and actions embody God's presence more transparently.

In its explicitly Christian manifestation, hope responds to all that God reveals in Jesus Christ, through the Holy Spirit. This revelation has the life, death, and resurrection of Jesus at its core, so it underlines that even the destructive force of death cannot supplant the life-giving God. The death of Jesus inverts expectations. After all, it seems reasonable to expect that the graced existence of human beings would engender a positive reception of God's boundless self-giving that Jesus incarnates in history. Nonetheless, the fact that God's love establishes human freedom even in relation to God, to recall the emphasis of chapter 2, means that human freedom can reject God. Human freedom can equally reject solidarity with other human beings, refusing to offer the forgiveness, compassion, justice, and generosity reflective of God's creative love. The fate of the prophets, a fate that Jesus shares (Matt 23:29-36), shows clearly that God's love, and those who represent it, do not advance from effortless triumph to effortless triumph.

Like the prophets, Jesus calls people to use their freedom constructively, to acknowledge their need for conversion, for a renewed relationship with God and life-giving commitment to others. Like the prophets, Jesus speaks for God, but does so uniquely, in his own name, amplifying his connection to the irruption of God's reign (Matt 5:44; John 13:34). As Jesus presents the choice for or against God and the choice for or against others, it is a choice for or against Jesus himself (Matt 7:24; Mark 8:34-38; Luke 9:23-27; 12:8-9). The death of Jesus marks the definitive choice against him.

The Death and Resurrection of Jesus in Relation to Hope

Jesus's death, Elizabeth Johnson contends, "is a consequence of the hostile response of religious and civic rulers to the style and content of his ministry, to which he was radically faithful with a freedom that

75. Pope Francis, *Fratelli Tutti*, On Fraternity and Social Friendship (2020), 55, http://www.vatican.va/content/francesco/en/encyclicals/documents/papa-francesco_20201003_enciclica-fratelli-tutti.html.

would not quit."[76] The identification between Jesus and God's reign might imply that the death of Jesus, the death that proceeds from injustice and violence that contradict his life and message, must be the death of the hope, the death of the future represented by Jesus's representation of the kingdom. Against such a possible interpretation, Walter Kasper, highlighting the paradoxical nature of God's relationship to humanity, argues that the death of Jesus is a revelation of the kingdom rather than the defeat of God or the rupturing of God's solidarity with humanity. For Kasper, the death of Jesus is "the form in which the Kingdom of God exists under the conditions of this age, the Kingdom of God in human powerlessness, wealth in poverty, love in desolation, abundance in emptiness, and life in death."[77] The death of Jesus, then, despite all contrary appearances, is not a victory for human sinfulness over God's kingdom.

Jesus's acceptance of his death is more than a profound act of solidarity with humanity: it encapsulates his radical trust in God's life-giving love, the love that is the unshakeable core of Jesus's life. The death of Jesus becomes an extraordinary expression of the kingdom: "Jesus goes to his death with clarity and confidence, faithful to God to the end and treating his death as an expression of service to his friends. . . . He saw that this is good and required of him, and that it is good, and so required, of others."[78] Jesus in his death refuses to grant the last word to the injustice that generates victims as the inevitable consequences of human sinfulness. Jesus's willingness to persevere in faithfulness to God and humanity even when facing death constitutes an element of "the dangerous memory of Jesus," a reminder that being his disciple is not a passport to a life of comfort that erases any need to be attentive to integrity and sacrifice for the sake of others.[79]

The circumstances of Jesus's death are particular to him, but death is a universal human phenomenon, the quintessential "interruption" and

76. Elizabeth Johnson, *She Who Is: The Mystery of God in Feminist Theological Discourse* (New York: Crossroad, 1993), 158.

77. Walter Kasper, *Jesus the Christ*, trans. V. Green (New York: Paulist, 1985), 118–19.

78. Jon Sobrino, *Christ the Liberator*, trans. P. Burns (Maryknoll, NY: Orbis, 2001), 203.

79. Johann Baptist Metz, *Faith in History and Society: Towards a Practical Fundamental Theology*, rev. trans. M. Ashley (New York: Crossroad, 2007), 169–85.

"experience" that human beings face. All analyses of the relationship between God's self-communication and humanity, consequently, must engage with the reality of death. In so doing, Karl Rahner describes death as the supreme expression of the inability of human beings and human planning to secure the fulfillment of history: "Death is not merely any kind of occurrence within our life, or coming at its conclusion. Rather, whether we suppress it or admit it, it is that in virtue of which we are continually discovering the nature of our own existence as finite."[80] In mocking all human pretensions to have achieved the high point of history, death confronts human beings, individually and communally, with the need to decide whether life is a chasm of absurdity or the revelation of "the infinitude of the mystery of love, the absolute future which is reached through death."[81]

The violent death of Jesus seems to imply that absurdity prevails, so could induce a loss of hope in the capacity of human beings to appropriate God's life-giving kingdom. Furthermore, the fact that human beings are capable of a fundamental rejection of God's love provides grounds for questioning whether any human action could unambiguously symbolize God's reign. The response to these concerns comes not from human beings, but from God. It comes in the climactic element in the story of Jesus Christ: the resurrection.

In the resurrection, God raises Jesus from the dead, raises the one who lives and dies with trust in God. The resurrection reveals the breadth and depth of God's creative love and faithfulness. It shows God's desire and capacity to give life is resolute and unequivocal, even when all human potentiality collapses or when human freedom chooses against God's love and damages life. Since it is Jesus, rather than a randomly chosen individual, whom God raises from death, the

---

80. Karl Rahner, "Ideas for a Theology of Death," in *Theological Investigations*, vol.13, trans. D. Bourke (New York: Crossroad, 1983), 180.

81. Karl Rahner, "The Experiment with Man: Theological Observations on Man's Self-Manipulation," in *Theological Investigations*, vol. 9, trans. G. Harrison (New York: Seabury, 1972), 222; see also his "The Quest for Approaches Leading to an Understanding of the Mystery of the God-Man Jesus," in *Theological Investigations*, vol. 13, trans. D. Bourke (New York: Crossroad, 1983), 195–200. For Rahner's fullest discussion of death, see his *On the Theology of Death*, trans. W. O'Hara (London: Burns and Oates, 1965).

resurrection is unquestionably linked to the life and death of Jesus. As Kasper suggests, the resurrection is "not a separate event after the life and suffering of Jesus, but what is happening at the most profound level in the death of Jesus: the act and suffering of a human being's bodily surrender to God and the merciful loving acceptance of this devotion by God."[82] In the death and resurrection of Jesus, the dynamics of the relationship between Jesus and his "*Abba*, Father" (Mark 14:36) come into relief.

Just as Jesus's self-surrender on the cross embodies his total trust in God and his comprehensive commitment to humanity, the resurrection symbolizes the steadfast faithfulness of God's creative love. The resurrection is not simply the final chapter in the life of Jesus, it is, as Rahner claims, an event of revelation: "The life of the exalted Lord is not the personal recompense for something which he did in his earthly life and which merely has 'consequences' which now persist in themselves after their cause is past. It is the very reality of the soteriological significance of his temporal life, accepted by God, set free to work, and actually effective."[83] The resurrection removes any ambiguity about the trustworthiness of God and God's commitment to humanity's thriving, just as it reveals the identity of Jesus as "Lord" and "savior," the one who is, permanently, "the gate and the door, the Alpha and Omega, the all-embracing in whom, as the one who has become [human], creation finds its stability."[84]

Integral to the proclamation of Jesus Christ as savior is the recognition that he is the incarnate Word of God, the "Son" who shares in divinity while being fully human: "This Savior who represents the climax of this self-communication, must therefore be at the same time God's absolute pledge by self-communication to the spiritual creature as a whole *and* the acceptance of this self-communication by the Savior."[85] Jesus's intimacy with God, his transparency to the will of

82. Kasper, *Jesus the Christ*, 150.

83. Karl Rahner, "Dogmatic Questions on Easter," in *Theological Investigations*, vol. 4, trans. K. Smyth (New York: Crossroad, 1982), 131.

84. Rahner, "Eternal Significance of the Humanity of Jesus," 43.

85. Karl Rahner, "Christology within an Evolutionary View of the World," in *Theological Investigations*, vol. 5, trans. K-H. Kruger (New York: Crossroad, 1983), 175–76; original emphasis.

God, his resolute commitment to serve God's kingdom by self-giving even to the point of death, and God's response in the resurrection, coalesce in the profession of the Christian community that "only God could be so human."[86]

Rahner's presentation of revelation argues that "the whole movement of this history of God's self-communication lives by virtue of its moving towards its goal or climax in the event by which it becomes irreversible, and hence precisely by virtue of what we are calling the absolute savior."[87] The risen Jesus as savior is also, as noted above, the revelation of God as the "absolute future" of all life, a future that frees humanity from the fear of death and from the limitations of sinfulness.[88] In Rahner's judgment, God is more than the source of the future: God *is* the future. Since "the original totality of the absolute future, towards which we project ourselves, can never really be expressed in the precise characteristics proper to it by determinations taken from intramundane, classifiable experience . . . God is the self-communicating future of humanity."[89] The resurrection identifies Jesus Christ as the agent of this absolute future.

Just as Jesus unites himself in his death with the whole of God's creation to reconcile creation with God, so God unites the whole of creation with Christ in his resurrection (Rom 8:15-17; 2 Cor 5:17-21; Col 1:20-22). The hope that derives from the resurrection, then, applies to the whole of God's creation. As a consequence of its foundation in Jesus Christ, "Christianity is eschatology, is hope, forward looking and forward moving, and therefore also revolutionizing and transforming the present."[90]

Christ's ascension extends the impact of Christ's resurrection on both the present and the future. The ascension, Anthony Kelly claims,

---

86. Leonardo Boff, *Jesus Christ Liberator*, trans. P. Hughes (Maryknoll, NY: Orbis, 1979), 179.

87. Karl Rahner, *Foundations of Christian Faith: An Introduction to the Idea of Christianity*, trans. W. Dych (New York: Seabury, 1978), 195.

88. Rahner, "Christian Humanism," in *Theological Investigations*, vol. 9, trans. G. Harrison (New York: Seabury, 1972), 199.

89. Rahner, "Marxist Utopia," 62–63.

90. Jürgen Moltmann, *Theology of Hope: On the Ground and the Implications of a Christian Eschatology* (London: SCM, 1967), 16.

highlights not only Christ's promise to return in glory at the end of time, but also the centrality of Christ to the relationship between God and creation in the present: "The ascension does not take Christ out of time, but is the condition for his complete immersion in it, as its fullness. Faith is the consciousness of having time 'in him,' so that he becomes the measure and goal of time. . . . Jesus in his ascent to the Father, brings time to its redemptive completion."[91] Christian hope, then, requires attention to the present as well as to the future, just as it has its foundation in the long history of God's self-communication.[92] This conviction that the past, present, and future of humanity and the whole of creation come together in Christ is fundamental to the life of the church.

As a response to grace, by which God sustains the whole of created life in the present and orients it toward "God's open future," hope weaves together the church's past, present, and future.[93] Trusting in God's promise that death will not ultimately triumph over life, hope neither holds the members of the Christian community prisoner to past failings nor legitimizes forgetfulness of those failings, thereby opening the possibility of "canonizing" a particular era of the church's history while ignoring its inevitable limitations. Rather, the commitment to forming the church as a witness to hope can facilitate the tilling that involves a graced reckoning with all that, left unaddressed, may be injurious to the future.

Hope sustains the efforts of communities and individuals to admit their limitations and enter freely into the process of conversion that grace prompts and that furthers fruitful participation in all that grace pervades. Hope underpins critically constructive receptions of the past and careful discernment of trends in the present. In freeing the ecclesial community to be self-critical, while empowering creative engagement with all that its mission requires at each moment of history, hope arouses the desire for a future that is more than the faint echo of

---

91. Anthony Kelly, *Upward: Faith, Church, and the Ascension of Christ* (Collegeville, MN: Liturgical Press, 2014), 144.

92. See Daniel Harrington, "The Future Is Now: Eternal Life and Hope in John's Gospel," in *Hope: Promise, Possibility, and Fulfillment*, ed. Richard Lennan and Nancy Pineda-Madrid (Mahwah, NJ: Paulist, 2013), 185–97.

93. Rahner, "Christian Humanism," 195.

a glorious past that has faded into a mediocre present. In these ways, hope supports the grace of conversion, the demanding effort to confront sinfulness and the willingness to learn, from all possible sources, the "best practices" that may further authenticity in a community's ways of proceeding. In all of these ways, too, a theology of ecclesial hope aligns well with the identification of the church as a project.

For human beings, sharing in the crucified, risen, and ascended Jesus Christ is a gift, but it is also an invitation. Human beings are not mere consumers or passive recipients of what God has done in Christ: they are people enabled by God to be the means, the symbols, by which the new life of Christ becomes more evident in the world (2 Cor 5:18-19; 1 Thess 1:2-8). In Gerhard Lohfink's assessment, God's revelation in Jesus Christ highlights God's "already," which prompts human beings to turn their experience of the "not yet" of God's reign into a more willing conversion to God and to the needs of others.[94]

In a related manner, Jon Sobrino contends that sustaining hope in the present requires that people of faith embody the mission of Christ in service of God's kingdom: "The course of action needed today to grasp Jesus' resurrection is nothing other than carrying out Jesus' mission, with the *form* of the impossibility of the Kingdom becoming real and the *content* of giving life to the poor."[95] Since hope "is not simply the attitude of one who is weak and at the same time hungering for a fulfillment that is yet to be achieved, but rather the courage to commit oneself in thought and deed to the incomprehensible and the uncontrollable which permeates our existence, and, as the future to which it is open, sustains it," a measure of hope is the constant choice to embrace the implications of Christian discipleship in the world.[96]

The Grace of Hope

The fact that hope is a response to God's revelation in Jesus Christ shows that hope is less an expression of self-assertion than of receptivity, which, as discussed earlier, has intimate associations with the

94. Gerhard Lohfink, *Jesus of Nazareth: What He Wanted, Who He Was*, trans. L. Maloney (Collegeville, MN: Liturgical Press, 2012), 306–7.

95. Sobrino, *Christ the Liberator*, 48; original emphasis.

96. Karl Rahner, "On the Theology of Hope," in *Theological Investigations*, vol. 10, trans. D. Bourke (New York: Crossroad, 1973), 251.

Holy Spirit. This receptivity is not akin to inaction and does not reflect a lack of imagination and initiative in the practitioners of hope. It is certainly true that hope looks toward a fulfillment that only God can accomplish, but hope motivates decisions and actions that counter the obstacles blocking a desired outcome, even as it moderates overconfidence in humanity's ability to finalize every plan. The intricacies of hope showcase its particularity: "[Hope] is less eloquent than either optimism or despair (both of which, knowing the outcome, confidently complete the story). Sometimes in silence, sometimes in more articulate agony or Job-like anger, the mood of the discourse of Christian hope is less that of assertion than request: its form is prayer."[97] Hope, then, is a lived spirituality.

As a response to grace, hope enacts the freedom that graced dependence on God conveys. The understanding of freedom as both "freedom from" and "freedom for," an understanding common in Christian theology, is applicable to the freedom that flows from hope. Hope is freedom from fear of irredeemable failure: "Only the great certitude of hope that my own life and history in general, despite all failures, are held firm by the indestructible power of Love . . . can free our life and the world from the poisons and contaminations that could destroy the present and the future."[98] Hope is also freedom for the love that expresses itself in compassion, justice, openness to forgiveness and reconciliation, and the practice of generosity. As a result of its grounding in God, hope enables all such efforts to transcend the danger of devolving into ways of acting that "either tire us or turn into fanaticism."[99] Through grace, hope can persist as a revelation of God's presence, even in circumstances that are far from congenial to the practice of hope.

For the church, hope, as the work of the Spirit, stimulates the community of faith to undertake an honest encounter with its own failures

97. Nicholas Lash, *The Beginning and End of 'Religion'* (Cambridge: Cambridge University Press, 1996), 229.

98. Pope Benedict XVI, *Spe Salvi*, Saved in Hope (2007), 35, http://www.vatican .va/holy_father/benedict_xvi/encyclicals/documents/hf_ben-xvi_enc_20071130_spe -salvi_en.html.

99. Ibid.

and sinfulness. In this way, hope supports and stimulates the ecclesial community's commitment to the forms of tilling evident in conversion, reform, and the embrace of possibilities for a more wholehearted witness to God's presence in the world.[100] This process is ongoing and always incomplete. It is also essential if the ecclesial community's faith and hope are to produce ways of living that express the love of the trinitarian God at the heart of the church.

Hope is not an instrument of prediction in relation to the church's future, but its role in furthering the church's conversion and empowering the willingness to engage with new questions does contribute to shaping that future. A theology of hope in relation to the church does not imply that the Christian community will enjoy a future free of difficulties, and so does not preserve members of the church from anguish, including anguish about their own failure to exemplify all that they endorse as the purpose of the Christian community. Such circumstances may appear to be inimical to the emergence of hope. Happily, it is a unique strength of hope, reflecting its foundation in Jesus and the Holy Spirit, that its operation does not depend on benign or even neutral conditions. Rather, hope "stirs when the secure system shows signs of breaking down," when circumstances make it difficult to maintain even the pretense of being able to ensure a desired outcome.[101] To return to Abraham: his "hoping against hope" (Rom 4:18) that God would be faithful to all that God had promised, despite the strength of the prevailing counter-indications, provides a model for all those who hope.

Building on this interpretation of hope, a key argument of this volume is that the tilling of the church, which can nourish hope for the church's future, embraces the acknowledgment of present-day difficulties facing the church. Hope fuels the tilling that engages with those difficulties, affirming that "our response to tragedy carries the

---

100. For an analysis of the relationship between the church and hope in terms of conversion, see Richard Lennan, "The Church as a Sacrament of Hope," *Theological Studies* 72 (2011): 247-74, and Richard Lennan, "The Church: Got Hope?" in *Hope: Promise, Possibility, and Fulfillment*, ed. Richard Lennan and Nancy Pineda-Madrid (Mahwah, NJ: Paulist, 2013), 42-54.

101. Anthony Kelly, *Eschatology and Hope* (Maryknoll, NY: Orbis, 2006), 5.

possibility of breaking open hope in history."[102] Hope, then, nourishes the practice of "obedience to what horrifies."[103] "Obedience" in this context conveys the acknowledgment and acceptance of all that characterizes the church's social and historical situation. Hope stimulates encounter with this reality, enabling members of the church to meet the fear that current circumstances may suggest that only decline and death will characterize the ecclesial future.

Facing the failures that hinder the witness of the Christian community in the early decades of the twenty-first century is uniquely demanding, as issues of racial, gender, and other forms of injustice, including all that "the sexual abuse crisis" summarizes, continue to scar the Catholic community. Hope buttresses the readiness to confront these truths in all of their ugliness: "If hope is not to belie its own essence, it can tolerate no definitive limits."[104] Without minimizing the scope of failure and the challenges of reform, hope generates the conviction that the church's future can be other than a portrait of "a few representatives left over as a sort of atavistic remnant from the past."[105] The commitment to following the paths that openness to the Spirit illuminates is the prerequisite for shaping the church as a community of hope. This hope does not promise a booming future, but is also not at ease in a community so discouraged by its own failure that it sees no alternative to looming extinction and the despair and inaction that such a "vision" brings to birth.

With the sustenance that hope provides, the ecclesial community as a whole, not simply its individual members or its leaders, can "live in waiting, in ambiguity, in something less than the full light of day."[106] Waiting captures something essential to hope, since "hope that is seen is

---

102. Nancy Pineda-Madrid, "Hope and Salvation in the Shadow of Tragedy," in *Hope: Promise, Possibility, and Fulfillment*, ed. Richard Lennan and Nancy Pineda-Madrid (Mahwah, NJ: Paulist, 2013), 116.

103. Paul Crowley, *Unwanted Wisdom: Suffering, the Cross, and Hope* (New York: Continuum, 2005), 61.

104. Karl Rahner, "Easter and Hope," in *The Great Church Year*, trans. ed. H. Egan (New York: Crossroad, 1993), 188.

105. Karl Rahner, *Free Speech in the Church*, trans. G. R. Lamb (London: Sheed and Ward, 1959), 47.

106. Crowley, *Unwanted Wisdom*, 55.

not hope. For who hopes for what is seen?" (Rom 8:24). It is important to reiterate here that the willingness to wait for the full flowering of all that derives from trust in God's providence does not equate to wishful thinking, and is certainly other than resignation or passivity. Authentic hope energizes the Christian community, stimulating the discernment that can flower in creative action: "Since, then, we have such a hope, we act with great boldness" (2 Cor 3:12). For this reason, there is an intimate relationship between hope and the work for justice that tills the world no less than the church: "Hope presumes a situation in which *human activity can make a difference* concerning the realization of the desired outcome."[107] Hope, in a word, acts.

Genuine hope promotes an outward-looking church, one seeking to embody God's love in the world, rather than one that is self-absorbed and anxious, especially about its future. For this reason:

> the church can be a sacrament of hope only if it succeeds in voicing its hope clearly and unequivocally for all to hear, if it avoids succumbing to dread of the future, and if it does not fall victim to a pale and paltry form of popular humanism lacking the decisive salt of Christian faith. The world does not need a duplication of its hope; still less does it need a duplication of its despair.[108]

It is evident that only a church able to entrust its own future to God, and draw the consequences of this trust for its present expressions of communal life, including in the liturgy and social action, can be a symbol of hope in the world. The enduring presence of grace mediated throughout history means that the church's future will not appear from a clear blue sky, as if independent of any ties to what has preceded it. This suggests that the future of the present, insofar as any point even in the near future is foreseeable, will be the product of the appropriation of grace in the myriad settings where the ecclesial community participates in the world of the twenty-first century. This book, taken as a

---

107. Bryan Massingale, *Racial Justice and the Catholic Church* (Maryknoll, NY: Orbis, 2010), 148; original emphasis.

108. Walter Kasper, "Individual Salvation and Eschatological Consummation," in *Faith and the Future: Studies in Christian Eschatology*, ed. John Galvin (New York: Paulist, 1994), 21.

whole, is an inventory and exploration of the graced resources available to the Christian community for all that "tilling the church" conveys, for all that being and remaining a community of hope requires.

These resources, which include the ecclesial community's self-understanding that is the product of the community's reflection on its experience of grace over its long history, are the church's graced patrimony. As such, they are tools for responding to the swirling complexity of the present moment, while keeping sight of the future. The ecclesial community in its manifold settings is to draw from this patrimony in the process of discerning the choices that it must make and remake if hope is to characterize its existence, both now and in the future.

The identification of the church as participating in a pilgrimage of hope specifies where the church begins—God's free initiative in Jesus Christ and the Holy Spirit—and where it will end—the fullness of God's reign. What the theology of the church's pilgrimage does not do, what is beyond its competence, is to assert a capacity to account for all that will happen between those points. The theology of pilgrimage affirms unequivocally the unpredictable nature of the church's existence in history. It allows for different experiences and for a variety of learning by not assuming that all pilgrimages resemble each other in every aspect. On the other hand, the theology of pilgrimage identifies grace, working through the discernment of individuals and communities, as the resource that enables and constantly renews the church's pilgrimage.

Grace, at work in manifold sources, illuminates possibilities for the church, but does not spare pilgrims the need to discern how to proceed creatively and faithfully. In this discernment, the graced insights that human wisdom can harvest from multiple settings coalesce with the deliberate endeavor to be attentive to the Spirit. The decisions that proceed from this discernment are, then, original and creative rather than readings of a blueprint. Building on this presentation of the church as a pilgrim, the next chapter will explore the church's engagement with history.

4

Engaging the Graced World

Pentecost is central to the story of the church. Catholic teaching is clear in its conviction that "the *era of the Church* began with the 'coming,' that is to say with the descent of the Holy Spirit on the Apostles gathered in the Upper Room in Jerusalem, together with Mary, the Lord's Mother."[1] Through their reception of the Holy Spirit at Pentecost, the followers of Jesus emerge as "the church," no longer a fearful group but the community of faith whose members take up their commission to proclaim Christ in word and action, even to "the ends of the earth" (Acts 13:47). Pentecost, like God's creative act in Genesis, "is not to be seen simply in the chronological sense of a one-off 'beginning,'" nor does it commemorate a random gift from an ephemeral muse.[2] Rather, the Spirit who launches the "era of the church" remains with the ecclesial community to deepen and sustain the faith and hope that fuels the church's engagement with the wider human community.

1. Pope John Paul II, *Dominum et Vivificantem*, On the Holy Spirit in the Life of the Church and the World (1986), 25; original emphasis; http://www.vatican.va /content/john-paul-ii/en/encyclicals/documents/hf_jp-ii_enc_18051986_dominum -et-vivificantem.html.
2. Ormond Rush, *The Eyes of Faith: The Sense of the Faithful and the Church's Reception of Revelation* (Washington, DC: Catholic University of America Press, 2009), 38.

The depiction of Pentecost in the Acts of the Apostles (Acts 2:1-13) captures vividly the transformative power of the Spirit that ignites the mission of the church. As compelling as such drama is, the more common setting for the Spirit's relationship to the church, and so for faithful responses to grace in service of God's reign, is the "everyday." In the latter context, the work of the Spirit is less spectacular than the events of Pentecost, but this does not reduce the Spirit's significance and efficacy. In remaining with the church, and in being the stimulus for its unity and mission, the Spirit prompts faithful responses to grace in the present, while orienting the ecclesial community toward the fullness of God's reign.[3]

The Spirit shapes the Christian story through a constancy of presence that supports clear-eyed discernment. Through grace, the Spirit sustains the commitments and self-sacrifice that are integral to fruitful discipleship in response to the ongoing reception of God's self-communication. Since "to each is given the manifestation of the Spirit for the common good" (1 Cor 12:7), the grace of God nourishes and guides all members of the community of faith in the life of discipleship, whose setting is the vicissitudes of every time and place.

The preceding chapters, through their analysis of sacrament and pilgrimage, as well as the exploration of faith and hope, have highlighted the church's presence in history, in the world, even as they acknowledged the church's movement toward the fullness of life in God. The present chapter examines more fully the church's engagement with history. This examination will be particularly attentive to the implications of this engagement for the existence of the church as a project in need of tilling. It will also focus on the role that the Spirit plays as the community of faith discerns and responds to its need for tilling.

In exploring its themes, the chapter concentrates on the resources proper to the church for its participation in history. These resources do not dictate the details of this participation in any specific circumstances, nor do they gesture toward a "one-size-fits-all" approach regarding how communities of faith should interact with the conditions

---

3. For the relationship between the Spirit, the reign of God, and the church, see James Coriden, *The Holy Spirit and an Evolving Church* (Maryknoll, NY: Orbis, 2017), 141–59.

unique to their time and place. More positively, the resources highlight the potential for fluidity both within the ecclesial community and in the manner of the community's activity in the wider society.

To give substance to its interpretation of the church's engagement with the graced world, the chapter will explore three distinct but related topics. To begin, there will be an overview of the relationship between the grace of the Holy Spirit and history, especially as it applies to the church as a body in history; the section will use the earliest Christian communities to illustrate this relationship. The second step is to canvass the warp and weft of the church's participation in the world beyond itself; "mission," which connects the church to both the life of Jesus and the ongoing movement of societies, frames this section. The final part of the chapter will present the church's communal existence in history as an "open system"; doing so will illustrate that the church's unfinished reality comes into ever-sharper view as the ecclesial community engages with the circumstances and questions of every time and place. Together, these themes set the stage for considering the dynamics of faithfulness in the church, especially as the ecclesial community navigates the relationship of preservation and change, dynamics that will feature in both chapters 5 and 6.

The Interweaving of Grace, History, and the Life of the Church

The thesis of this section is that the Christian community's identity as a sacrament of grace, as a particular expression of the presence of the Holy Spirit, binds the church to history. Establishing this thesis lays the foundation for the analysis of "mission" in the following part of the chapter. Since the church lives among the complex realities of everyday life in the world, it is in history, with its myriad unpredictable occurrences, that all expressions of the church are to symbolize the Spirit. In so doing, the church speaks to the deepest reality of the world, which is graced rather than being a godless wasteland that the church alone can transform.

The graced world is already a pointer to the presence of the Holy Spirit. The history of the Spirit in the world does not begin at Pentecost and is far more than a collection of cameo appearances. In fact, it is permanence of presence that is most characteristic of the Holy Spirit. Long before Pentecost, the "spirit" of God (Ps 104:30) was integral to creation.[4] It is also the Holy Spirit who "overshadows" Mary (Luke 1:35), confirming her election by God and nurturing her unique contribution to the fulfillment of God's promises to Israel. In "alighting" on Jesus at his baptism (Matt 3:16), the Spirit reveals the unity of God's trinitarian love at the heart of the incarnation, the love that communicates itself through the life, death, resurrection, and ascension of Jesus.

It is certainly true that God becomes incarnate only in Jesus Christ, but it is the Spirit "who brings about the acceptance by the world in faith, hope and love of [God's] self-communication" in Christ.[5] The inextricable relationship between the Spirit and the church means, as chapter 2 discussed under the heading "sacrament," that "the true image of the Holy Spirit is the church, the Christian community with its assemblies."[6] Even as the church makes the Spirit "visible," the Spirit prompts the church's ongoing conversion and creativity so that the ecclesial community might express more wholeheartedly God's commitment to the whole of creation. In this vein, Vatican II describes the Spirit as the one "who moves the heart and converts it to God," a movement that enables God's trinitarian revelation to be "more and more deeply understood" (*Dei Verbum*, 5).

The interweaving of Christ and the Spirit within God's self-communication in history establishes each of them as "the co-instituting principle" of the church.[7] Accordingly, as Sandra Schneiders argues, an appreciation of the Spirit's role is simultaneously an affirmation of the church's relationship to the trinitarian God: "As the Spirit constitutes the unity of Jesus with God, so the Spirit is the unity between Jesus

---

4. For the "pre-history" of the Holy Spirit before the revelation that the New Testament chronicles, see Andrew Davis, "Spirit, Wind, or Breath: Reflections on the Old Testament," in *The Holy Spirit: Setting the World on Fire*, ed. Richard Lennan and Nancy Pineda-Madrid (Mahwah, NJ: Paulist, 2017), 63–72.

5. Karl Rahner, *The Trinity*, trans. J. Donceel (London: Burns and Oates, 1970), 86.

6. Gerhard Lohfink, *Prayer Takes Us Home: The Theology and Practice of Christian Prayer*, trans. L. Maloney (Collegeville, MN: Liturgical Press, 2020), 18.

7. Yves Congar, *I Believe in the Holy Spirit*, vol. 2, trans. D. Smith (New York: Seabury, 1983), 9.

and the Church. The indwelling Spirit as constitutive of the Church's identity with Christ was bestowed by Jesus in the context of his paschal mystery."[8] For this reason, discussion of the Spirit reinforces rather than detracts from the identity of the church as the "body of Christ" and "the people of God," terms that highlight the church's relationship to God's self-communication.

The fact that the grace of the Spirit tends toward the building up of relationships is fundamental for the health of the ecclesial community. Without impairing individuality, grace does not stoke the type of individualism that would reduce "the ecclesial community" to a meaningless term. The portfolio of the Spirit in the life of the church includes deepening the ecclesial community's faith in Christ, enlivening its worship and prayer, supporting its common life, and empowering the church for the mission of Christian discipleship in the wider world. In these ways, the Spirit is the primary agent of the church's tilling, working through all baptized members of the church who share in the grace of the Spirit.

Acknowledging the centrality of the Holy Spirit and grace to ecclesiology does not mean that the discipline will inevitably "spiritualize" the church. The "incarnational tendency" of God's revelation, to recall Karl Rahner's emphasis on the embodied nature of grace, means that faithfulness to God's self-communication requires the church to embrace its own graced participation in history. A further corollary of this theology of grace is that the church enjoys no immunity to the complexity, and messiness, evident in the world. The focus on the church's embodiment and its engagement with the world aligns with earlier explorations of the ecclesial community as a project and as a pilgrim. Each of those depictions has also demonstrated that the church's existence as a sacrament in history does not secure its perfection.

Beyond anchoring the church in history, the omnipresence of the Spirit in the church also means, to anticipate a point that will be significant in the final section of this chapter—and especially for chapter 6—that there can be in the church no privileged group that alone has access to the Spirit. To determine how the ecclesial community ought

---

8. Sandra Schneiders, *The Revelatory Text: Interpreting the New Testament as Sacred Scripture*, 2nd ed. (Collegeville, MN: Michael Glazier, 1999), 72.

to engage with the world or what facets of the church's life might require tilling is a task for *the church*, not simply for its leadership. This is especially so when such discernment requires engagement at the local level rather than being an activity that a centralized authority carries out on behalf of all groups in the church, irrespective of their situations, questions, and needs.

Along with showcasing the universality of grace and the Spirit's role in promoting the church's continuing conversion, Vatican II insists in *Ad Gentes* (AG), its decree on the church's mission, that the Spirit, at work in all the baptized, plays a multifaceted role in the church's mission: "[the Spirit] at times visibly anticipates apostolic action, just as in various ways [the Spirit] unceasingly accompanies and directs it."[9] This emphasis of the council highlights that the life of the church, the life that the Spirit nurtures and sustains, is life in history, life amid the ever-changing realities of societies and cultures.

The church's setting in history repeatedly confronts the ecclesial community with its incompleteness; with the sinfulness, unknowing, and need for conversion that are all characteristic of being a pilgrim. This status makes plain that the "citizenship" (Phil 3:20) of the disciples of Christ is in heaven, that their home is not "the earthly tent" but "a building from God, a house not made with hands, eternal in the heavens" (2 Cor 5:1). No less decisively, the pilgrimage of the followers of Christ takes place in and through "the present age," where they are "to live lives that are self-controlled, upright, and godly" (Titus 2:12), a prescription that requires the gifts of the Spirit for its completion. The church's pilgrimage in history, then, is the workplace of the Holy Spirit. It is the Spirit who guides the church through and within the graced world of God's creation, enabling the church to live in the tension of its setting in the "not yet . . . but already" of God's reign.

The designation of the church as a pilgrim is especially fitting for the circumstances of the world as its history is unfolding in the twenty-first century. Numerous facets of contemporary experience—from the repercussions of climate change and the effects of corrosive racial inequality, to the displacement of unfathomably large numbers of refu-

9. The Second Vatican Council, *Ad Gentes* (AG), Decree on the Church's Missionary Activity (1965), 4.

gees, the profound disparity in levels of wealth that not only reflects but exacerbates the radical devaluing of labor, and the reverberations of the COVID-19 pandemic—are symptoms of a world adrift, "unmoored" from any unity of purpose, as chapter 1 discussed.[10] It is in these circumstances that the discipleship of the pilgrim church, even as it attempts to weather its own forms of dislocation, is to symbolize hope for the present and future.[11]

In response to the love of God shared through Christ and the Spirit, discipleship is the voluntary choice to "do nothing from selfish ambition or conceit, but in humility regard others as better than yourselves" (Phil 2:3). This choice mirrors what Paul Crowley refers to as God's own voluntary "dislocation" that takes place in the incarnation.[12] The possibility that such discipleship might become a defining attribute of the church is unimaginable without grace. Nor would a church resistant to the graced tilling of its own life be able to represent grace, especially in a world where grace can seem elusive, even absent.

It is in the shifting contours of history that the disciples of Christ are to embody the gospel through their witness to faith, hope, and love, which are constitutive of ecclesial spirituality in its most cogent form. These Spirit-stamped virtues are to season the daily activities of Christians within the wider society that extends beyond the boundaries of the church. The flourishing of such a spirituality is a core aspect of what grace enables for the Christian community, but, as with all that pertains to ecclesial life, humanity's response to grace is far from being a peripheral factor in this flourishing.

The Holy Spirit "speaks" to the Christian community through Scripture, sacraments, and the everyday life in the world of countless women and men of faith. These sources, drawing again on chapter 2's presentation, are not conduits for information about God, but symbols of

10. For the notion of the "unmooring" of society from much that once offered security, including religious faith, see Paul Crowley, *The Unmoored God: Believing in a Time of Dislocation* (Maryknoll, NY: Orbis, 2017).

11. For a helpful analysis of the possibilities for mission even in the midst of social complexity, see Robert Schreiter, "Mediating Repentance, Forgiveness, and Reconciliation: What Is the Church's Role?," in *The Spirit in the Church and the World*, ed. Bradford Hinze (Maryknoll, NY: Orbis, 2003), 51–67.

12. On discipleship as voluntary dislocation, see Crowley, *Unmoored God*, 74–87.

the Spirit's presence, graced mediators of encounters with the creator God. As such, they invite a response, especially as they challenge the ecclesial community, Pope Francis contends, to allow the Spirit to "enlighten, guide and direct us, leading us wherever [the Spirit] wills," a choice that is possible only through renouncing "the attempt to plan and control everything to the last detail."[13] These encounters can enliven the church with God's vision for greater justice in history, while also prompting the Christian community to look toward what exceeds even the deepest aspirations of the human spirit.

The church cannot ignore the world, or at least can do so only by ceasing to live the discipleship that defines the ecclesial community. This assertion is more than an obvious consequence of the church's existence in history: it is a direct outcome of the church's foundation in God's revelation through Jesus Christ and the Holy Spirit. Since the grace that initiates and sustains the church does likewise for the whole world, grace implicates the ecclesial community in history, just as it implicates humanity in responsibility for the whole of God's creation. A fruitful theology of the church's presence in history will support the Christian community's vocation to nurture positive connections to the world beyond the church. This emphasis is consistent with affirming the particularity of the church.

Building on the presentation of the church as sacrament, the church's particularity derives from being "where salvation from God is thematized or put into words, confessed explicitly, proclaimed prophetically and celebrated liturgically."[14] This identity resonates with the movement of grace through the church's historical reality; it likewise illuminates various dimensions of the church's mission, the theme on which the next section of the chapter will elaborate. This grace-given particularity proscribes collapsing the church into the world, but is congruent with the possibility that the ecclesial community might learn from the vast array of sources in the wider world that can also be symbols of grace. True, this learning requires discernment as not everything in the world is necessarily reflective of grace, but discernment and self-critical reflec-

13. Pope Francis, *Evangelii Gaudium*, 280.

14. Edward Schillebeeckx, *Church: The Human Story of God*, trans. J. Bowden (New York: Crossroad, 1980), 13.

tion are equally applicable within the ecclesial community's own life as a body that never outgrows its need for conversion to grace.

The Formative Role of History

From its beginnings, the ecclesial community has been part of a world more familiar with flux than permanence. During this same length of time, the church itself has been neither an inert object nor a body following a program designed to ensure the unfailing and unambiguous faithfulness of the ecclesial community. As is evident in the long narrative of ecclesiastical history, the Christian community's surrender to grace is far from being an automatic and seamless event. An enthusiastic embrace of the lack of control that pilgrims hold over their situation is not the default mode of the ecclesial community in all of its manifestations.

Since grace is not destructive of human freedom, the Spirit furnishes no guarantees that the church will be either unfailingly consistent in its response to grace or blissfully free of uncertainty, conflict, inconsistency, and even duplicity. Likewise, the omnipresence of the Spirit in the church offers no assurance to the Christian community that it will progress, inexorably and triumphantly, through the various eras of history toward its goal of eternal blessedness. For this reason, the church's history differs from a chronicle of unimpeachable holiness—a qualified assessment that could well be too mild to reflect adequately many phases and figures in ecclesiastical history. The church's irreducible complexity is evident in the earliest Christian communities, in every later period of ecclesiastical history, and, yes, in the present day.

Emphasizing that the presence of the Spirit does not inoculate the church against its own complexity is crucial for clarifying that the presence of the Spirit is not a form of magic. It is no less important, on the other hand, to clarify how the Spirit inspires and sustains the formation of the church in history. One way to illustrate both principles is via a survey of the first Christian communities, a survey that focuses on the multifaceted role of the Holy Spirit.

It would be wildly inaccurate to depict the first communities of Christians through an idyll claiming them as paradigms of perfect unity and sterling commitment. The New Testament itself records the tensions and divisions that these communities experienced—"'I belong to Paul,' or 'I belong to Apollos,' or 'I belong to Cephas,' or 'I belong to Christ'" (1 Cor 1:12). Yet, many facets of those same communities are testimony to the effectiveness of grace—"I have heard of your faith in the Lord Jesus and your love towards all the saints" (Eph 1:15). Through the Spirit, communities of disciples proclaimed the crucified and risen Christ and formed a common life, even as they experienced, at every turn, circumstances that carried the potential for partisanship and rancor at odds with the gospel.[15]

From the obligation to decide whether the law of Moses applied in its fullness to gentiles who became Christians (Acts 15:1-29), to the task of determining appropriate admonition and guidance for their members who were "living in idleness, mere busybodies, not doing any work" (2 Thess 3:11), the communities needed to construct the path on which they were to walk. There was, of course, no blueprint that mapped a solution for every exigency. What did provide direction for members of the church was not only their individual relationship to God, but their participation in a community of faith in Christ and the Spirit. This community, which could be intimately personal and affirming—"a faith that lived first in your grandmother Lois and your mother Eunice" (2 Tim 1:5)—but also adamant and challenging—"You foolish Galatians! Who has bewitched you?" (Gal 3:1). Both aspects ensured that authentic Christian life was dynamic.

As they formed their responses to all that confronted them, the communities intended to discern what "has seemed good to the Holy Spirit and to us" (Acts 15:28). This goal could sound breathtakingly hubristic. What preserves it from such a designation is the fact that those doing the discernment drew on their existing relationship to the grace of the Holy Spirit. In the process of discernment, it was their lived familiarity with grace that facilitated creative decisions.

Discernment took place within communities already seeking, through their prayer and worship, to be attentive to the Spirit—"Let

---

15. For an overview of the individual communities represented in the New Testament, see Coriden, *The Holy Spirit and an Evolving Church*, 30–65. See also the chapters in part 2 of *The Oxford Handbook of Ecclesiology*, ed. Paul Avis (Oxford: Oxford University Press, 2018), 55–160.

the word of Christ dwell in you richly . . . and with gratitude in your hearts sing psalms, hymns, and spiritual songs to God" (Col 3:16).

Beginning with the Acts of the Apostles, the New Testament connects efficacy in responding constructively to the challenges of discipleship with reliance on the Spirit. Through this reliance, the members of the churches developed their receptivity to grace at work in the world and in their own communities. Faith in the Spirit's guidance sustained local communities as they encountered manifold difficulties inherent in both the work of proclamation and the process of fashioning a common life—"Guard the good treasure entrusted to you, with the help of the Holy Spirit living in us" (2 Tim 1:14). It was the same faith on which they relied to guide actions dedicated to the gospel more than to self-interest and to transcend predetermined ideas about who could participate in their community, and even minister within them—"I commend to you our sister Phoebe, a deacon of the church at Cenchreae, so that you may welcome her in the Lord as is fitting for the saints" (Rom 16:1-2).

In the light of God's free gift of grace that sustained the community of faith, the self-understanding of the church revolved around the call to trust that the Spirit was with the community, as its guide and the anchor that preserved its connection to Christ. The Spirit, then, was reliable, even if the community's response to the Spirit was not always consistent.

As a pilgrim, the life of the church in every era and setting is part of the flow of history. It is not surprising, then, that the confrontation with urgent internal and external matters that began in the church's first generation did not end there. The struggle to be faithful to the Spirit in the midst of the contingencies proper to every time and place has shaped the church's history as something other than the endless repetition of a single experience. The differences evident between various periods of that history emerged as Christian communities sought to clarify their faith, refine their structures, and learn from failures, in the particular circumstances of their historical setting. Nor are such efforts finally complete.

Developments that occurred over two millennia of history have moved the church beyond anything imaginable in the experience of first-century Christians. Over the span of the church's history, ministerial structures, sacramental practices, instruments of governance, and processes for settling disputes about the faith of the ecclesial community have become more settled and less malleable. As a result, further adaptation becomes difficult—"[The church] often places more value on the bureaucratic apparatus of the Church than in the enthusiasm of her Spirit; she often loves the calm more than the storm, the old (which has proved itself) more than the new (which is bold and daring)."[16] The preference for life in the ecclesial community to be predictable and assured, a preference manifest often through the church's history, can discourage questioning and even provoke active resistance to possibilities that the Spirit might be enabling. This is especially so when these possibilities offer alternatives to established ways of proceeding.

It would be simple to conclude here that the inertia characteristic of structures weighs against any merit for the institutional reality of the church, and especially for any connection between the Holy Spirit and the church's institutions. The final section of this chapter will argue, however, that the various elements of the church's institutional apparatus are a mixed reality. They are neither an unalloyed good nor indisputable proof of the church's decay and resistance to the Spirit. What is unambiguously true is that this ineradicable complexity testifies to the church's abiding need for tilling.

The record of the church's checkered openness to grace in history notwithstanding, the imperative to address even the unanticipated events of every time and place remains one from which the ecclesial community can claim no exemption. The invocation of the Spirit as "the soul of the Church," then, mandates attention to the church's presence in history, rather than rendering such attention redundant.[17] This obligation likewise fuels the work of ecclesiology.

Theological reflection that is part of the church's engagement with history contributes to the formation of the church on its pilgrimage, to reiterate another of this book's main convictions.[18] It does so in part by highlighting the boundless mystery of God that encompasses

16. Karl Rahner, "Thoughts on the Possibility of Belief Today," in *Theological Investigations*, vol. 5, trans. K-H. Kruger (New York: Crossroad, 1983), 16.

17. Pope John Paul II, *Dominum et Vivificantem*, 26.

18. For a survey of the interweaving of the church's theology and practice with the events of multiple times and places, see Frederick Cwiekowski, *The Church: Theology in History* (Collegeville, MN: Liturgical Press, 2018).

the church throughout its history. It is this grace of God that generates multiple occasions and means for the tilling of the church. Theology's affirmation of the symbiosis between history and grace recognizes that the Spirit is present through the diversity of contexts in which the ecclesial community encounters grace. The church depends on grace, but this reliance on God's activity does not diminish the relevance of the historical experience of the church between Pentecost and the consummation of God's reign.

As the community of faith navigates history, the ecclesiology that accompanies and supports it must plot a path between two extremes. At one end, there is the temptation to present the church as an unchanging and unchangeable reality. This perspective tends to imbue artifacts of the past with an aura of grace, making them wondrously applicable to present circumstances without even the need for interpretation, and obviating any possibility of innovation. The contrasting extreme denies permanence to any products of the past, and even devalues them as the work of those who lack the sophistication evident in the present day. Although "permanence" is a notion in need of the elaboration that chapter 5 will offer, refusing to accept that it is a possibility in any form would condemn each generation of the church to imprisonment in the present. Such a stance would deprive all historical epochs of both ancestors and descendants, while also implying that grace is episodic rather than continuous. Within the spectrum that the two extremes delineate, the area is vast. In this space, ecclesial practice and theological reflection have always intersected, and continue to intersect.

As chapter 5 explores the relationship between the church's past and present, it will do so with an eye to the future. A related element of both chapters 5 and 6 will be their consideration of the conflict that the prospect of "change" so often generates in the ecclesial community. This conflict reflects the tension between the perception of the church as a future-oriented body—one open to conversion, reform, and multiple possibilities—and the invocation of "tradition" as an impermeable and insurmountable barrier to such activities.

Exploring that conflict will lay a path for chapter 6's consideration of "reception," which is "the lively process of the Church drawing from the resources of the past to seize and accept the present activities of its loving Lord," a context that, because it inevitably differs from what applied in the original home of those resources, opens the possibility of change.[19] The examination of reception will take into account the distinction between what is primary and what is less central in all that the church, in every era, receives from the past. Both chapters 5 and 6 will stress that doing justice to the movement of grace in history and in the life of the church requires rejecting all one-dimensional approaches in favor of the richness that the Sprit generates.

The health of the church at every period of its history depends largely on the willingness of its members to accept that their community is never fully at the disposal of human desires, let alone human whims. As the product of God's initiative, the church cannot change "into something or other at will, arbitrarily, but only into a new presence of its old reality, into the present and future of its past, of the Gospel, of the grace and truth of God."[20] This obligation has implications for theological consideration of the church's present and future.

A principal task of engagement with the present and future is to seek ways to reconcile faith in the grace that has formed the church over its long history with openings to a future that is no less graced, even if it differs from the past. In this context, discernment of the Spirit's call and movement is crucial as it can clarify possibilities for the future without implying a comprehensive repudiation of the past. This discernment, in which creative reception of what has come from the past plays an indispensable role, applies to all components of the church's life, but preeminently to the church's mission in the world. It is "mission," as the following section of this chapter will illustrate, that most accentuates the church's engagement with the fluidity of the world and its history.

Graced Mission in a Graced World

The Second Vatican Council describes the pilgrim people of God as being "by its very nature missionary since, according to the plan of the Father, it has its origin in the mission of the Son and the Holy Spirit"

---

19. William Rusch, "The Landscape of Reception," in *Seeking the Truth of Change in the Church: Reception, Communion and the Ordination of Women*, ed. Paul Avis (New York: T. and T. Clark, 2004), 4.

20. Karl Rahner, *The Christian of the Future*, trans. W. J. O'Hara (London: Burns and Oates, 1967), 36.

(AG 2). This description aligns the church with God's creative self-communication in history. Building on this foundation, the council teaches that the mission of the church in the world is that "of proclaiming and establishing among all peoples the kingdom of Christ and of God" (LG 5). The missionary mandate, framed by the command of the risen Jesus to "Go therefore and make disciples of all nations" (Matt 28:19), has been integral to the church's self-understanding from the apostolic era onward. The church's methods of evangelization have changed during that long span of time, but so, too, has the church's perception of "the world" in which it is to fulfill its mandate. As the latter perception has shifted, practices of mission have also evolved to reflect the prevailing attitude in the church.

In the two centuries before Vatican II, the church's approach to the world revealed both a deep suspicion toward the modern form of the nation-state and an intense commitment to evangelization in "mission lands" beyond Europe, as chapter 1 discussed. Catholic teaching and practice in this period desired the conversion of the world, but was largely innocent of any awareness that the Catholic Church, too, might stand in need of conversion, let alone that it could be possible for the church to learn from the world. Rather, the church's leaders in particular understood themselves as empowered to teach and correct civil societies, while protecting Catholics from the deleterious influences of those societies. The best-known illustration of this attitude is the condemnation that Pope Pius IX issued in 1864 against the "current errors" evident in liberal democracies.[21] By depicting the church as morally superior to civil societies, this stance reflected the interpretation of "perfect society" that elevated the church above all lesser groups.

Perceptions of the church's unique position in relation to God's grace also influenced the methods of evangelization that missionaries applied in many nations. In theologies of evangelization during this period, the logic often ran thus: the Catholic Church is a privileged fount of grace, so it has the responsibility to baptize those who would

21. Pope Pius IX, *Quanta Cura*, Concerning Current Errors, in *The Papal Encyclicals 1740–1878*, ed. Claudia Carlen (1864; repr., Wilmington, NC: McGrath Publishing, 1981), 380–85.

otherwise lack all access to the grace of God's salvation.[22] The possibility of alternatives to this constricted interpretation of the church's mission requires a broader canvas for theologies of both grace and the church, one that can enable a more positive attitude toward the world beyond the church.

Since the uniqueness of the relationship between grace and the church is central to ecclesial faith, acknowledging the universality of grace in the world can complicate the church's self-understanding. If grace can be effective always and everywhere, if it is a gift to all people, transcending any possible containment within an explicitly religious casing, the ecclesial community must be other than the sole beneficiary of grace, just as it must be other than the sole fount of grace for those who are not part of the church. This truth can serve to till the ecclesial community by deflating any tendency within the church to understand itself as an exclusive community of the saved. The same recognition can leave the Christian community uncertain about its place in the world.

The universality of grace, if viewed positively, can elucidate the expanse of the church's mission. Since grace is present within the vast array of the complex and oft-perplexing realities of human history and culture, the ecclesial community, too, must be in relationship with those same realities. Constructive engagement with the graced inhabitants of diverse cultures does make demands on the Christian community. One such demand is the self-restraint required to avoid the misrepresentation of faith that occurs "when we speak more about law than about grace, more about the Church than about Christ, more about the Pope than about God's word" (EG 38). In this way, engagement with the world can free the church from succumbing to a limited vision of grace.

Without compromising the particularity of the church in God's self-communication, Vatican II connected the church's mission to what it suggests are humanity's common longings. From this perspective, the council teaches that "in manifesting Christ, the church reveals to men and women their true situation and calling, since Christ is the head and

22. For an overview of emphases in the theology of mission prior to Vatican II, see John Sivalon, *God's Mission and Postmodern Culture: The Gift of Uncertainty* (Maryknoll, NY: Orbis, 2012), 19–34, and Francis Anekwe Oborji, *Concepts of Mission: The Evolution of Contemporary Missiology* (Maryknoll, NY: Orbis, 2012), 59–71.

exemplar of that renewed humanity, imbued with that familial love, sincerity and spirit of peace to which all women and men aspire" (AG 8). In today's context of decolonialism in social thought and pluralism in religious thought, the council's formulation could sound problematic, an expression of Christian exclusivism that has often been the driver of forced conversions. While Vatican II is not the final word on the church's mission, the council's contribution to the topic remains significant, especially because it commits the Catholic Church to dialogue with the world at large, including other faiths.[23]

Vatican II promotes a "dialogical openness" in the church.[24] In the decades since Vatican II, "dialogue," has become a key element of the church's inculturation in, and engagement with, the world. In *Ecclesiam Suam* (ES), Pope Paul VI seeks "to demonstrate with increasing clarity how vital it is for the world, and how greatly desired by the Catholic Church, that the two should meet together, and get to know and love one another" (ES 3).[25] The encyclical claims that dialogue embodies the conviction that "the world cannot be saved from outside" (ES 87). As a more constructive alternative to standing outside the world, the pope promotes friendship and service as expressions of what God offers all people, and as a way to acknowledge that "every good value in the world" (ES 98) bears a relationship to the life-giving God. Walter Kasper, consistent with the emphasis of *Ecclesiam Suam*, sees a preparedness to engage in dialogue as so fundamental to the church that he classifies the church as a "dialogistic sacrament."[26] Dialogue, then, is more than an option for the church: it is intrinsic to the church's

23. For an assessment of the present-day relevance of the council's teaching on mission, see Stephen Bevans, "The Church in Mission," in *The Cambridge Companion to Vatican II*, ed. R. Gaillardetz (Cambridge: Cambridge University Press, 2020), 136–54.

24. Ormond Rush, *The Vision of Vatican II: Its Fundamental Principles* (Collegeville, MN: Liturgical Press, 2019), 226. For an evaluation of the council's understanding of "dialogue" and its present-day implications, see James McEvoy, *Leaving Christendom for Good: Church-World Dialogue in a Secular Age* (Lanham, MD: Lexington, 2013), 163–75.

25. Pope Paul VI, *Ecclesiam Suam* (1964), On the Church, http://www.vatican.va/holy_father/paul_vi/encyclicals/documents/hf_p-vi_enc_06081964_ecclesiam_en.html.

26. Walter Kasper, *Theology and Church*, trans. M. Kohl (London: SCM, 1989), 140.

mission in the world—the role of dialogue in the inner life of the church is a theme that chapter 6 will address.

In a related way, Ian Linden connects the manner of the church's presence in the public sphere, especially the behavior of those who represent the church officially in that arena, with the likelihood that the church will be perceived as a life-giving possibility. Linden contends that if the church's bishops act as "the shop stewards of Catholicism," as representatives of a vested interest who direct their attention primarily to preserving the church's privileges, "Catholic interventions in the public domain can be marginalized as special interests, rather than listened to—not necessarily heeded—as the expression of a wider claim to be a universal religion and a moral teacher."[27]

The "not necessarily heeded" makes plain that the church will not always "win," will not always be the determinative voice in society, and certainly not be able to impose its principles and convictions. In this circumstance, which differs strikingly from the church's dominant place in the era of Christendom and the expectation that "perfect society" fosters, the willingness to enter into dialogue can be part of the church's witness to hope. Dialogue can be a way for the church to bear witness to what Pope Francis names in *Fratelli Tutti* (FT), his encyclical On Fraternity and Social Friendship, as the "grand ideals that make life more beautiful and worthwhile" (FT 55).

Entering into dialogue with the world, with other religions as well as with the panoply of social groups that might not always welcome the Catholic voice in any form, contributes to the tilling of the church. It does so, argue Steven Bevans and Roger Schroeder, in the context of dialogue with other religions, by providing "a way to discover the fullness of our own faith, so that, paradoxically, we can offer it to others with a bolder humility and a humbler boldness."[28] This is so as dialogue with "otherness" prompts the self-critical questioning of the ecclesial community's priorities and practices, not to undermine them but to seek how they might connect to those who do not share them.

27. Ian Linden, *Global Catholicism: Diversity and Change Since Vatican II* (New York: Columbia University Press, 2009), 263.

28. Stephen Bevans and Roger Schroeder, *Constants in Context: A Theology of Mission for Today* (Maryknoll, NY: Orbis, 2011), 379–80.

This possibility distinguishes dialogue from the "parallel monologues" (FT 200) characteristic of the age of social media.

Jesus and the Reign of God

In the process of self-critical reflection on the priorities and methods of the church's mission, the contours of Jesus's own mission on behalf of God's reign can guide the ecclesial community. The kingdom of God is at the heart of Jesus's preaching. The gospels do not give a precise definition of the kingdom, but refer to it through images, such as a mustard seed flowering into a large tree (Matt 13:31; Luke 13:18), yeast leavening bread (Matt 13:33; Luke 13:20), a treasure that makes a claim on one's whole life (Matt 13:44), a seed growing unseen (Mark 4:31), or an invitation to a wedding feast, an invitation to which not all the recipients respond appropriately (Matt 22:2-14). Common to these images is the stress on both abundance and gift.

As vivid as those images are, Jesus does not merely talk about the kingdom: he enacts it. The miracles of healing, for example, symbolize the life-giving love of God that is not subject to the limits imposed by human corporeality (Mark 5:22-43; Luke 8:41-56). Similarly, the miraculous feeding of the great crowds (Matt 14:13-21, 15:32-38; Mark 6:35-44, 8:1-6; John 6:1-14) witnesses to God's desire and capacity to respond to humanity's needs. In the miracles, as in the parables, abundance and gift are primary.

In Jesus, God reveals the kingdom as "a gracious gift from God, who comes with unconditional love to seek out humankind and to offer ultimate salvation to all. It is a gift which people can only receive in gratitude and awe. God is coming toward us as unconditional love, seeking communion and intimacy."[29] This element of "gift" is evident in the Jesus who "went about doing good and healing all who were oppressed by the devil, for God was with him" (Acts 10:38). It is present, too, when Jesus challenges both superficial and disingenuous religious observance that sought to lay an obligation on God (Mark 7:1-23). Jesus's appreciation of God's reconciling love as a gift enabled him to associate with outcasts, an association that affronted the upholders of

---

29. John Fuellenbach, *The Kingdom of God: The Message of Jesus Today* (Maryknoll, NY: Orbis, 2002), 97.

the socio-religious order (Luke 15:2). The gospels even present Jesus as growing in his recognition of God's gift, as when faith in God that came from unexpected quarters surprised Jesus (Matt 8:5-13; Mark 7:24-30). All of these facets of Jesus's own mission have implications for ecclesial practice.

Jesus's words and actions associate the kingdom, as Gustavo Gutiérrez maintains, with hope for the victims of social injustice and inequality, the hope that "opens us, in an attitude of spiritual childhood, to the gift of the future promised by God."[30] Jon Sobrino also underscores the importance of the hope that flows from Jesus's proclamation of the kingdom: "The Kingdom of God is a utopia that answers the age-old hopes of a people in the midst of historical calamities; it is then, what is good and wholly good. But [the Kingdom] is also something liberating, since it arrives in the midst of and in opposition to the oppression of the anti-Kingdom."[31] Intrinsic to this hope is the presence of Jesus with those who are victims.

As the agent of the kingdom, Jesus invites people to recognize God as the God of unconditional love, which shows itself particularly in merciful forgiveness: "With a tenderness which never disappoints [Jesus] makes it possible for us to lift up our heads and to start anew" (EG 3).[32] Jesus, through words and actions that heal, reconcile, and establish possibility where none was taken to exist, highlights the link between the kingdom and the vanquishing of both a crippling fear of God and ways of living that exploit others.

Even though everything about Jesus declares God to be loving and merciful, trepidation has often characterized humanity's response to Jesus's invitation to perceive the reign of God as an expression of unconditional love:

30. Gustavo Gutiérrez, *A Theology of Liberation*, rev. ed., trans. C. Inda and J. Eagleson (Maryknoll, NY: Orbis, 1988), 139.

31. Jon Sobrino, *Jesus the Liberator: A Historical-Theological Reading of Jesus of Nazareth*, trans. P. Burns and F. McDonagh (Maryknoll, NY: Orbis, 1993), 72; see also O. Ernesto Valiente, "From Utopia to *Eu-topia*: Christian Hope in History," in *Hope: Promise, Possibility, and Fulfillment*, ed. Richard Lennan and Nancy Pineda-Madrid (Mahwah, NJ: Paulist, 2013), 198–210.

32. See also Walter Kasper, *Mercy: The Essence of the Gospel and the Key to Christian Life*, trans. W. Madges (Mahwah, NJ: Paulist, 2014), 61–82.

People expect that if they were to give themselves to God completely and to concern themselves only with God's cause, nothing
would be left but God . . . and that they would have to do without themselves and the whole of the marvelous world of God's
creation. That the cause of humanity is God's cause and that *this*
is what Jesus means when he talks about the kingdom of God,
transcends all our human expectations of God.[33]

Jesus's response to human sinfulness, the area of life where anxiety
before God can be most acute, typifies the way in which he embodies
the God who desires the freedom and thriving of all people. Jesus calls
people to repentance (Matt 7:21; Mark 1:15), but that repentance is
more than an acknowledgment of failings, and profoundly other than
a declaration of self-loathing in the face of one's sinfulness or of ter-
ror that God's mercy has been exhausted. The gospels are replete with
examples of Jesus mediating God's forgiveness to those who sought it,
including those whom "public opinion" judged to be beyond the reach
of God (John 8:1-11). As with the tax collector Zacchaeus (Luke 19:1-
10), Jesus responds to true repentance, which manifests a longing for
what God enables and promises, with encouragement and the invitation to a new beginning. The only harshness evident in the portraits
of Jesus in the gospels aims not at repentant sinners, but at those who
paraded their own righteousness and styled themselves as people whose
virtues entitled them to affirmation from God (Luke 11:37-52).

The intimacy with God to which Jesus invites people has its foundation in the intimacy with God that is central to Jesus's own life.
Jesus's proclamation of the reign of God and his actions on behalf of
that reign are not simply his obligations to fulfill, they reveal who he
is: "My food is to do the will of him who sent me and to complete his
work" (John 4:34). Who Jesus is accords fully with what Jesus does.
In his prayer, Jesus is transparent to God (Matt 14:23; Mark 1:35). It
is this relationship with God that enables Jesus to carry out his mission with "authority" (Mark 1:26; Luke 4:32), which establishes him
as good news for those who suffer.

33. Edward Schillebeeckx, *Interim Report on the Books* Jesus *and* Christ, trans. J.
Bowden (New York: Crossroad, 1982), 130; original emphasis.

In Gerhard Lohfink's assessment, Jesus represents a "revolution," not in a political sense, but in a way that "presupposed faith, joy in God, becoming his followers, discipleship, a radical understanding of Torah, a new community, new family."[34] Francis Schüssler Fiorenza, likewise, makes the case for the newness of Jesus, represented by his inclusivity, solidarity with those who suffer, reverence for creation, and the nurturing of a vision for a future that is beyond all that human beings are capable of dreaming.[35] Through those features, Jesus illustrates the creativity proper to the reign of God.

Significantly for the life of the church, Jesus does not understand his activity on behalf of the kingdom as a private enterprise or his individual undertaking. Rather, Jesus calls certain people into a more intimate relationship with him, a relationship in which they become his disciples (Matt 4:18-22; Luke 6:12-16). Through their relationship to Jesus, those disciples learn how to pray, they struggle to appropriate the broader vision of God and humanity that he represents, and they are sent out as apostles to carry his good news to others (Mark 6:7-13). All of this, the disciples do together.

The practice of Jesus in calling, mentoring, and commissioning disciples makes clear that discipleship for the sake of God's kingdom "requires a dedicated community, a form of life into which it can enter and be made visible."[36] The disciples themselves become a symbol of God's kingdom: "The circle of men and women who followed Jesus, their solidary community, their being-together with one another, was to show that now, in the midst of Israel, a bit of 'new society' had begun. . . . [Disciples] witness also by their believing life together."[37] This "new society" indicates that God's reign is already operative in human history, but it also looks beyond the present to a future that God alone can determine.

The Church and the Reign of God

As the preceding two chapters of the book have stressed, the church exists to symbolize all that "the reign of God" expresses. In this mission,

---

34. Lohfink, *Jesus of Nazareth*, 37.
35. Francis Schüssler Fiorenza, "Thy Kingdom Come," *Church* 10 (1994): 6–7.
36. Lohfink, *Jesus of Nazareth*, 90.
37. Ibid., 90.

the church is doing far more than trying to keep alive the memory of Jesus or invoking Jesus as a model. Through the Holy Spirit, the church is the sacrament in history of God's reign: the ongoing presence of God's transformative grace that comes as a gift to all of creation through the life, death, and resurrection of Jesus. "Sacrament" offers a way to situate the church in relationship to both the message of the kingdom and the world in which God's reign has already begun.

Like any sacrament, the church "is to manifest what it embodies."[38] Since such a manifestation involves a presence in history, the church is part of the world. What is crucial for the shape that the church's mission takes in the world, and for the potential of that mission to promote change in the church itself, is how the church understands itself in relation to God's reign and God's relationship to the world. As the history reviewed above demonstrates, not only has the church's understanding varied over time, but, as Pope Francis recognizes in *Christus Vivit*, developing a healthy relationship to the world, while also being faithful to the church's specificity, is an abiding challenge for the whole community of faith:

> Let us ask the Lord to free the Church from those who would make her grow old, encase her in the past, hold her back or keep her at a standstill. But let us also ask him to free her from another temptation: that of thinking she is young because she accepts everything the world offers her, thinking that she is renewed because she sets her message aside and acts like everybody else. No! The Church is young when she is herself, when she receives ever anew the strength born of God's word, the Eucharist, and the daily presence of Christ and the power of his Spirit in our lives. The Church is young when she shows herself capable of constantly returning to her source.[39]

For the church's engagement with the contemporary world to be genuinely sacramental of the Spirit's presence, it must embody the self-critical

---

38. Susan Wood, "Continuity and Development in Roman Catholic Ecclesiology," *Ecclesiology* 7 (2011): 160.

39. Pope Francis, *Christus Vivit*, Post-Synodal Apostolic Exhortation to Young People and to the Entire People of God (2019), 35, http://w2.vatican.va/content/francesco /en/apost_exhortations/documents/papa-francesco_esortazione-ap_20190325 _christus-vivit.html.

attitude that has been a recurring theme through this book. One dimension of that self-criticism is the willingness to acknowledge the difference between the church and the fullness of God's reign, even as the ecclesial community proclaims its faith in the connection between the two: "It is true that the Church is not an end unto herself, since she is ordered toward the kingdom of God of which she is the seed, sign and instrument. Yet, while remaining distinct from Christ and the kingdom, the Church is indissolubly united to both."[40]

The ecclesial community, then, can understand itself as the venue for "the grateful welcome to what is as it were the anonymous, concealed and modest coming of God into the world," while appreciating that the grace of God extends beyond the church.[41] This connection between the explicit dependence of the church on grace as the source of its own life and the "anonymous" presence of grace sustaining the whole of creation echoes Rahner's analysis of the relationship between the specificity of created grace and the more vast, but largely unnamed presence of uncreated grace.

Michael Himes offers a helpful way to affirm the church's link to both God's reign and to the world. His approach suggests depicting the church as *tertium quid*, a "third thing" that is neither fully the kingdom nor fully the world, but inseparable from both:

> The church is the community of those who accept that they are loved and engraced in faith and give thanks for the fact. It is the public expression of grateful receptivity; that is why its fundamental and constitutive act is always Eucharist. . . . It is the community with and in the world that acknowledges and celebrates what is true of the whole world, although the whole world does not know it. It is the sacrament of what the world really is and what it will be when the world is transformed by God into God's kingdom. It is the world publicly and openly being transformed, and as such, it is both still world and already kingdom.[42]

40. Pope John Paul II, *Redemptoris Missio*, On the Permanent Validity of the Church's Missionary Mandate (1990), 18, http://www.vatican.va/holy_father/john_paul_ii/encyclicals/documents/hf_jp-ii_enc_07121990_redemptoris-missio_en.html.

41. Schillebeeckx, *Church*, 14.

42. Michael Himes, "The Church and the World in Conversation: The City of God and 'Interurban' Dialogue," *New Theology Review* 18 (2005): 34.

In order for members of the church to be able to "'sniff [the kingdom] out,' raise people's awareness of it, and celebrate it where it makes itself present," they must continue to grow in their own awareness and experience of God's reign.[43] The grace already at work in the world can free the ecclesial community from the temptation to act "as arbiters of grace rather than as its facilitators" (EG 47). As an alternative to this danger, Pope Francis promotes a church that embraces "a missionary option" (EG 27), that looks beyond its internal concerns to representing the gospel in the world. The likelihood that the church can fulfill such a commitment is inseparable from the ongoing conversion of all members of the ecclesial community. Openness to conversion contributes to reshaping the church's mission in the world by freeing the members of the church from the illusion of controlling grace in the world.

In the world, the church can perform a "critical liberating task," a task that reminds all people of humanity's orientation to God's kingdom.[44] This task, which belongs to the community of faith as a whole, not simply to particular individuals or designated groups within the church, is one that promotes hope in the world. If all the church's members and all its institutions are to manifest the hope that witnesses to God's reign, while also keeping in view the distinction between the church and that reign, then, argues John Fuellenbach, no aspect of the church's life will act as if "cut off from real history and its traumas."[45] Similarly, Fuellenbach stresses that the basis for the church to engage with history is in order to "connect the historical liberation of the oppressed in this world with the eschatological kingdom still to come in fullness at the end."[46] In this way, the ecclesial community manifests both the "not yet . . . but already" that define humanity's experience of God's reign.

Although the church's engagement with the world confronts it with circumstances where "human dangers and errors" come into conflict with the gospel, such circumstances do not legitimate any reduction of

43. John Fuellenbach, "The Church in the Context of the Kingdom of God," in *The Convergence of Theology: A Festschrift Honoring Gerald O'Collins SJ*, ed. David Kendall and Stephen Davis (Mahwah, NJ: Paulist, 2001), 237.

44. Johann Baptist Metz, *Theology of the World*, trans. W. Glen-Doepel (New York: Seabury, 1969), 141–47; see also his *Faith in History and Society: Towards a Practical Fundamental Theology*, rev. trans. M. Ashley (New York: Crossroad, 2007), 115.

45. Fuellenbach, "Church in the Context of the Kingdom of God," 232.

46. Ibid., 231.

the church's willingness to build relationship beyond its own borders.[47] In a claim consistent with the emphasis on the church's sacramentality, the Orthodox theologian John Zizioulas argues, "What we used to call 'mission' is better rendered with notions and nuances of reception, because 'mission' is loaded with ideas of aggressiveness, whereas the Church should be *offering herself to the world for reception* instead of *imposing* herself on it."[48] Zizioulas's argument converges with the realization that the church is no less complex a mix of transparency to grace and resistance to grace than is the world. A church that the world might receive in ways that help the world to appreciate its own sacramentality is not likely to be one that either courts cheap popularity or proclaims its own virtue, but one seeking to "bear fruit in every good work" (Col 1:10). Self-critical tilling can contribute to nurturing possibilities for this outcome.

Pope Francis in *Fratelli Tutti* envisages social dynamics that would serve the well-being of everyone, rather than of a fortunate few who separate themselves from others. The pope has in mind society at large, but his vision is certainly germane to the church. As a means to shared flourishing, the encyclical promotes "the growth of a culture of encounter" in which "no one is useless and no one is expendable" (FT 215). In such a culture, as with a "polyhedron," "differences coexist, complementing, enriching and reciprocally illuminating one another, even amid disagreements and reservations" (FT 215). This image can guide the church in its relationship to the world.

Since the church does not possess its own "autonomous faith culture," but is part of the world, it must seek to express the gospel of Jesus Christ in ways that resonate with people in a plurality of cultures.[49] The processes of inculturation buttress the need for responsiveness to the

47. Pope Benedict XVI, "A Proper Hermencutic for the Second Vatican Council," in *Vatican II: Renewal within Tradition*, ed. Matthew Lamb and Matthew Levering (New York: Oxford University Press, 2008), xiv.

48. John Zizioulas, "The Theological Problem of 'Reception,'" *One in Christ* 21 (1985): 189; original emphasis.

49. Richard Gaillardetz, *Ecclesiology for a Global Church: A People Called and Sent* (Maryknoll, NY: Orbis, 2008), 68. See also Anthony Gittins, *Living Mission Interculturally: Faith, Culture, and the Renewal of Praxis* (Collegeville, MN: Michael Glazier, 2015).

presence of the Spirit beyond the church itself. As Pope John Paul II acknowledges, the endeavor to inculturate the gospel is integral to the life of the church: "Through inculturation the Church makes the Gospel incarnate in different cultures and at the same time introduces peoples, together with their cultures, into her own community. . . . Through inculturation the Church, for her part, becomes a more intelligible sign of what she is, and a more effective instrument of mission."[50] Authentic inculturation—a theme to which chapter 6 will return—is, then, a core element of a culture of encounter.

"Encounter" captures a dimension of the church's presence in the world that has not always been prominent in analyses of mission: the relationship with the world can be a means of grace for the life of the church. In its involvement with diverse cultures and nations, the church can be a beneficiary, not only a benefactor.[51] The church not only shares its good news, it hears that good news more fully in proclaiming it. No less importantly, the ecclesial community can learn from the ways in which individuals and cultures have already responded to grace, responses that can lead members of the church to reflect on their own responses to grace.

The church in the world, as Vatican II acknowledged in *Gaudium et Spes*, receives from sources beyond itself: "It profits from the experience of past ages, from the progress of the sciences, and from the riches hidden in various cultures, through which greater light is thrown on the nature of humankind and new avenues to truth are opened up" (GS 44). As Fuellenbach phrases it, a church that "feasts" on the presence of grace in the Eucharist can learn to do likewise on the grace at work in the world.[52]

As it remains alert to the presence of grace in the world, the church must continue to reflect on how and whether its own life witnesses to all that it proclaims. For this self-critical attitude to be and remain characteristic of the ecclesial community, engagement with what Pope Francis names "the peripheries" (EG 20) is urgent. Among those who dwell beyond the neat and ordered structures of societies and the

---

50. Pope John Paul II, *Redemptoris Missio*, 52.
51. Himes, "Church and the World in Conversation," 32.
52. Fuellenbach, "Church in the Context of the Kingdom of God," 236–37.

church, the poor and marginalized have "a privileged epistemological perspective from which to evaluate 'reality.'"[53] Encounters with those on the periphery of the world's interest can enable members of the church to rediscover, and appropriate continually, the truth that is central to Christian faith: that God's presence and action transcends the church, even as grace gives life to the church.

The same grace that calls for a church willing to encounter God beyond itself also provides the impetus for the church to reflect on its "inner" life, on the encounters with the Spirit that differences within the community of faith can facilitate. Here, the goal is to ensure that the mechanisms of the church's communal existence support rather than stifle the "missionary dynamism" (EG 81) that the Spirit furthers.

Grace and the Church as an Open System

The church is to act in the world as an authentic witness to the abundant life that Christ promises (John 10:10). The extent to which the church fulfills this brief depends on the continuous conversion of the ecclesial community. As Pope Francis acknowledges, one element of the commitment to pursue authenticity in the church must be a willingness to interrogate the church's current practices. Doing so involves, for example, asking whether parishes have become "a useless structure out of touch with people or a self-absorbed cluster made up of a chosen few" (EG 28).

Likewise, Pope Francis links witness to the joy of the Gospel with inquiring whether particular customs in the church "no longer serve as means of communicating the Gospel," even if the customs are themselves "beautiful" (EG 43). In the context of the church's structures, Pope Francis warns that "excessive centralization" in the church "complicates the Church's life and her missionary outreach" (EG 32). The pope amplifies his observation with the specific contention that bishops must ensure that "those who would tell him what he would like to hear" (EG 31) do not monopolize episcopal attention.

53. Roberto Goizueta, "To the Poor, the Sick, and the Suffering," in *Vatican II: A Universal Call to Holiness*, ed. Anthony Ciorra and Michael Higgins (Mahwah, NJ: Paulist, 2012), 65–66.

Just as Pope Francis argues against assuming that all aspects of the church's communal life function effectively for everyone, so Johann Baptist Metz claims that for the church to be a site of "critical freedom" in society, the same freedom must characterize the community of the church.[54] Similarly, Gustavo Gutiérrez asserts that the church's structures represent a crucial test for the authenticity of the church's sacramentality: "The church should signify in its own internal structure the salvation whose fulfillment it announces. Its organization ought to serve this task. As a sign of the liberation of humankind and history, the Church itself ought to be a place of liberation."[55] The fact that this liberation is not permanently evident in the church gives unambiguous witness to the church's unfinished reality. It also confirms the need for ecclesial community to undertake the ongoing discernment of how best to respond to grace in the specific circumstances of the church's present.

To encapsulate this unfinished state of the church, Rahner, employing a term from sociology, classifies the church as "an open system."[56] As such, the church is not simply incomplete at any moment in its history, but can and must continue to change in response to the Spirit. None of these features would apply if the church were a "closed" or totalitarian system. Yet, even as an open system, the church is particular: it has a profession of faith that makes a claim on those who are members of the church and it also has structures that the tradition of faith associates with grace. Being unfinished, then, does not equate to being totally fungible.

Rahner summarizes the uniqueness of the church's communion by depicting membership of the church as being, paradoxically and simultaneously, humbling and liberating. It is humbling because all members must come to terms with the fact that they are not the sole source of the church's beliefs and priorities, but liberating because membership of the community of faith bestows on all believers access

54. Metz, *Faith in History and Society*, 94.

55. Gutiérrez, *Theology of Liberation*, 147.

56. Karl Rahner, "Observations on the Factor of the Charismatic in the Church," in *Theological Investigations*, vol. 12, trans. D. Bourke (New York: Seabury, 1974), 88–90. For the notion of "open systems" in social structures, see W. Richard Scott and Gerald F. Davis, *Organizations and Organizing: Rational, Natural, and Open Systems Perspectives* (Upper Saddle River, NJ: Prentice Hall, 2007).

to a body of faith and experience that no individual could accrue in a single lifetime.[57] These interwoven dimensions of ecclesial life will feature further in the following two chapters.

As an open system, the church will need to practice discernment and make decisions about how to carry out its mission in ways that embody the depths of its own identity and respond to the needs of specific contexts. As the ecclesial community seeks to live by the openness that grace facilitates, the primary criterion shaping the church's life cannot be simply what is most popular or cost-effective, nor can it be a retreat into "we have always done it this way" (EG 33). Rather, the standard must be a commitment to respond to the promptings of the Spirit, who continues to form the church as a sacrament and pilgrim whose mission extends into the world beyond the church. Faithfulness, in other words, is inseparable from renunciation of all that could be an obstacle to the Spirit—"We must repudiate all exclusionary symbols, values, criteria, and practices."[58] The renunciation necessary for faithfulness has its complement in the commitment to follow where the Spirit might be leading—"We must support creative initiatives in the development of new symbols and practices, in the articulation of new values and criteria for a life of human flourishing."[59]

In drawing out the implications of "the people of God," Kasper associates the presence of the Spirit with both the capacity of the church for change and the existence of the church as an ordered, stable body. In relation to the latter, Kasper connects the Spirit to "decency and order" rather than "charismatic and enthusiastic disorder," while for the former he echoes Rahner by describing the Spirit-led church as "an open system that cannot be directed or even manipulated from one point or by one instance."[60] A Spirit-led church, then, if it is to be faithful to its foundations, must take its inspiration only from what

---

57. Karl Rahner, "Dogmatic Notes on 'Ecclesiological Piety,'" in *Theological Investigations*, vol. 5, trans. K-H. Kruger (New York: Crossroad, 1983), 347.

58. M. Shawn Copeland, "Knit Together by the Spirit as Church," in *Prophetic Witness: Catholic Women's Strategies for Reform*, ed. Colleen Griffith (New York: Herder and Herder, 2008), 22.

59. Ibid.

60. Walter Kasper, *The Catholic Church: Nature, Reality and Mission*, trans. T. Hoebel (London: Bloomsbury, 2015), 139–41.

is in accord with all that grace empowers—a criterion that, of course, requires the discernment of the community.

Openness to grace is crucial as the church in its various locations contemplates new circumstances and questions, all of which bring with them the possibility of change in the ecclesial community's self-understanding and practice. This possibility is one for which the church's relationship to the Spirit is especially relevant: "If the church were just a creation of Jesus [it] would not change, nor could it. . . . If the church proceeds from the Holy Spirit, however, its condition is different. It springs up in an infinite variety of human situations, as a community made up of communities of faith, hope and mutual love."[61] One element of the Spirit's constitutive presence in the church is that the Spirit does not impose the "one-size-fits-all" approach mentioned above, but guides the church as it discerns what constitutes authentic discipleship in unique cultural and historical contexts.

The Catholicity and Communion of the Church

"Catholicity" is the theological category that best captures the capacity of grace to be at home in a diversity of experiences in the one church. Although a theme integral to the Christian community's creedal confession of the Spirit's presence in the church, catholicity is more complex than typical interpretations suggest. Usually, "catholicity" appears as synonymous with the "universality" of the church, indicating either dispersal over the globe or as reaching the sum total of humanity—"The Church is catholic because she has been sent out by Christ on a mission to the whole of the human race."[62] Since geography and numbers are not categories that apply specifically to the Spirit, defining catholicity by those classifications does not account adequately for its graced quality.[63] Nor is the church's catholicity reducible to the worldwide application of a product that emanates from the "export firm" that this volume has referenced a number of times.

---

61. José Comblin, *The Holy Spirit and Liberation*, trans. P. Burns (Maryknoll, NY: Orbis, 1989), 89

62. *Catechism of the Catholic Church*, 831.

63. For an overview of contemporary approaches to "catholicity," see Richard Lennan, "Catholicity: Its Challenge for the Church," *New Theology Review* 24 (2011): 36–48.

Yves Congar offers a distinctly theological analysis of catholicity by depicting the church's catholic dimension as wholeness, as an effect of the Holy Spirit that ensures that the one church is, simultaneously, one and diverse. Far from being reducible to uniformity, argues Congar, catholicity requires Spirit-generated variety that is fully reconcilable with Spirit-generated unity: "The church is catholic because it is particular, and it has the fullness of gifts because each person has their own gifts."[64] It is precisely the "particular" aspect of the church that comes into relief through considering the various contextual ecclesiologies that have emerged in recent decades. These ecclesiologies underscore that "when plurality is approached from the perspective of catholicity, it is accepted as richness" rather than as a threat to unity.[65]

The Spirit's capacity to hold together unity and diversity applies not only to the multiple expressions of the Roman Catholic Church that emerge from a variety of social and cultural situations. It applies, too, to the relationship between different ecclesial traditions, and, in yet another way, to the whole panoply of humanity's religious forms. As the Christian churches seek to overcome their historical divisions in order to achieve the unity that alone does justice to the followers of Christ (John 17:20-21). they seek also to manifest a truly catholic church—that is, a church whose unity does not require the dissolution of particular identities.

Achieving catholic unity within the church necessitates more than the willingness to negotiate and compromise. Since ecclesial unity is properly "the dominion of the divine Spirit," Gesa Elsbeth Thiessen contends that its realization depends on cooperation with the Spirit, who enables "a certain openness, freedom and respect for otherness which in itself constitutes a healthy antidote to any attempts to constrict dialogue and to explore untrodden paths in ecumenism, in interfaith dialogue and in the theology of religions."[66] Here too, then, the image of the church as a pilgrim toward a fulfilment that God

---

64. Congar, *I Believe in the Holy Spirit*, 26.

65. Gemma Tulud Cruz, "A New Way of Being Christian: The Contribution of Migrants to the Church," in *Contemporary Issues of Migration and Theology*, ed. Elaine Padilla and Peter Phan (New York: Palgrave Macmillan, 2013), 114.

66. Gesa Elsbeth Thiessen, "Seeking Unity: Reflecting on Methods in Contemporary Ecumenical Dialogue," in *Ecumenical Ecclesiology: Unity, Diversity and Otherness in a Fragmented World*, ed. Gesa Elsbeth Thiessen (London: T. and T. Clark, 2009), 41.

alone can accomplish is an apt one, as is the notion of the church as an "open system."

In order to be a catholic body that reflects the Spirit's role as the agent of God's unity no less than of the multiplicity that is also reflective of God (1 Cor 12), the diversity of voices in the church must become more symphony than cacophony. The realization of this goal requires all members of the church to be attentive to how the Spirit might be moving in their own context. Just as importantly, the possibility of an authentically catholic church necessitates the willingness to engage in dialogue with those who are similarly listening to the Spirit, but doing so in their own unique setting.

These voices include those from the past as well as the present, and the voices of those who are officeholders in the church as well as those who do not exercise formal authority but in whom grace is no less at work. Such dialogue, as chapter 6 will reinforce, is itself a work of the Spirit. As Clare Watkins acknowledges, it is the Spirit who promotes "a theological articulation that has more in common with the pedagogy of conversation than with the monologues of the academy, or of the magisterium, or of practice itself."[67]

Within her analysis of the church's multiple voices, Watkins recognizes the divergence that is often present between the beliefs and principles that members of the church might profess—the "espoused" voice—and the motivations revealed through people's actions, rather than their words—the "operant" voice.[68] In other words, the proclamations of individuals and groups can lay claim to expressing the Spirit, while their actions may show an absence of receptivity to grace. For that reason, Paul Murray suggests that ecclesiology necessarily involves "the testing for and searching out of that which, in theological terms, signifies grace and that which is culturally, organizationally, and practically discordant."[69] By so doing, ecclesiology demonstrates that all aspects of the church stand in need of tilling, of ongoing conversion.

67. Clare Watkins et al., "Practical Ecclesiology: What Counts as Theology in Studying the Church?," in *Perspectives on Ecclesiology and Ethnography*, ed. Pete Ward (Grand Rapids, MI: Eerdmans, 2012), 180.

68. Ibid., 178.

69. Paul Murray, "Searching the Living Truth of the Church in Practice: On the Transformative Task of Systematic Ecclesiology," *Modern Theology* 30 (2014): 270.

A commitment to conversion can sensitize members of the church, both as individuals and groups, to the danger of reducing their community to what Stanley Grenz characterizes as the "social contract" view of the church. In this framing, the church is a gated community or a "lifestyle enclave," whose members come together on the basis of shared interests.[70] Within such an enclave, there can be exchanges among those who are similar in attitudes and background, but without the members being at risk of the disturbances that arise from "difference." Parishes in the Catholic Church can fall into this trap if they become "enclaves of the like-minded" to which people of similar worldviews migrate because they "feel less challenged by teachings or people that make them uncomfortable."[71] Members of these communities remain fixed in their views and untroubled by anything that originates from beyond their borders. The church's Spirit-formed catholicity and openness, consequently, dissipate or even disappear.

For the church to be authentically catholic, its communal life must witness to all that grace enables. This is possible only if the church itself does not suppress or attempt to disguise, even hide, its own complexities. Diverse communities, then, are neither something to endure or to bypass, but can be a means of grace, part of the way in which the church manifests the reign of God. For members of the church, this relationship to God's reign can never be independent of their shared faith, with all of its challenges: "Believers realize that they *really* believe (i.e. that they burst through their knowledge and pass into the uncomprehended Comprehending Being) by believing with the faith of the Church and by surrendering themselves to the faith of all the witnesses beginning with Abel the Just right up to the last believer at the end of time."[72]

The communal reality of the church was a key focus of Vatican II.[73] The council paid due attention to the church's structures and the par-

70. Stanley Grenz, "Ecclesiology," in *The Cambridge Companion to Postmodern Theology*, ed. Kevin Vanhoozer (Cambridge: Cambridge University Press, 2003), 257.

71. Michael Peppard, "Can the Church Transcend a Polarized Culture?," in *Polarization in the US Catholic Church: Naming the Wounds, Beginning to Heal*, ed. Mary Ellen Konieczny, Charles Camosy, and Tricia Bruce (Collegeville, MN: Liturgical Press, 2016), 149.

72. Rahner, "Dogmatic Notes on 'Ecclesiological Piety,'" 347; original emphasis.

73. See Rush, *Vision of Vatican II*, 200–229.

ticular responsibilities of its ordained leadership, but situated these within its presentation of the church as a communion. The ecclesiology of communion, another aspect of the pre-conciliar *ressourcement*, has been prominent in Catholic circles in recent decades, building on Vatican II's recovery of the trinitarian grounding of the church's life and the council's emphasis on the church as the "People of God."[74] Pope John Paul II, in *Novo Millennio Ineunte* (2001), not only describes the church as "the home and school of communion," but asserts that the church's structures could become "mechanisms without a soul" unless they operated within "a spirituality of communion."[75]

Communion ecclesiology contends that as the Trinity is a unity of difference with a common mission, so the members of the church, made one in their shared baptism into the trinitarian life of God, have particular roles and responsibilities that serve their one mission. Gerhard Lohfink makes the case that the communal identity of the church reinforces in a specific way that the church is a symbol of the risen Jesus. Lohfink's argument is that those who follow Christ, those heading to the fullness of life in Christ, cannot be isolated and self-enclosed individuals, since "the Risen One is not alone; he is surrounded by the saints, those who have reached the completion of their lives. And I as a believer am not alone. I could not believe at all without the others."[76] In addition, and even more remarkably, Lohfink claims that the church's communal life is the necessary means for enabling appreciation of God's trinitarian existence: "Where Christians share

74. For the historical background and content of the ecclesiology of communion, see Denis Doyle, *Communion Ecclesiology* (Maryknoll, NY: Orbis, 2000), and Jean-Marie Tillard, *Flesh of the Church, Flesh of Christ: At the Sources of the Ecclesiology of Communion*, trans. M. Beaumont (Collegeville, MN: Pueblo, 2001); see also Susan Wood, "The Church as Communion," in *The Gift of the Church: A Textbook on Ecclesiology*, ed. Peter Phan (Collegeville, MN: Michael Glazier, 2000), 159–76, and Richard Lennan, "Communion Ecclesiology: Foundations, Critiques, and Affirmations," *Pacifica* 20 (2007): 24–39.

75. Pope John Paul II, *Novo Millennio Ineunte*, 43, http://www.vatican.va/content/john-paul-ii/en/apost_letters/2001/documents/hf_jp-ii_apl_20010106_novo-millennio-ineunte.html.

76. Gerhard Lohfink, *No Irrelevant Jesus: On Jesus and the Church Today*, trans. L. Maloney (Collegeville, MN: Liturgical Press, 2014), 200.

their lives with one another they can at least surmise that there is also a shared life in God, a mutually self-giving life. When these experiences are no longer present there is a danger that confession of the Trinity will become purely formulaic."[77]

Louis-Marie Chauvet is another theologian who describes the church's communal existence in striking terms. Chauvet asserts that the "true scandal" of the church is that "the path to our relation with God passes through our relation with human beings and most especially through our relation with those whom the judgment of the mighty has reduced to 'less than nothing.'"[78] Chauvet locates both the primary connection of the Christian community to Christ and the primary expression of the church's life as a community in the liturgical assembly gathered for the celebration of the Eucharist:

> As the first sacramental representation of the Risen One, this *ecclesia*-assembly shows that the truth of the bond with him not only requires that we not ignore *the presence of others*, but on the contrary demands that we make our *way* through them. . . . The Sunday *ecclesia* denounces as *illusory* this *individualism* by which we would believe ourselves to be more Christian the more we achieve immediate contact with God in the silent conversation of meditation.[79]

The communal existence of the church provides the essential framework for considering the role of the church's structures. Rahner presents the church's institutional dimension as itself functioning in a way that is analogous to a sacrament: "Christianity is the religion of a demanding God who summons my subjectivity out of itself only if it confronts me in a church which is authoritative . . . a church which confronts me in a mission, a mandate and a proclamation which really make the reality of salvation present for me."[80] Understood in this

---

77. Lohfink, *Prayer Takes Us Home*, 19.

78. Louis-Marie Chauvet, *Symbol and Sacrament: A Sacramental Reinterpretation of Christian Existence*, trans. P. Madigan and M. Beaumont (Collegeville, MN: Pueblo, 1995), 187.

79. Ibid., 188; original emphasis.

80. Karl Rahner, *Foundations of Christian Faith: An Introduction to the Idea of Christianity*, trans. W. Dych (New York: Seabury, 1978), 344.

way, institutions contribute positively to the life and mission of the Christian community: "Institutional authorities give the community members the tools to work with, to coach them in their practices, and to discern what constitutes good practice in the school of discipleship that is the local community. . . . Institutional authorities, especially bishops and theologians, serve the bearers of the tradition, the participants in the community."[81] Of course, not all the news about the church's institutions is good, especially when the structures foster the perception of the church as "a clerical, religiously camouflaged kind of totalitarian system."[82]

Chauvet acknowledges that the structures of the church, which are an integral element of the church's sacramental identity, represent a distinct challenge for the appropriation of sacramentality:

> The recognition of the institutional Church as the "fundamental sacrament" of the reign always requires a conversion—either because believers, too comfortably ensconced in the institution, forget that it is *only* a sacrament and overlook the distance between it and Christ or because their critical suspicions towards the institution result in their not seeing that it *is* indeed a sacrament.[83]

Even though the church's institutional forms are regularly judged to be primarily responsible for obscuring the life of the Spirit in the church, the sacramentality of the whole communion of faith underscores that every member of the church, not simply officeholders, can obstruct what God's Spirit enables, just as they can also witness to what grace makes possible. An emphasis on the universal need in the church for conversion recognizes that as no single group has a monopoly on being "the church," so no single group bears exclusively the church's need for conversion.

The danger that aspects of the ecclesial community, including its structures, can degenerate into the opposite of what the Spirit enables,

---

81. Terrence Tilley, "Communication in Handing on the Faith," in *Handing on the Faith: The Church's Mission and Challenge*, ed. Robert Imbelli (New York: Herder and Herder, 2006), 163.

82. Karl Rahner, "Freedom in the Church," in *Theological Investigations*, vol. 2, trans. K-H. Kruger (New York: Crossroad, 1983), 99.

83. Chauvet, *Symbol and Sacrament*, 186; original emphasis.

Chauvet associates with three particular temptations. Those temptations, which he labels collectively as "necrotic," as death-dealing, induce the community of faith "to capture Christ in our ideological nets or in the ruses of our desire."[84] The three temptations—to use religious knowledge to assert control over "the unmanageability of the Spirit"; to use ritual as "magic" that guarantees God's action, while bypassing the encounter with God that is the primary aspect of the liturgy; and to use good works "to obtain leverage" over God—represent the shadow side of the word, sacrament, and ethics that, as chapter 2 illustrated, Chauvet identifies as giving shape to the church's presence in the world.[85]

What is common to the temptations that Chauvet details, what constitutes them as likely to imperil the church's sacramental identity and its mission, is that they subvert the proper relationship between the community of faith and grace. By promising that the community of the church will no longer need to receive grace as a gift, but can regulate grace, the temptations can obscure the church's dependence on the life-giving Spirit of Jesus Christ. Accordingly, a church deformed by such temptations ceases to point toward the fullness of life in the kingdom as that which exceeds anything that humanity can imagine or design. The lure of the necrotic temptations testifies to the importance of *Lumen Gentium*'s acknowledgment that the church can be what God enables it to be only if it "follows constantly the path of penance and renewal" (LG 8).

Chauvet's analysis demonstrates that the efficacy of grace in the individual members of the church, in their common life, and in the structures that support their life and mission is not guaranteed, the church's constitution in grace notwithstanding.[86] Since grace does not function mechanistically, the members of the church never outgrow the need for tilling, for remaining open to conversion, which is itself both a stimulus that comes from the Spirit and an irreducible dimension of

84. Ibid., 173.
85. Ibid., 174.
86. For discussion of the efficacy of grace in the church and the implications of the church's failings for its designation as "holy," see Karl Rahner, "The Sinful Church in the Decrees of Vatican II," in *Theological Investigations*, vol. 6, trans. K-H. Kruger and B. Kruger (New York: Crossroad, 1982), and Francis Sullivan, *The Church We Believe In: One, Holy, Catholic and Apostolic* (Dublin: Gill and Macmillan, 1988), 76–83.

faithfulness to the Spirit. This conversion involves turning away from whatever is opposed to the Spirit, while also embracing what the Spirit enables. Clearly, the effectiveness of both actions is inseparable from discernment of the Spirit. Chapter 5 will take up questions about the status and function of tradition as part of this discernment, homing in on the role of tradition in the manifestation of the church as a sacrament of the reign of God.

As sacrament, Chauvet contends, the church "radicalizes the vacancy of the place of God. To accept its mediation is to agree that this vacancy will never be filled."[87] This principle can attune the church to the importance of being self-critical, of being attentive to the ways in which the community of faith obscures, rather than symbolizes, the Spirit of Christ. The ecclesial sacraments, especially the Eucharist, model what the Spirit enables for the church and work as catalysts for the conversion of all expressions of the church's communal life. Thus, Gutiérrez stresses that "without a real commitment against exploitation and alienation and for a society of solidarity and justice, the Eucharistic celebration is an empty action."[88]

Here again, being self-critical is "a primary condition enabling the Church to exercise a critical function with regard to society."[89] The word and sacrament through which the Spirit shapes the church's mission in the world, therefore, are also the means by which the Spirit promotes the ongoing conversion of the church. It is the Spirit who leads the members of the church to recognize the ways in which their lives as church can "constitute a counter-testimony to Christianity . . . and that our sin has impeded the Spirit's working in the hearts of many people."[90] The self-critical stance embodies a refusal to assert control over the Spirit and a willingness to remain open to the Spirit's prompting. More specifically, a self-critical atmosphere in the church reflects an appreciation of the difference between the church and God.

87. Chauvet, *Symbol and Sacrament*, 178.

88. Gutiérrez, *Theology of Liberation*, 150.

89. Karl Rahner, "The Function of the Church as a Critic of Society," in *Theological Investigations*, vol. 12, trans. D. Bourke (New York: Seabury, 1974), 237.

90. Pope John Paul II, *Incarnationis Mysterium*, Bull of Indiction of the Great Jubilee of the Year 2000, 11, in *Origins* 28 (1998): 450.

This acceptance includes an appreciation of the church's existence as sacrament, rather than as the fullness of God's reign.

Rahner stresses that self-criticism is inseparable from recognition that the church's self-understanding, as a result of its foundation in Christ and the Spirit, "is always wider, freer, and more exalted than that which is *de facto* realized in the form which she assumes in history, and is in fact wider in scope than that which we have formulated to ourselves about her at the level of speculation and theory."[91] In addition, a self-critical attitude, which all members of the church can embrace, frees members of the church from the presumption that they will always do precisely what effective mission requires at every moment of history.

Without a self-critical attitude, so Rahner contends, the church, like any institution, would be in danger of becoming an end in itself and an increasingly conservative body that would "lose living contact with other social realities."[92] There is, then, a permanent need for the members of the church to inquire into whether their response to the world in which they live is a trustworthy reflection of where the Spirit might be moving: "If the Church can never end up outside the truth of Christ, does that also mean that the Church proclaims this truth with that strength, with that topicality and always newly appropriated form which would make it salutary and which one might long for?"[93]

The tilling that can help to form a more faithful church often meets resistance that invokes "tradition" as a defense against any forces of change. Chapter 5 will address this resistance by considering whether faithfulness to tradition is compatible with all that "tilling" suggests. This inquiry is certainly pertinent to the relationship between the church's past and present, but also to grasping more fully what it means for the church to be a body whose orientation is to God's ever-new future.

91. Rahner, "Function of the Church as a Critic of Society," 233.
92. Ibid., 231.
93. Rahner, "Dogmatic Notes on 'Ecclesiological Piety,'" 339.

5

The Future-Oriented Past

The digital age is heir to the passion for innovation that sparked the Industrial Revolution. Today, this passion animates countless "start-ups," the "big tech" firms of Silicon Valley, and the world of "e-sports," just as it underpinned the growth of factories and manufacturing in the machine age. To feed the insatiable appetite of consumers for "the next big thing," entrepreneurs and engineers of hardware and software must avoid the complacency that regards past achievements as the pinnacle of possibility. Unless companies continue to imagine, design, and develop products that are faster, more versatile, and more user-friendly than anything presently available, they face the fate of the fax machine and cassette player. Without a stream of updates, today's "leading edge" becomes tomorrow's "superseded," a designation fatal to market share.

Even though all innovations depend in part on existing systems, commercial pressure mandates that "forward" is the only direction that is significant for today's technology. In society at large, on the other hand, there is a growing demand that the makers of "smart" products address concerns about the impact of such devices on personal privacy, the "digital divide" between rich and poor communities, and even national security. The tension between the two perspectives makes evident that innovation has cultural implications. Since technological development is a human reality, it does not simply affect the present and the future, but has consequences for inherited values and ways of acting. In generating resistance to change, the desire to protect the past can be as potent a motivator as is anxiety about the future.

The "culture wars" of recent decades, especially in the United States, further complicate the narrative of change. Characteristic of this phenomenon is the conflict between competing versions of what constitutes desirable social goals.[1] In today's polarized atmosphere, every proposed change can become a battleground. When, for example, protagonists present policies that they believe extend human rights, protect the environment, or increase safeguards for vulnerable sections of the population, their ideas face summary dismissal from those who perceive the same proposals as assaults on cherished institutions, economically foolhardy, or subterfuges masking a plot to remake society on the basis of a presently fashionable ideology.

These divergent interpretations ensure that disagreements broaden into chasms, preventing balanced assessments of any proposed change. This is especially so when "culture warriors" are allergic to conversation with each other and unsympathetic to efforts at reconciliation between their differing hopes and fears. A corollary of this division, and symptomatic of the lack of nuance often evident on both sides of a dispute, is that measured evaluations of the past become impossible. The past becomes either the best of times or the worst of times, judgments equally lacking in light and shade.

In many forms of human activity, then, receptivity to innovation can be delicately in balance with the potential for its rejection. Even in circumstances free of the ideological baggage of the culture wars, an elevated esteem for the past, a general inertia, or the cozy familiarity of the status quo tends to douse fervor for "change." When the church is the setting for possible innovation, the reluctance to embrace what is new regularly intensifies. In part at least, this reluctance reflects the manifestation in the church of the polarization emblematic of contemporary society—a reminder that the church is inseparable from the graced and complex world—but it also has sources in all that gives the church its specificity.

---

1. For an analysis of the origins and issues characteristic of the "culture wars" in the United States, see Jill Lepore, *These Truths: A History of the United States* (New York: Norton, 2018), 646–718.

The perception of change as the substitution of human preferences for what is God-given might well be the root cause of resistance to change in the church. Change, then, whether it takes shape as reform or innovation, becomes the rejection of God's revelation mediated through history, and even a potential rebellion against God. This assessment leads ultimately to the conviction that the church is not free to change.

With this perception in mind, the earlier chapters of this book have presented the tilling of the church as a Spirit-initiated imperative. They have stressed the connection between the Holy Spirit and an openness to movement that is proper to the unfinished project that is the church, and conducive to the well-being of the ecclesial community. As part of their focus on grace, the preceding chapters have argued that the Spirit sustains the ecclesial community as it redresses past failures, faces the challenges that confront its mission in the present, and presses on with the pilgrimage into the ever-new future of God. The multidimensional presence of the Spirit suggests that obdurate resistance to all possible changes could itself equate to resistance to grace, and so to the conversion that grace prompts.

A clear understanding of the movement of grace through the church's past, present, and future can reduce the fear that any change in the church comes at the cost of the wholesale rejection of the past. Even so, what is perhaps ineradicable is anxiety in the ecclesial community about specific changes, about "this" change. Such anxiety drives the desire for a clear-cut and reliable technique for distinguishing between what Yves Congar named "true and false reform in the church."[2] Addressing this anxiety and desire is a task for chapter 6. That chapter, the final one in the book, will engage directly with the specificities of change in the context of the ecclesial community's tradition of faith and its place in a restless world. More specifically, chapter 6 will explore the reception of tradition and the dialogue, discernment, and decision-making that play a critical role in the ecclesial community's endeavor to be faithful to God's self-communication that encompasses the church's past, present, and future.

The present chapter provides a key building block for chapter 6. The particular goal of this chapter is to make the case that the church's

---

2. Yves Congar, *True and False Reform in the Church*, trans. P. Philibert (1950; revised in 1968; repr. Collegeville, MN: Michael Glazier, 2011).

tradition is a driver of change. To build its paradoxical argument that a comprehensive understanding of tradition affirms its potential to support movement in the church, the chapter first profiles "the past" as both a human phenomenon and a site of God's self-communication. An appreciation of the two aspects is critical for establishing why a comprehensive appreciation of the past must take account of its links to the present and future, links that underscore that the past, like the present and the future, is not a hermetically sealed unit.

Following the exploration of "the past," the next two sections of the chapter will offer a theology of "apostolicity" and "tradition," respectively. The analysis of these key themes, which will include a review of nineteenth- and early twentieth-century theologies that were seminal for the Second Vatican Council's understanding of "tradition," will establish that preservation and innovation are complementary. The relationship between preservation and innovation in the life of the church is multilayered and complex, but also graced. The grace that unites the past, present, and future guides the ecclesial community as it seeks to embody in an ever-changing world the faithfulness that testifies to its foundation in Christ and the Holy Spirit and continues its heritage of discipleship.

The emphasis on grace, which always interweaves with the mystery of human freedom, attests to the church's status as an ongoing project, and as a work that can never be independent of the Spirit. This emphasis also reinforces that "tilling," a theme with intimate links to notions of change, expresses the faithfulness of the ecclesial community to the Spirit, rather than an unjustifiable disturbance of the church's prevailing order.

The Past as Present and Future

The belief that the past could be a fertile source of guidance for the present and future was once a truism. Trust in the past, however, has not fared well in the last few centuries. Since the Enlightenment's characteristic commitment to human autonomy and reason-driven "progress" began to dominate social discourse, interest in the past as a source of enrichment for the present has waned considerably. The popular perception of science, especially the sense that current trends in technology will shepherd humanity inexorably toward new frontiers, has been detrimental to esteem for any direction and inspiration that the past might offer.

When endorsed without reserve, the vision of a grand future can induce the myopia that is an obstacle to the perception of reality in all its dimensions. The climate crisis illustrates what can occur when the myth of endless progress, free of any possible deficits, takes hold in society. This danger increases exponentially when the all-consuming stress on progress marries the profit motive of modern capitalism: "The economy accepts every advance in technology with a view to profit, without concern for its potentially negative impact on human beings."[3] A renewed appreciation of history offers a remedy for this shortsightedness, and for its ill-effects.

Although reference to "history" naturally conveys an allusion to the past, a broader sense of the term, one that has been important for this volume, encompasses the awareness that human beings live within the flow of time. "History," then, can refer simultaneously to the past, present, and future. This usage connects different epochs without abolishing what is particular to each one and without implying that any one era is superior to the others, especially since each is unique in its conditions. The human beings who populate any one epoch will have much in common with those of other periods, but each group must live in its inimitable present. While each "present" is unique, it is not self-contained: it receives an inheritance from previous ages and leads to the unknowable future.

The interweaving of past, present, and future defines each period of history. No society, whether it is a family, a nation, or a church, can thrive if it isolates itself from the circumstances, needs, and questions specific to its own time and place, but attention to the present need not imply rejection of the past or a lack of interest in the future. Learning from the past, learning that can come via problematizing the unquestioned assumptions of the past and analyzing its dysfunctions, can be a gift to the present and future of all communities. This gift might

3. Pope Francis, *Laudato Si'*, On Care for our Common Home (2015), 109, http://www.vatican.va/content/francesco/en/encyclicals/documents/papa-francesco_20150524_enciclica-laudato-si.html.

include the appropriation of insights from the past that challenge the prevailing wisdom of the present.

Conversely, the wholesale rejection of the past can endanger, even shatter, a society. The turmoil resulting from China's "Cultural Revolution" and the human catastrophe that followed the attempt by Pol Pot's Khmer Rouge to restart Cambodia from "year zero," two comparatively recent—albeit extreme—examples, illustrate this principle. Both instances confirm that a vital future depends on a constructive relationship between the past and present, rather than favoring one period over the others.

Three features of the past are particularly noteworthy when considering how it might contribute to the present, in the digital age no less than in any other era. First, the past has its most significant impact on the present by providing to would-be innovators the proverbial shoulders of giants. Even the most revolutionary of today's satellite-linked devices, which exceed the dreams of previous generations of science-fiction authors, would not exist without earlier, less spectacular forms of technology. As a base on which newcomers can stand, then, the past influences the future that results from innovation in the present. Second, on a different plane, lessons from the past can illuminate the hazards inherent in presuming that progress equates to perfection or that all movement leads triumphantly onward and upward, such that there is no possibility of decay or regression. This presumption is often the prelude to future missteps that are likely to be analogous to the missteps that the very same presumption wrought in the past. Third, a deep familiarity with the past, especially with the fact that not everyone benefited from its riches, can challenge the tendency that stands at the opposite end of the spectrum to a fixation on today and tomorrow: assuming that the past was so much grander than the mediocrity of the present or of the anemic future that today presages.

The church, a community composed of complex human beings rather than robots, shares with civil societies the challenges inseparable from being a body that inherits a past, lives in the present, and looks toward the future. For the church, it is the presence of the Holy Spirit at work in all members of the community of faith that links the three periods of history. The integrating role of grace in the church can counter any tendency toward "existential actualism," which concentrates only on what human beings experience at this moment, without any reference to what has been and what is yet to be.[4] Not only does the constancy of grace ensure that the ecclesial community is other than ephemeral, it sustains the church as a dynamic, fluid body. Thus, grace stimulates movement in the church, but does so without a detrimental impact on the ecclesial community's grounding in the past. Through the inexhaustible activity of the Spirit, the church is a community that endures, one with a history but also one capable of adaptation, of the movement that embodies openness to God's future.

An appreciation of the relationship between the various phases of history within the one movement of God's Spirit makes imperative the pursuit of a balanced perspective on the past. Necessary for such balance is the avoidance of what Rowan Williams classifies as "bad history." Practitioners of this flawed approach are likely to eliminate complexity "by giving us a version of the past that is just the present in fancy dress or by dismissing the past as a wholly foreign country whose language we shall never learn and which can only be seen as incomprehensible and almost comic in its savagery and ignorance."[5] "Good history," conversely, is a source of freedom from "the crippling imprisonment of what we can grasp and take for granted, the ultimate trivializing of our identity."[6]

In the context of the church, "good history" aligns with the emphasis on grace and the mystery of God as the source and sustenance of ecclesial faith. This emphasis differentiates the church from "what we can grasp," but is also alert to the fact that the ambiguities of the human response to grace have not shrunk over time. At the turn of the twentieth century, Maurice Blondel captured strikingly the goal of "good history:" "With the help of the past [the Church] liberates the future from the unconscious limitations and illusions of the present."[7]

---

4. Karl Rahner, "History of the World and Salvation-History," in *Theological Investigations*, vol. 5, trans. K-H. Kruger (New York: Crossroad, 1983), 107.

5. Rowan Williams, *Why Study the Past?: The Quest for the Historical Church* (Grand Rapids, MI: Eerdmans, 2005), 24.

6. Ibid.

7. Maurice Blondel, "History and Dogma," in *The Letter on Apologetics* and *History and Dogma*, trans. A. Dru and I. Trethowan (1904; repr., New York: Holt, Rinehart and Winston, 1964), 281–82.

Blondel's formula reverences the gifts of each period, without implying either that the past was the apogee of the community of faith or that the church has become progressively more able to develop a definitive response to grace.

The unfolding of the Christian story through manifold generations demonstrates unambiguously that every age in the life of the church is a mixed reality, as this book's focus on tilling has insisted throughout. Each period of the church's history has witnessed humanity's capacity for altruism, wisdom, and holiness existing alongside the tendency toward cupidity, indifference, and sinfulness. Such a condition has been evident in the past, applies presently, and is no less likely to be palpable in the future.

The Christian community shares the links between the past and present common to all human endeavors, but has a unique warrant for highlighting the importance of the past: the structure of God's self-communication in history. As a community of faith, the church locates itself in relation to God's once-for-all historical revelation in Jesus Christ through the Holy Spirit. If it is to symbolize in an enduring manner the hope and possibility that the life, death, and resurrection of Jesus Christ enable for humanity and the whole of creation, the church must transcend confinement in any one place or time. "The church," then, always conveys the church with a past, the church that seeks to live faithfully amid the questions and circumstances of the present, and the church on pilgrimage to the fullness of life in the future that belongs to God alone. Significantly, the church's Spirit-driven capacity to be part of more than one phase of history does not require the church to be unchanging. What is necessary, and necessary as far more than an externally imposed obligation, is faithfulness to all that the Spirit enables. Satisfying this condition is compatible with both preservation and modification to the vast array of elements that constitute the church.

Since God's self-communication unites the past, the present, and the future, a specific temptation for members of the church is to isolate one of those periods as being supremely the province of the Spirit, and so the apotheosis of ecclesial life. Succumbing to this temptation means that members of the church cannot do justice to either the human reality of the church as a body in history or the church's place in the mission of God, the mission that transcends any single period of history.

In its dysfunctional form, reverence for the past can become an archaism whose indifference to the present distorts both the movement of grace and the church's reality—"in the desire to retain will always linger the residual danger of a collapse into fundamentalism."[8] Equally, when enthusiasm for the present and future is insufficiently attentive to the most ancient layers of the church's identity-forming witness to Christ and the Holy Spirit, what can result is a version of Christian faith lacking in roots. At its worst, a scant regard for the past can "assail the identity of the Church's memory and replace it with a different mentality."[9]

The Church's "Memory" and the Dynamism of the Spirit

In tandem with recognizing God's self-communication as taking place in history, the prominent role of "the Church's memory" underlines why change in the church can be fraught with tension. From its beginning, the community of faith has emphasized its foundation not in a human initiative, but in God's trinitarian love, held in a "memory" that extends back through the life of the church to God's covenants with the people of Israel.[10] It is this foundation that continues to shape the church. For this reason, Pope Francis refers to memory in the church as "a grace which we constantly need to implore."[11] The status of memory as a grace underlines the connection that the church of today has to "so great a cloud of witnesses" (Heb 12:1) from the past. Drawing on this memory is integral to the church's present-day proclamation of the gospel. Clearly, proposals for change that seem to devalue this memory or, worse, to erase it are likely to arouse strong resistance.

The church's memory does more than recall events in the past: in interpreting the past in the light of God's presence, it affirms that the past has an enduring value, that it can contribute to the present and the future. This attitude to the past requires nuance if it is to avoid

8. John Rist, *What Is Truth?: From the Academy to the Vatican* (Cambridge: Cambridge University Press, 2008), 326.

9. Joseph Ratzinger, *Called to Communion: Understanding the Church Today*, trans. A. Walker (San Francisco: Ignatius Press, 1991), 20.

10. For the role of "memory" as key to the church's past, present, and future, see Gerhard Lohfink, *No Irrelevant Jesus: On Jesus and the Church Today*, trans. L. Maloney (Collegeville, MN: Michael Glazier, 2014), 147–59.

11. Pope Francis, *Evangelii Gaudium*, 13.

canonizing every aspect of the church merely on the basis of its being a certain age. Nonetheless, ecclesial faith does make the radical claim that what comes from the past, if it reflects God's life-giving grace, can remain essential to the life of the church in every age. As Vatican II's *Dei Verbum* states, "God graciously arranged that what he had once revealed for the salvation of all peoples should last forever in its entirety and be transmitted to all generations" (DV 7). In light of this conviction, it is scarcely wondrous that the prospect of change to forms of ecclesial life that have a significant grounding in history generates a charged atmosphere in the ecclesial community.

In the self-understanding of Catholics, especially as the church's official teaching articulates it, "God-given" applies not simply to particular aspects of the church's faith and structure, but to the very existence of the ecclesial community. Not surprisingly, then, the invocation of "God-given" in relation to any elements of the church can militate against openness to human creativity as a potential shaping force in the church. For this reason, disputes over possible changes in the church's way of proceeding are almost as old as the church itself. As chapter 4 discussed, the baptism of gentile converts was contentious for the first generation of Christians, as it represented the overturning of what was already conventional wisdom about the background that potential disciples of Jesus Christ would share (Acts 15:1-29).

The combination of inescapable inertia and the invocation of God's will for the church gradually ensured that the inheritance of the past assumed the aura of being final. As the church's structures developed during the first millennium, fluidity in the church's practices receded. The threefold ministry of bishop, presbyter, and deacon, which could claim the endorsement of divine law, became more dominant and the variety of other ministries that had been formerly evident all but disappeared.[12] After the trauma of the Reformation, the theology of

---

12. For the theological issues central to the threefold ministry, see Neil Ormerod, "On the Divine Institution of the Three-fold Ministry," *Ecclesiology* 4 (2007): 38–51. For detailed surveys of the history of ministry in the church, see Kenan Osborne, *Priesthood: A History of the Ordained Ministry in the Roman Catholic Church* (Mahwah, NJ: Paulist, 1988), and Kenan Osborne, *Ministry: Lay Ministry in the Roman Catholic Church* (Mahwah, NJ: Paulist, 1993).

"perfect society," especially when buttressed by the "hierarchology" that later became its loyal attendant, left little room for regarding any aspect of the ecclesial community's structure as other than complete. It also left no room at all for doubting that existing structures embodied God's will for the church. This framework of "perfect society," which, as chapter 1 indicated, was itself an innovation alien to earlier periods of ecclesiastical history, facilitated the centralization of many aspects of ecclesial life. A centralized church, acting as if all local ecclesial communities were identical, helped to form the myth of an unchanging and unchangeable church, a view regnant immediately prior to Vatican II:

> In the form in which it had been inherited, the Christian tradition related the true narrative about God, humanity and the world, and this was valid for everyone, past, present, and future. This truth was unassailable, revealed and entrusted to humanity in the Bible and the tradition and not simply placed at humanity's disposal. The Church, and more specifically the Magisterium, was responsible for protecting the integrity of this salvific truth. The result was a sustained and inflexible dogmatization of the historical form of the anti-modern Christian master narrative.[13]

The historian John O'Malley argues that the bishops at Vatican II, which is surely the major portal of change in the modern history of the Catholic Church, perceived themselves to be proceeding in ways that would ensure "that no substantial change was being made in the patrimony of the past."[14] It is far from extraordinary, then, that Catholics, lacking a shared memory of endorsing and negotiating change, have experienced tensions in the wake of the council. These tensions, which have become most familiar in response to changes in numerous aspects of the church's liturgy since the 1960s, are currently evident in, for example, proposals for greater recognition of gay people in the church and for expanding access to the reception of the Eucharist for Catholics in "irregular" marriages. In a related way, theological inquiry,

13. Lieven Boeve, *Interrupting Tradition: An Essay on Christian Faith in a Postmodern Context*, trans. B. Doyle (Louvain: Peeters, 2003), 47.
14. John O'Malley, "Reform, Historical Consciousness, and Vatican II's Aggiornamento," *Theological Studies* 32 (1971): 576.

an activity that resonates with stirrings toward possibilities, has often been subject to the accusation that it was subverting the church's dependence on God's revelation. This form of accusation was most virulent between the Modernist crisis of the early twentieth century and the Second Vatican Council, but has also featured in more recent times.[15]

The suspicion that innovation in any area of the church's life is a rejection of what comes from God is likely to proliferate when the changes appear to reflect values dominant in "the world," when that term carries the implication of hostility to God (John 15:15-19; 17:9-19). Efforts at innovation and reform in the church often wither if bearing the stigma of being no more than an echo of the values that incite the world's flux, or of an ideology popular in a particular moment in history and culture. This perception encourages the refutation of change, as well as its depiction as a harbinger of the disintegration sure to follow the church's departure from the ways of God.

It can certainly be the case that would-be innovators in the church are dismissive of the past as less enlightened than the present, but this judgment is rarely the principal or sole motivation driving advocates of change. Seen in a more favorable light, the willingness to grapple with the possibility of change can reflect the church's orientation toward the eschatological future, the orientation intrinsic to Rahner's description of the church as an "open system," the notion that chapter 4 introduced. From this perspective, change can accord with the status of the church as an unfinished project. The implications of the church's existence as a Spirit-led pilgrim, which chapter 3 presented as highlighting the need for the ecclesial community to engage with the unexpected, are also germane to the discussion of change. No less importantly, an appreciation of the church's sacramentality, which, as chapter 2 stressed, can likewise contribute to the formation of an environment receptive to change, whether as innovation or as reform. This is so as the church's sacramentality does not equate to the church mastering grace or being beyond the tilling by which grace inspires more authentic discipleship.

---

15. For discussion of various aspects of the response to contemporary theologians from authorities in the church, see Richard Gaillardetz, ed., *When the Magisterium Intervenes: The Magisterium and Theologians in Today's Church* (Collegeville, MN: Michael Glazier, 2012).

As a pilgrim, the church encounters a variety of historical impulses that are never simply repetitions of what the Christian community has experienced previously. Responding to these circumstances calls for the exercise of graced creativity and imagination. Pope Francis, even as he endorses the necessary preservation of the church's memory, connects the gospel itself with generating "new paths of creativity" that enable the church to proclaim its faith "with different forms of expression, more eloquent signs and words with new meanings for today's world" (EG 11). Notably, the pope identifies God as the source of these possibilities: "The real newness is the newness which God himself mysteriously brings about and inspires, provokes, guides and accompanies in a thousand ways" (EG 12).

The emphasis on God's newness supports Werner Jeanrond's claim that a church unwilling to change is at risk of becoming a museum that houses what is no longer living, while obscuring God's life-giving presence that history has mediated to the present:

> The primary Christian concern cannot be the mere survival of an old tradition—the church as museum—but the actualization of a challenging message in our generation according to our best abilities—the church as a community of responsive and responsible fellow builders. Only if Christian faith is lived today, only if the center of this faith, that is the presence of God in Christ and in all of our lives, is experienced today, only if the universal call of God to all people is freed again from the legalistic deposits which have been distorting its proclamation, and only if the hope for the fullness of the experience of God provokes us to change our lives and so the fate of this world, will authentic Christianity continue.[16]

Pope Francis similarly cautions the church against the danger of separating itself from its own time and place. He warns that if the church "stops listening to others" and "leaves no room for questions," it is likely that the ecclesial community "loses her youth and turns into a

---

16. Werner Jeanrond, *Theological Hermeneutics: Development and Significance* (New York: Crossroad, 1991), 173–74.

museum."[17] An intransigent commitment to preservation that opposes or ignores what might be arising in the present may well be detrimental to the manifestation of a living church, and so to the church's faithfulness to its eschatological orientation. In this regard, John Henry Newman offers a helpful principle: "One cause of corruption in religion is the refusal to follow the course of doctrine as it moves on, and an obstinacy in the notions of the past."[18] If a lack of regard for the past damages the church's faith and hinders its mission, a refusal to move beyond the past can effect a similar deleterious outcome.

Rather than an uncritical approach endorsing or rejecting all that has come from the past, members of the ecclesial community in every time and place can interrogate the church's current practices and structures, along with their own lives, to discern whether they are serving, rather than obscuring, the manifestation of God's reign. Members of the church, then, must continue to engage in the tilling inseparable from the call to conversion. Doing so includes the need to distinguish between "cultural and anthropological frameworks" and "the content of divine revelation."[19] Prioritizing one of these two categories over the other fails to acknowledge the complex relationship between them—a relationship that will claim attention in chapter 6's exploration of "reception." This failure can prevent the ecclesial community from responding to the movement of the Spirit in the circumstances of the present, just as it can hinder faithful reception of what the past has mediated to the present for the sake of the future.

The ecclesial community, in order to be faithful to the ongoing summons of grace, must confront the challenge of determining how to do justice to the movement of the Spirit in both the past and present, movement that always leads to the future. When there is disagreement in the ecclesial community over the legitimacy of change, be it

---

17. Pope Francis, *Christus Vivit*, Post-Synodal Apostolic Exhortation to Young People and to the Entire People of God (2019), 41, http://w2.vatican.va/content/francesco /en/apost_exhortations/documents/papa-francesco_esortazione-ap_20190325 christus-vivit.html.

18. John Henry Newman, *An Essay on the Development of Doctrine*, 3rd ed., (1878; New York: Cosimo, 2007), 176–77.

19. Elisabeth Schüssler Fiorenza, *Discipleship of Equals: A Critical Feminist Ekklesia-logy of Liberation* (New York: Crossroad, 1993), 101.

in relation to opening access for women to the church's ordained ministry or reconsidering the church's stance on disputed ethical issues, partisans of every stripe are likely to conscript the Spirit in support of their convictions. As a result, the Spirit becomes attached to opposing, sometimes contradictory, claims.

An alternative to internecine struggles over ownership of the Holy Spirit requires attention "to what the Spirit is saying to the churches" (Rev 2:7). This attention is also critical as a corrective to equating faithfulness to the Spirit with either one's own preferences or the predilections of one's "party." Individual and communal efforts to listen to the Spirit are essential for the church's discernment, but not sufficient on their own. What is also crucial are venues where different "listenings" can engage and enter into dialogue with each other in the hope of echoing the earliest Christians in their consensus regarding what "has seemed good to the Holy Spirit and to us" (Acts 15:28)—this, too, is a theme that chapter 6 will consider.

The Christian community has learned through its history to associate the Spirit not only with continuity, but also with change. It is certainly true that the Spirit, like the wind, "blows where it chooses" (John 3:8), but Jesus's description of the Spirit as "Advocate" for his followers (John 14:16), makes plain that the Spirit is neither eccentric nor capricious, but promotes the well-being of Christ's disciples and their mission in the world. The church's lack of control over the Spirit is evident not simply in the complexity of discernment, but in the fact that the need for such discernment arises in specific historical circumstances, for which the church cannot prepare itself in advance.

The specifics of the Spirit's activity might not be predictable, but the church is able to profess, in the light of its long history of engagement with the Spirit, that the movement of the Spirit is invariably toward the building up of God's reign, a process that differs from an endless repetition of "the same." Since the ecclesial community cannot validly domesticate the Spirit, the sources through which the Spirit draws the church into an ever-deeper encounter with the incomprehensible mystery of God transcend the church's regulation. This truth exists alongside the church's affirmation that the Spirit is integral not only to the community of the baptized, but also to the church's structures and its officeholders—a well-documented locus of tension that will find a place in chapter 6's list of topics for discussion.

A church striving to practice faithfulness to the Spirit through being not only "one" but also "catholic" must be the venue for a variety of voices, while being alert to the danger of dissolving into sectarianism. The challenge inseparable from meeting these requirements reinforces the truth at the heart of the church's creedal profession: that the unity, catholicity, holiness, and apostolicity of the ecclesial community are gifts of the Spirit, rather than human achievements. The Christian community must appropriate those gifts continually, but that appropriation, too, takes place through the Spirit. The following sections on apostolicity and tradition, therefore, will engage with the movement of the Spirit and with what might best reflect God's reign in relation to possibilities for change.

Apostolicity and the Permanence of the Past

The church's unity, holiness, and catholicity, three of the four characteristics or "marks" that have been part of the church's creed since the Council of Constantinople in 380, have been a topic of discussion at different points in this book.[20] This section examines the remaining mark: "apostolicity." In the context of building an argument to establish the possibility of change in the church, a discussion of apostolicity might appear to be misplaced. Even the surface-level meaning of the term itself seems to champion the past over the church's present and future. First impressions, then, would not connect apostolicity with receptivity to innovation in the church.

It is certainly true that apostolicity has as its primary referent the foundational period of the church's life. "The apostolic era" designates the years in which those believers who had known Jesus prior to his death became the first to confess the risen Jesus as the Christ and Lord. During those years, believers began to articulate their faith in Jesus Christ as part of making him known to others. This period also witnessed efforts to clarify the connotations of discipleship in light of questions and circumstances that emerged after Pentecost, and to

---

20. For an overview of the "marks," see Werner Löser, "Attributes of the Church," in *Handbook of Catholic Theology*, ed. Wolfgang Beinert and Francis Schüssler Fiorenza (New York: Crossroad Publishing, 1995), 38–39.

structure the community of faith for the sake of its mission, worship, and unity. The church's apostolicity is inseparable from these roots, even though the "apostolic era" is no more repeatable than any other period of history. "Apostolicity," however, denotes a property particular to the church in every age rather than a harkening back to the past.

The Faith and Order Commission of the World Council of Churches, in a document it published in 2005, identifies the defining feature of apostolicity as "the continuity in the permanent characteristics of the Church of the apostles."[21] The document presents the elements emblematic of this continuity—"witness to the apostolic faith, proclamation and fresh interpretation of the Gospel, celebration of baptism and Eucharist, the transmission of ministerial responsibilities, communion in prayer, love, joy and suffering, service to the sick and needy, communion among the local churches and sharing the divine gifts which have been given to each"—as other than relics from the church's earliest years.[22] The items on the list, which are not the exclusive preserve of any single moment of ecclesial life, indicate how apostolicity can be applicable to the community of faith across multiple times and places.

What, then, of "permanent"? Does its connection to apostolicity suggest something more than an excessive elevation of the respect due to the first generation of Christians? In addressing these questions, it can be instructive to compare the status of what derives from the apostles to those features of civil society associated with "the founders," the pioneers who loom large in both the myths and constitutions of various nations, especially in the United States. While those who lay foundations perform a unique task, the work of secular founders is often superseded, sometimes even erased. Civil constitutions are usually open to later amendments, which can both modify the vision embodied in the original document and add provisions in the light of circumstances that the founders could not have anticipated. More dramatically, it is possible to abrogate a state's constitution in favor of

21. The World Council of Churches, *The Nature and Mission of the Church*, 71 (Faith and Order Paper 198), in *Receiving "The Nature and Mission of the Church": Ecclesial Reality and Ecumenical Horizons for the Twenty-First Century*, ed. Paul Collins and Michael Fahey (2005; repr., London: T. and T. Clark, 2008), 130.
22. Ibid.

an entirely new concept that refashions a society, and so produces a new set of "founders."

Far from being merely a theoretical possibility, the overturning of a state's foundations is a constant of political history: democratic systems replace absolute monarchies, including those that asserted their origin in "divine right," while democratic societies can become dictatorships, and vice versa. The century since the First World War (1914–18) offers manifold examples, from across the world, of the shattering of constitutions and the remaking of the sociopolitical order. In some instances, particularly in Eastern Europe, but also in parts of Africa and Asia, individual nations have experienced such changes more than once. Ironically, then, "permanence" in the political sphere can be a quality with a limited life span.

The church's existence in such a volatile world notwithstanding, the ecclesial community "is called to be ever faithful to its apostolic origins," to remain always the church built on the faith of the apostles, rather than transmogrify into a community with a different foundation.[23] Clearly, the church's profession of its apostolic faith intends "permanent" to stand without equivocation, and certainly without any sense that something more desirable or convenient will ultimately displace it.

The commitment to guard against any dilution of the church's apostolicity does not exclude any role for hermeneutics in identifying and clarifying the nuances proper to apostolicity. In fact, the association between apostolicity and permanence gives rise to questions that lend an urgency to interpretation: Is "permanent" a synonym for "unchanging"? How can anything from the past enjoy the status of permanence when the members of the first generation of Christians were no more immune to the limits and distortions of their time than are Christians in every subsequent generation? How, to raise an explicitly theological question, is the emphasis on permanence reconcilable with the church's eschatological orientation? In light of those questions, the primary task for the remainder of this section is to provide a hermeneutic of "permanent," doing so with an eye to the chapter's focus on the legitimacy of change and innovation in the church.

23. The World Council of Churches, *The Church: Towards a Common Vision*, Faith and Order Paper 214 (Geneva: World Council of Churches, 2014), 23.

Interpreting "Permanent"

As part of this hermeneutical endeavor, the first requirement is to establish why the earliest history of the ecclesial community receives the honor it does. The insistence that the church's apostolic foundations are of enduring significance could be an arbitrary imposition that divinizes the past, while also failing to respond to the movement of the Spirit in the present, and refusing the possibility of a future beyond inherited imaginings. An alternative interpretation, one that claims a thoroughly theological grounding, is that "the Church of the apostles" is integral to God's self-revelation, such that the church can be faithful to God, and fulfill its mission as sacrament, only through the preservation of its apostolic faith. Rahner argues that the latter is the inference proper to the profession of the church's apostolicity:

> It would not be correct to say that God's founding of the Church consists simply in conserving it in existence; rather we must say that an essential part of God's conserving it in existence consists in God having founded it at a particular moment in time. God, then, as founder of the Church, has a unique, qualitatively non-transmissible relationship to the first generation, one which God does not have in the same sense to other periods of the Church's history, or rather has to the latter only through the former.[24]

The existence of a "unique, qualitatively non-transmissible relationship" between God and the first generation of Christians need not suggest that God discriminates arbitrarily between believers in different eras. Rather, the uniqueness of this relationship aligns with the unique mission of those believers. The historical nature of God's self-revelation in Jesus Christ and the historical reality of the church are key to appreciating the particularity of the mission proper to the earliest Christians. Their mission centers on the identification of Jesus. The first Christians witnessed the life, death, and resurrection of Jesus; their testimony that "Jesus Christ is Lord" (Phil 2:11) emerged from their direct experience. This experience is not within the domain of later generations,

---

24. Karl Rahner, *Inspiration in the Bible*, trans. H. Henkey, rev. trans. M. Palmer (New York: Herder and Herder, 1964), 45.

all of whom receive the testimony of the original witnesses. Rahner even suggests that decisions in the apostolic age about the shape and operation of structures in the church might be irreversible if they, too, have a grounding in Jesus's words and action. Crucially, Rahner argues, too, that "irreversible" is not synonymous with "unchangeable," that it does not imply a future that is closed rather than open.[25]

While apostolicity "means being continuously and vitally the same Church as the Church of the apostles, led through history by the same Holy Spirit to proclaim the same Good News and to bring the same salvation," it does not imply that the faith of the earliest believers was perfect, or at least of a higher quality than that evident in subsequent eras.[26] Nor does the notion require the depiction of the apostolic era as a time when Christians were people who sailed untroubled on a sea of faith that was itself always calm.

Indeed, the fact that forgiveness is a principal aspect of apostolic faith demonstrates that the first Christians recognized the Spirit of Christ as the expression of God's merciful love because they themselves had experienced the need for God's mercy: "Forgiveness is only possible in the power and at the prompting of God's saving activity in Christ (Rom 3:25f). It is possible only in light of the statement that God has reconciled us to himself while we were still enemies (Rom 5:10)."[27] Rather than it being the case that believers in the apostolic era were people of incomparable virtue, it was the grace of the relationship with God that enabled flawed and fallible human beings to be agents of the reign of God in the apostolic era. This grace is the same grace from which the church lives in every age. Through the same Spirit whose outpouring at Pentecost was the immediate catalyst for the proclamation of faith in Christ, the church continues to profess the apostolic faith, to engage the mission of the first apostles, and to look towards the fulfillment of God's reign, as the ecclesial community has done in every age.

---

25. Karl Rahner, "The Church's Redemptive Historical Provenance from the Death and Resurrection of Jesus," in *Theological Investigations*, vol. 19, trans. E. Quinn (New York: Crossroad, 1983), 35–36.

26. John Wright, "The Meaning and Structure of Catholic Faith," *Theological Studies* 39 (1978): 709.

27. Walter Kasper, *Mercy: The Essence of the Gospel and the Key to Christian Life*, trans. W. Madges (Mahwah, NJ: Paulist, 2014), 139.

All believers after the first century depend on the earliest generation not for their own experience of the Spirit, but for their ability to identify and name the Spirit of Christ as being the Spirit of Christ. The Holy Spirit inspires faith, but believers do not intuit for themselves all that "Jesus Christ" encompasses. Rather, all believers learn about Jesus through the faith and teaching of the ecclesial community, faith and teaching that have their foundation in the apostolic witness that the same grace of the Spirit inspired.

The Spirit-inspired faith of those who were the first to believe that "in Christ God was reconciling the world to himself" (2 Cor 5:19) shapes the ecclesial community in every subsequent era. All those who enter into the Christian community "come to faith in Jesus with the apostles, but it is also *through* their faith that we come to faith."[28] Those who were the first to experience that the Spirit is able to transform fear into courageous discipleship continue to enlighten all believers, challenging them to embrace "a spirit of power and of love and of self-discipline" (2 Tim 1:7) at the heart of faith.

This inextricable link between the first Christians and their successors underscores vividly the communal nature of faith. As the discussion of "faith" in chapter 3 detailed, a major feature of the apostolic profession that reverberates through the church's history is its emphasis on faith as communal rather than as the exclusive possession of individuals. Vatican II likewise emphasizes the connection between the Spirit and the community of faith: "All the faithful scattered throughout the world are in communion with each other in the Holy Spirit" (LG 13). The relationship with God proper to each Christian is not in competition with communal faith, since the grace of that relationship is one that all members of the church share equally through their baptism— "For in the one Spirit we were all baptized into one body" (1 Cor 12:13).

Through the community's profession of faith, each member of the church in every age comes to know the core of Christian faith. It is also the ecclesial community, through the Spirit that animates it, that is the conduit for the grace at work through the church's proclamation of the gospel and celebration of the sacraments. The communal

---

28. Pamela Dickey Young, *Feminist Theology/Christian Theology: In Search of Method* (Minneapolis: Fortress, 1990), 84; original emphasis.

setting of these primary supports for Christian discipleship reinforce that "the Church, for the believer, is not so much an object believed as an extension of the believing subject. The faithful comprise the community of those who view reality, under its religious aspects, through the eyes of the Church, convinced that in that way they will see more and see better than they otherwise could."[29] This belief exists together with the recognition of the community's ongoing need for conversion toward ways of proceeding more responsive to the gifts of the Spirit that all members share.

The primacy of the church's apostolic faith identifies the Christian community as being, permanently, "a community of reception."[30] Since the community of faith exists in history, it is always in the position of receiving what comes from the past. Reception includes understanding, interpreting, and applying Scripture, all of which are activities that take place through the Holy Spirit.[31] Since reception contributes to the tilling of the church for the sake of its future, chapter 6 will examine more fully the dynamics of reception, especially in relation to the church as a structured communion of faith, one in which all members, not simply officeholders, are capable of graced discernment.

As a community of reception, the church's experience of the Spirit in the past lives on through the continued appropriation of its apostolic heritage. The biblical, liturgical, and theological *ressourcement* that were essential to the achievements of Vatican II, as chapter 1 explained, illustrates dramatically the interweaving of reception and creativity. At the council, the re-reception of the apostolic memory did not confine the church to repetition of any one phase of its past, but stimulated the creativity that enabled responses to present exigencies that were already influencing the church's future.

Without reception of the apostolic witness, the church in any time or place would be a community whose shared faith, lacking a connec-

---

29. Avery Dulles, *A Church to Believe In: Discipleship and the Dynamics of Freedom* (New York: Crossroad, 1982), 44.

30. For the origins and implications of the description of the church as "a community of reception," see Ormond Rush, *The Eyes of Faith: The Sense of the Faithful and the Church's Reception of Revelation* (Washington, DC: Catholic University of America Press, 2009), 42–46.

31. Ibid., 72–78.

tion to the originating experience of Christianity, would not exceed the limits of its particular moment of history. Jean-Marie Tillard expresses this conclusion forcefully using a theme that has already featured in this chapter: "memory." Tillard contends that "the apostolic 'memory' is the sphere outside of which the Church cannot live. This memory is her constant yardstick. She neither believes, nor confesses, nor preaches, nor prays, nor puts the forces of the Kingdom at the service of humanity, she neither celebrates today nor will celebrate in eternity the living God, except *in communione Apostolorum*."[32] The permanence of this memory, the fact that the church does not begin from nothing in every new time and place, binds communities through time, while also being integral to the unity between diverse churches at each moment of the church's history.

In order to develop further how the permanence of the church's apostolic memory can be an ongoing source of enrichment for the ecclesial community, it will be helpful to consider memory as *anamnesis*. This approach, which is prominent in sacramental theology, understands memory as "making present" what has come from the past, not simply looking back at it.[33]

Anamnesis *and the Church's Liturgy*

In every time and place, the church's liturgy "recalls" the great events of God's once-for-all self-giving in Christ—"For I received from the Lord what I also handed on to you" (1 Cor 11:23). This *anamnesis* does not add to Christ's action, as if the grace at work through the life, death, and resurrection of Jesus Christ was not definitive, but nor is the liturgy simply a ritual of looking back or, even less, a reenactment. Rather, sacramental liturgy, through the Holy Spirit, makes present God's self-communication in Christ as the event through which God gives life today, not merely in the past. *Anamnesis* underscores that

32. Jean-Marie Tillard, "Ministry and Apostolic Tradition," *One in Christ* 25 (1989): 17.

33. See Allan Bouley, "*Anamnesis*," in *The New Dictionary of Theology*, ed. Joseph Komonchak et al. (Wilmington, DE: Michael Glazier, 1987), 16–17; see also Karl Rahner and Herbert Vorgrimler, "*Anamnesis*," in *Dictionary of Theology*, 2nd ed., trans. R. Stachan et al. (New York: Crossroad, 1985), 9–10.

the revelation of God is for every time and every place. Tillard refers to this "once-for-all" dimension of God's revelation in Christ as *kairos*, not simply a moment in the flow of moments (*chronos*) that constitute history, but as a decisive moment, one that God alone can accomplish, one that "recapitulates" what God has done over time, and includes what God will do in the future.[34]

In making present God's self-giving in Christ, *anamnesis* is distinct from any exercise of memory that is only the retrieval of a past that has faded from view, a past whose elements were once vital but are now devoid of any potential to influence today and tomorrow. The church's remembering of the events of God's revelation in Jesus Christ through the Holy Spirit, a remembering that takes place liturgically in word and symbol, renews the worshipping community in its relationship to Christ. It is this relationship, which the Holy Spirit sustains, that is, always and everywhere, the source of the church's identity and its mission to proclaim and embody the gospel.

Underpinning the theology of *anamnesis* is the church's faith that God's revelation in Christ is the enduring—permanent—center of the church. Louis-Marie Chauvet expresses the dynamism inherent in this emphasis when he declares that the church "cannot 'narrate' Jesus as Christ and Lord without being itself taken in the present into what it narrates in the past. The church holds its identity by constantly receiving itself from him."[35] Similarly, David Power, in an analysis that is congruent with the approach to revelation and the church in the earlier chapters of this book, employs "event" to expound the "memorial" aspect of the Eucharist and its effect on the life of the Christian community:

> Through the narrative Christ events again in the community, within the aspirations of its ritual expressions, transforming them into new being. The community itself events within its time and society, as a proclamation and witness of this way of God's being among humans and on the earth. . . . The sacramental celebration is not faithful to the event of the *pasch* that it represents un-

---

34. Jean-Marie Tillard, "Tradition, Reception," in *The Quadrilog: Tradition and the Future of Ecumenism*, ed. Ken Hagen (Collegeville, MN: Michael Glazier, 1994), 333.

35. Louis-Marie Chauvet, *The Sacraments: The Word of God at the Mercy of the Body*, trans. M. Beaumont (Collegeville, MN: Pueblo, 2001), 135.

less it remains faithful to its own eventful character. . . . As far as [Christ's] body on earth is concerned, the eucharistic memorial is a power to be and to become, to event again in sacrament in new places, incorporating persons and things into the communion of God's love.[36]

Power's analysis makes clear that the creative potential of the church's memory, the potential "to be and to become," has its source in God's self-communication, the very same self-communication that constitutes the permanence of the church's apostolicity. Accordingly, when the church celebrates the liturgy, especially the eucharistic liturgy that recalls the central events of God's life-giving in Christ, it does so as a community formed by the one Spirit of Christ. The words and actions of the liturgy are the means by which the church both affirms and experiences anew that Christ, in the Spirit, is the source of its life: "By such ritual memorial, participants experience themselves as contemporary with the group's origin and so are plunged together more deeply into its core identity."[37] In being "plunged" into its origins through the liturgy, the Christian community in every time and place shares the same faith and receives the same mission as that of the first Christian communities.

As remarkable as is the link between the past and the present that is integral to the recalling of the apostolic memory, the yet-more-remarkable aspect of the church's liturgical *anamnesis* is the connection it makes between the church's memory and the future. Since the grace of God's self-revelation is always oriented to the future, to the fullness of God's reign, the *anamnesis* of the great acts of that revelation enables the church to share already, in an anticipatory but not final manner, in the future that belongs to God. This future is what the foundational events of God's revelation both initiate and guarantee: "In sharing, as it were, in the foundational event through the keeping of memorial, the people share in what it has given and in what it promises for the

36. David Power, *The Eucharistic Mystery: Revitalizing the Tradition* (New York: Crossroad, 1992), 311–12; for a detailed discussion of various approaches to "memorial," see 304–16.

37. John Laurance, *The Sacrament of the Eucharist* (Collegeville, MN: Liturgical Press, 2012), 122–23.

future."[38] Gerhard Lohfink's description of the biblical word that the church proclaims in the liturgical setting highlights the paradoxical combination of memory and the focus on the future:

> On the basis of its biblical tradition, [the church] has a memory that retains all the experiences of the past, and it has an assembly in which its saving knowledge is handed on from generation to generation and constantly becomes new. . . . And for that very reason the church is in a position to be always new, always younger and more modern than any other society, because radical memory gives a future and causes the church, insofar as it takes its own experiences seriously, always to be ahead of its time.[39]

At the heart of this complex interweaving of the past, present, and future is the "simple" fact of God's self-revelation in Jesus Christ through the Holy Spirit. Recapitulating four aspects of Rahner's theology of grace can assist the effort to map the connection between the various elements of the revelation in Christ and the Spirit and the church's memory. First, the self-communication that is God's creative grace present in Jesus Christ brings the community of faith into being, sustains it, and guarantees its future fulfillment. Second, through sacramental symbols, including the biblical word, the church's memory "recalls" God's saving acts. Third, the biblical word and the ecclesial sacraments are the means for the community to encounter in the present the God of humanity's past, present, and future. Fourth, this encounter not only renews the call to discipleship in all Christians, it empowers communities and individuals to make decisions about how best to respond to grace in their unique settings. In these ways, grace weaves between, and weaves together, the past, present, and future.

The shared experience of the Spirit promotes unity in faith, attention to God's word, and shared worship. It stimulates, too, engagement with the world beyond the Christian community. As this volume has stressed often, every encounter with the God of Jesus Christ conveys

---

38. David Power, "Eucharist," in *Systematic Theology: Roman Catholic Perspectives*, 2nd ed., ed. Francis Schüssler Fiorenza and John Galvin (Minneapolis: Fortress, 2011), 519.

39. Gerhard Lohfink, *No Irrelevant Jesus: On Jesus and the Church Today*, trans. L. Maloney (Collegeville, MN: Michael Glazier, 2014), 154.

an invitation to discipleship. The focus on discipleship suggests that the connection between the church's memory and the church's mission for the future must be more than a matter of orthodox faith, believing what the apostles believed; it must also involve "the right praxis of lived discipleship," doing what the apostles did, for the sake of God's reign.[40] The context for the church's action varies between eras and cultures, but the mission remains the same. Still, there is no single way that the ecclesial community, in different times and places, must fulfill its mission.

Consistent with the centrality of discipleship for the faithfulness of the church, Vitor Westhelle identifies apostolicity primarily with the church's mission in the present for the sake of the future: "The church is apostolic when it is reminded of Jesus and awakened through the Spirit by the witness of those who testified to the life, passion, death, and resurrection of Jesus the Christ, and where he now is as the community in its eschatological experience of being on the front, where there is no *safety*, but the bursting out of *salvation*."[41] In other words, a church faithful to its apostolic inheritance will be a church attentive to enacting whatever service God's reign might require of it. Since the willingness to serve God's reign is inseparable from a concern for the future, the church must remain attuned to the needs and questions of the present, needs and questions that are not only the building blocks of the future, but also require the church to grapple with the relationship between the past, the present, and the future.

A further implication of the connection between apostolicity and discipleship is that faithfulness to the church's apostolic dimension must be an aspect of the mission common to all the baptized, rather than being applicable only to a cross-section of the whole church. This conclusion is especially relevant in the context of interpreting "apostolic succession."[42] When the understanding of that term limits its reach only to the church's bishops, and even then as only a measure of valid

---

40. John Burkhard, *Apostolicity Then and Now: An Ecumenical Church in a Postmodern World* (Collegeville, MN: Michael Glazier, 2004), 34.

41. Vitor Westhelle, *The Church Event: Call and Challenge of a Church Protestant* (Minneapolis: Fortress, 2010), 123; original emphasis.

42. For discussion of "apostolic succession," see Burkhard, *Apostolicity Then and Now*, 35–39.

ordination, it suggests that bishops alone represent the church's apostolicity. When, on the other hand, the term designates the relationship
and responsibility characteristic of the whole church, it highlights both
the communal identity and shared mission of the entire Christian community. The latter emphasis underlines the need for mechanisms in the
church that enable the speaking and listening of the entire community,
a theme that is a subset of the church's discernment that chapter 6 will
explore more fully.

The challenge integral to holding together the church's foundations,
its mission, its communal life, and its eschatological orientation suggests that, correctly understood, even the church of the apostolic age
itself faced the task of becoming "apostolic." Rather than emerging fully
formed as exemplars of faith and discipleship, Christians in the first
century, no less than those in the twenty-first, struggled to embody
in their daily lives the radical demands of the faith in Christ that they
came to profess. Since there was "no primitive period of immediate and
unambiguous clarity," in either the belief or practice of the first Christian communities, what the church now affirms as "apostolic faith" was
never a sharply defined object that those communities possessed with
absolute ease and certainty.[43]

The churches of the apostolic era had to draw on the memory of
Jesus living in their members, a memory empowered by the same Spirit
at the heart of the church in the present day, to clarify its "doctrine,
life, and praxis."[44] There can be, then, no valid expectation that the
Christian community in every subsequent age will be exempt from
a similar process. If, as Avery Dulles argues, the church's historical
existence means that "changes in the cultural climate thus introduce
a certain discontinuity in the self-understanding and self-expression
of the Church," becoming "apostolic" is an enduring task for every
ecclesial community.[45]

In summary, the fact that the church is a community that claims
apostolicity as a defining feature is neither justification for a rosy-hued

---

43. Stephen Sykes, *The Identity of Christianity: Theologians and the Essence of
Christianity from Schleiermacher to Barth* (London: SPCK, 1984), 15.
44. Burkhard, *Apostolicity Then and Now*, 32.
45. Avery Dulles, *The Catholicity of the Church* (Oxford: Clarendon Press, 1985), 101.

nostalgia nor a brake applied to the church's development. Rather, it can be a stimulus for change and growth toward a more authentic discipleship across the community of faith. As a work of the Spirit for the sake of the fullness of life in Christ, apostolicity is both a gift to the church and a task for the church: it requires and facilitates the church's engagement with the challenges of the present, including the challenges presented by the church's sinfulness.

Far from being an assertion of perfection, affirmation of the church's apostolicity is a potent motive for the ongoing conversion of the church whose "battered, bruised and sinful" state does not negate God's presence: "Christ did not promise to keep the church free from sin. He promised to remain with it. He also asked the Father, who sent another Advocate, the Holy Spirit, to be with it."[46] For this reason, Sandra Schneiders contends that the continuity proper to apostolicity can include "not only deeper insight, but also new insight, and even correction and purification."[47] The ecclesial community, therefore, must continue—permanently—to appropriate the gift of the Spirit through multiple channels in order to become, be, and remain faithful to all that "apostolicity" implies.

The recognition that apostolicity encompasses the present and future, as well as the past, indicates, yet again, the role of the Spirit. As *Dei Verbum* phrases it, it is the Spirit "through whom the living voice of the Gospel rings out in the church—and through it in the world—leads believers to the full truth and makes the word of Christ dwell in them in all its richness" (DV 8). The link between the Spirit and apostolicity has resonances with the role that "tradition" plays in the ecclesial community, specifically with the capacity of the Christian tradition to guide the community of faith in responding creatively to the circumstances of the present for the sake of the future. Since the invocation of "tradition" in many facets of human experience regularly imposes a requirement for the preservation of what is unchangeable, it is necessary to investigate

46. Mary Ann Donovan, "The Church Is Apostolic," in *The Many Marks of the Church*, ed. William Madges and Michael Daley (New London, CT: Twenty-Third Publications, 2006), 55.

47. Sandra Schneiders, *The Revelatory Text: Interpreting the New Testament as Sacred Scripture*, 2nd ed. (Collegeville, MN: Michael Glazier, 1999), 78.

whether such an association is an accurate reflection of all that the term implies for the church.[48] "Tradition," then, will be the centerpiece of this chapter's final section.

Tradition and the Living Faith of the Church

The Council of Trent (1545–63) situated its teaching on tradition within the larger field of considering God's revelation, especially in relation to the Bible. Trent mandated the church's bishops "to check the lack of discretion by which the words and sentiments of sacred scripture are turned and twisted to scurrilous use."[49] The council noted explicitly the misuse of the Bible in "magical formulae, fortune telling, lotteries, and also scandalous pamphlets," but its larger anxiety centered on the likely ill effects of any general access to Scripture free of direction and control by the church's bishops. This freedom was an aspect of the Reformers' stress on making Scripture, as the primary source of revelation, available to all believers. As part of its commitment to preserve in the church "the purity of the gospel, purged of all errors," Trent strongly opposed the unfettered availability of the Bible.[50]

The bishops at Trent expressed their "feeling of piety and reverence" for the Bible, but insisted that Scripture alone did not exhaust God's revelation, which the council located "in written books and unwritten traditions which were received by the apostles from the mouth of Christ himself, or else have come down to us, handed on as it were from the apostles themselves at the inspiration of the holy Spirit."[51] For this reason, Trent insisted on the need for the church's officeholders to "pass judgment on the true meaning and interpretation of the sacred scriptures."[52] The bishops extended this control by seeking to restrict even the activities of printers, "who, thinking they have a right to do what they wish without restraint and without the permission of ecclesiastical superiors, print the

---

48. For discussion of the role of "tradition" as a human and sociological phenomenon, see Gerald O'Collins, *Tradition: Understanding Christian Tradition* (Oxford: Oxford University Press, 2018), 20–34.

49. Council of Trent, Session 4, in Norman Tanner, ed., *Decrees of the Ecumenical Councils*, vol. 2 (1546; repr., Washington, DC: Georgetown University Press, 1990), 665.

50. Ibid., 663.

51. Ibid.

52. Ibid., 664.

texts of sacred scripture with added notes and commentaries of anyone at all."[53] The efforts of Trent to counter any separation of Scripture from the tradition over which the church's bishops maintained their guardianship stamped Catholic life into the twentieth century.

From the sixteenth century to Vatican II, the "Scripture or tradition" contest divided the Christian Church. If depicted as a sporting contest between rival clubs, Protestants supported "team Scripture," while Catholics rallied behind "team Tradition." Sadly, this division, and the rivalry it fed, applied not only in Europe but in all the countries to which the churches of Europe spread Christianity during the centuries of Western colonialism. Defense of the primacy of tradition mediated through the church's authoritative structures thus became a badge of Catholic orthodoxy in settings far removed in space and time from sixteenth-century Trent.

The polemic quality of the standard Catholic interpretation of tradition meant that it was scarcely open to ascribing legitimacy to change or innovation in the life of the church. In fact, until Vatican II, Catholics generally understood that tradition functioned as "a heavy gold rock. It is a weighty object mined in the past that is passed unchanged from one generation to the next."[54] The centrality of the church's bishops as the primary defenders of this orthodoxy perpetuated ecclesiologies that reinforced the hierarchology discussed in earlier chapters. In this environment, the invocation of "tradition" conveyed the end of every argument, even when, as Congar notes, this practice could smother "the most urgent pastoral adaptations."[55] It likewise eliminated, as mentioned in the previous section of the chapter, any need to take account of the faith of the whole church rather than simply that of the bishops—a deficit that affected Catholic understandings of "reception," as the following chapter will detail.

Nineteenth-Century Theologies of Tradition

While Vatican II is pivotal for the reassessment of tradition, stirrings toward a more comprehensive understanding of the concept had begun in the nineteenth century. Johann Sebastian Drey (1777–1853) and

---

53. Ibid.

54. Terrence Tilley, *Inventing Catholic Tradition* (Maryknoll, NY: Orbis, 2000), 25. For a review of the theological history of "tradition" between Trent and Vatican II, see O'Collins, *Tradition*, 1–19.

55. Congar, *True and False Reform in the Church*, 38.

Johann Adam Möhler (1796–1838), both of whom were theologians at the University of Tübingen, were the first to explore faithfulness in the church in relation to the potential for creativity, not simply preservation. The writings of "the Tübingen school" were influential on the person who continues to be important for the church's thinking about tradition: John Henry Newman.[56]

Drey made the case for "the spirit of Christianity" that supported developments in the church's faith while excluding "any modification contrary to this spirit as *de facto innovation* (the invasion of what is foreign and not originally posited in the spirit of Christianity)."[57] In terms reminiscent of the focus on "memory" in this chapter's discussion of apostolicity, Drey stressed that this "spirit" was not a theory, a set of objective facts, or the personal possession of individuals in the church, but what "is always present in the community, in the church."[58] Drey contended that the "mutually explanatory" relationship between the doctrine that the Christian community professed and its ethics and worship held the key to determining authentic expressions of the church's faith as it engaged in the world.[59] The living faith of the living church, then, was no less important than formulations of that faith in the past.

Möhler similarly identified "tradition," which he classified as "the living word, perpetuated in the hearts of believers," with the life of faith.[60] The link between God's revelation and the community of faith in history suggested that the church's doctrine could appear "in a much al-

---

56. For details of the Tübingen school, see James Livingston, *Modern Christian Thought: The Enlightenment and the Nineteenth Century*, vol. 1, 2nd ed. (Minneapolis: Fortress, 2006), 185–98, and Donald Dietrich and Michael Himes, eds., *The Legacy of the Tübingen School: The Relevance of Nineteenth-Century Theology for the Twenty-First Century* (New York: Crossroad, 1997).

57. Johann Sebastian Drey, *Brief Introduction to the Study of Theology*, trans. M. Himes (1819; repr., Notre Dame, IN: University of Notre Dame Press, 1994), 90; original emphasis.

58. Ibid.

59. Ibid.

60. Johann Adam Möhler, *Symbolism: Exposition of the Doctrinal Differences between Catholics and Protestants as Evidenced by Their Symbolical Writings*, trans. J. Robertson (1832; repr., New York: Crossroad, 1997), 278.

tered form" through history while remaining "the same in substance."[61] Changes, then, did not necessarily undermine doctrine, but could even make the doctrine more clear. Since "free-will and grace" worked together, since "the one and the same undivided deed is at once divine and human," changes were not tantamount to human beings rejecting revelation.[62] Faithfulness, as a result, was reconcilable with the legitimacy of change in what the ecclesial community in particular times and places had inherited.

A guiding principle of Newman's theology of tradition was that the church is always "in its substance the very religion which Christ and His Apostles taught in the first (century), whatever may be the modifications for good or for evil, which lapse of years, or the vicissitudes of human affairs, have impressed upon it."[63] Newman acknowledged freely the church's history of change, but also asserted vigorously that the church in his time remained what it had been from its beginnings: the church of Jesus and the apostles. As an Anglican and later as a Roman Catholic, the two phases of Newman's life that encompass the first edition of his landmark *An Essay on the Development of Christian Doctrine* in 1845 and its definitive third edition in 1878, respectively, Newman defended the continuing apostolicity of a changing church.

Newman recognized that the ecclesial community in the mid-nineteenth century, as well as that of the many intervening eras from Pentecost onward, was not a facsimile of the church as it had been in the first century. In light of the undeniable differences, Newman developed a theology that argued for the maintenance of the church's identity through the changes of history. This enduring identity was far more than the merely formal continuity of a body that lacked any substantive connection to the church as it was during the apostolic era. Consequently, Newman differentiated the church from an object that continued to bear the title "knife" even as it acquired over time new handles and new blades that bore no relationship to its original parts. [64]

61. Ibid., 289.
62. Ibid., 290.
63. Newman, *An Essay on the Development of Christian Doctrine*, 5.
64. Ibid., 6.

Central to Newman's thesis was an extended analogy between the church and all living organisms that grow over time. For an organism, Newman stressed, its beginnings are not the sum total of its possibilities. These possibilities can develop through changes in history, changes that can be consistent with their source even when "appearances" suggest otherwise: "A representation which varies from its original may be felt as more true and faithful than one which has more pretensions to be exact."[65] This line of argument issued in one of Newman's most famous aphorisms: "In a higher world it is otherwise, but here below to live is to change, and to be perfect is to have changed often."[66]

In portraying Christianity as a "universal religion," Newman contended that since it was "suited not simply to one locality or period, but to all times and places, it cannot but vary in its relations and dealings towards the world around it, that is it will develop."[67] Newman's aim was to show that the church could change, not through natural evolution but through human decisions made on the basis of engagement with history, yet remain the church of Christ. For Newman, the application to the Catholic Church of his convictions about change and continuity had a decidedly apologetic purpose: to provide "an explanation of so many of the reputed corruptions, doctrinal and practical, of Rome, as might serve as a fair ground for trusting her in parallel cases where the investigation had not been pursued."[68] In other words, Newman sought to demonstrate that a history of change in the Catholic Church was compatible with a history of faithfulness.

"Tradition" in the Twentieth Century: Blondel, Congar, and Vatican II

Earlier in this chapter there was a reference to Maurice Blondel's linking of the church's past, present, and future. Blondel also offered a formula for bringing together the elements that established the church's faith: "When it is a question of finding the supernatural in Sacred History and in dogma, the Gospel is nothing without the Church, the

---

65. Ibid., 176.
66. Ibid., 40.
67. Ibid., 58.
68. Ibid., 32.

teaching of Scripture is nothing without the Christian life, exegesis is nothing without Tradition—the Catholic Tradition which is now seen to be not a limitative and retrograde force, but a power of development and expansion."[69] Blondel's understanding of tradition provides a perspective on all the elements that could contribute to the church's effort to conform its life to the movement of grace through history.

The inclusion of "the Christian life" among the factors that Blondel nominated as aiding the church's discernment of the truth of Christianity gave voice to his conviction that "what Jesus desired and obtained was not to be elucidated like a theological theme, but loved above all things."[70] Those who loved Jesus and sought to live as his disciples could witness to the truth that depended radically on "the practical obedience of love."[71] For this reason, Blondel contended, the health of Christian faith required more than the repetition of doctrines: it required a community of active disciples "nourished by the sources of the moral life and by the suggestions of the invisible Spirit present in every age and in every civilization."[72]

The writings of Drey, Möhler, Newman, and Blondel prioritized the church's living faith in Jesus Christ as the heart of the Christian tradition. Blondel framed this priority by stressing that "one goes from faith to dogma, rather than from dogma to faith."[73] This sequence helps to establish that the community of faith, from which dogma arises, is the proper home of tradition, which does not have an existence independent of believers. The insights of Drey, Möhler, Newman, and Blondel offered the church a way to think about its existence in history, specifically about how change could be a vehicle for faithfulness. What the four theologians shared was not a calculus for the exact determination of what could be a legitimate development in the church, but attention to the lived faith of the church as the indispensable source of insight into what was or was not reconcilable with the faith of the apostles.

69. Blondel, *History and Dogma*, 275–76.
70. Ibid., 246.
71. Ibid., 274.
72. Ibid., 275.
73. Ibid., 279.

On the eve of Vatican II, Yves Congar, who would be influential on the council's own interpretation of tradition, published both a major historical review and a theological analysis of the Catholic understanding of tradition.[74] Congar identified tradition "as a principle that ensures the continuity and development of the same attitude through successive generations . . . it enables them to remain the same human race and the same people as they go forward throughout history, which transforms all things."[75] In ways that echo Blondel, Congar associated tradition not simply with doctrine, but with "a whole communication" that encompassed sacraments, ecclesiastical institutions, powers of ministry, customs, and liturgical rites.[76] Consistent with this perspective, Congar paralleled the communication of tradition to raising a child: an undertaking that owes more to "immersion in an environment" than to "explicit instruction."[77]

As is the case throughout his theology, Congar's understanding of tradition highlights the role of the Holy Spirit in guiding the church to an ever-deeper relationship with Christ. The Spirit, as the "transcendent subject of tradition," animates the Christian community "to announce Jesus Christ, not only as a historical event, but as the meaning of the present, each day, today and tomorrow until the end of time."[78] Significantly, Congar stressed that faithfulness to Christ was the work of the entire community of the baptized, of all those who sought to live by the

74. The French version of Congar's historical study appeared in 1960 and the theological study in 1963; the two appeared together in a single English-language volume in 1966 as *Tradition and Traditions*. In 1964, a condensed version of the two studies appeared in English as *The Meaning of Tradition*. For the background to Congar's development as a theologian, see Gabriel Flynn, "*Ressourcement,* Ecumenism, and Pneumatology: The Contribution of Yves Congar to *Nouvelle Théologie,*" in *Ressourcement: A Movement for Renewal in Twentieth-Century Catholic Theology*, ed. Gabriel Flynn and Paul Murray (Oxford: Oxford University Press, 2012), 219–35.

75. Yves Congar, *The Meaning of Tradition*, trans. A. Woodrow (San Francisco: Ignatius Press, 2004), 2.

76. Ibid., 13.

77. Ibid., 22. For a later analysis of the role that absorption in a community plays in communicating and deepening the tradition of faith, see Avery Dulles, "Tradition and Creativity: A Theological Approach," in *The Quadrilog: Tradition and the Future of Ecumenism*, ed. Kenneth Hagen (Collegeville, MN: Michael Glazier, 1994), 312–27.

78. Congar, *Meaning of Tradition*, 52.

church's apostolic faith: "Tradition is living because it resides in minds that live by it, in a history that comprises activity, problems, doubts, opposition, new contributions and questions that need answers."[79] In furthering the church's faithfulness, there was a definite role for bishops, but Congar also asserted that "it is the Christian parents, much more than priests and preachers, who really transmit the faith."[80]

Congar's insistence that all the members of the church could play a role in preserving the church's unity in faith and witness reflected his conviction that "tradition is not disjunctive; it is unity and harmony."[81] This principle of integration guided Congar's approach to the divisive topic of the relationship between Scripture and tradition. Congar was unequivocal that "Scripture is always the supreme rule and is never submitted to any other objective rule," but recognized the Spirit as enabling the church to draw from Scripture what deepened its life of faith.[82] As if to underline the differences between his presentation and the post-Reformation controversies, Congar emphasized that "there is not a single point of belief that the Church holds by tradition alone, without any reference to Scripture; just as there is not a single dogma that is derived from Scripture alone, without being explained by tradition."[83]

Congar was equally clear that not only must the church respond to the emergence in history of new questions and new challenges, but that the Spirit working through both Scripture and tradition together could enable the church to do so. Again finding inspiration in Blondel, Congar emphasized the capacity of the community of faith to recognize an "analogy of faith" between what the community received from the past and its determination of authentic faith in the present, "such that new statements, not made explicitly in the documents of revelation, appear possible and even necessary."[84]

The theology of tradition that Congar produced is a strong alternative to narrow understandings that limited tradition to a body of

79. Ibid., 77–78.
80. Ibid., 72–73.
81. Ibid., 98.
82. Ibid., 100.
83. Ibid., 39–40.
84. Ibid., 120.

past knowledge that the magisterium, the church's teaching authority, had defined and then protected zealously. In place of this truncated interpretation, Congar contends that, like "the church's awareness," tradition "cannot be limited to what has been expressed by certain people in the past."[85] Rather than being a one-dimensional object, tradition for Congar resembles the church's liturgy in being "the action of a subject who loves, prays, meditates, and, in so doing, progressively reaches a deeper understanding of what it holds and practices each day."[86] Congar's portrayal of tradition showcases it as a process— "traditioning"—not simply a fixed body of content. As such, the fullest possible understanding of tradition requires a theology of reception, a theme that, as indicated already, chapter 6 will develop at some length.

The insights of the theologians profiled above moved from the margins of the church's life to its center as a result of their influence, both direct and indirect, on Vatican II's understanding of revelation. Before detailing the council's approach to tradition in *Dei Verbum*, it is important to acknowledge that Vatican II's text coincided with a document on the same theme from the World Council of Churches.[87] Together, the two texts provided a foundation for the ecumenical convergence that bridged the divisions over "Scripture or tradition" that had become fossilized in the sixteenth century.

The document from the World Council of Churches presents tradition as passing on "the Christian faith, not only as a sum of tenets, but as a living reality transmitted through the operation of the Holy Spirit."[88] In a way that aligns with the ongoing work of tilling the church, this document stresses that the living tradition, if it is to find a home in the full panoply of cultures in which the church is present, challenges the church to unity that is more than sameness, a unity that is properly catholic.[89] This means that the church must constantly be attentive to proclaiming its faith in a living way, even though the

85. Ibid., 154.
86. Ibid., 139.
87. The document from the World Council of Churches is "Scripture, Tradition, and Traditions," in *Documentary History of Faith and Order: 1963–1993*, ed. Günther Gassmann (1963; repr., Geneva: WCC Publications, 1993), 10–18.
88. Ibid., 46.
89. Ibid., 69–72.

particularities of each new context make it inevitable that doing so will not repeat the past in every detail.

Vatican II's declaration that Scripture and tradition "make up a single sacred deposit of the word of God, which is entrusted to the church" (DV 10) was a major step toward reconciling the post-Reformation divisions. In the context of this chapter's consideration of how the church can be both faithful to what it has received from the past and open to new possibilities, the council's invocation of the Holy Spirit is particularly relevant. *Dei Verbum* connects the Spirit to a spectrum of activities that includes the formation of the Bible, the "growth in insight into the realities and words that are being passed on" (DV 8), the communication of the "living voice of the Gospel" (DV 10) in the church and the world, the faithful transmission of the truth of the Scriptures, and responsiveness to those same Scriptures.

The bishops at Vatican II also highlighted the connection between tradition and the Christian community's faith. In this vein, *Dei Verbum* taught that "what was handed on by the apostles comprises everything that serves to make the people of God live their lives in holiness and increase their faith" (DV 8).[90] In the council's presentation, this "everything" certainly has a central place for doctrine, but also for the "life and worship" of the ecclesial community; in fact, "everything" embraces "all that [the church] itself is, all that it believes" (DV 8). The council's formulation underlined the dynamism of the church's faith rather than presenting it as an inert object that doctrine preserved in an univocal manner.

Vatican II's presentation of tradition in the light of revelation helped to stimulate a rethinking of the relationship between the church's bishops and the wider community of the baptized. Without diminishing the responsibility of bishops for the church's unity in faith, the council acknowledged the "unique interplay between the bishops and the faithful" that is necessary for "maintaining, practicing and professing the faith

---

90. For a detailed analysis of Vatican II's understanding of "tradition," including in relation to Scripture, see Ormond Rush, *The Vision of Vatican II: Its Fundamental Principles* (Collegeville, MN: Liturgical Press, 2019), 141–64; see also Avery Dulles, "Vatican II and the Recovery of Tradition," in *The Reshaping of Catholicism: Current Challenges in the Theology of Church* (New York: Harper and Row, 1988), 75–92.

that has been handed on" (DV 10). In so doing, *Dei Verbum* reflected *Lumen Gentium*'s view of the church as a believing community, one in which all members, because they share the gift of the Holy Spirit, share a common faith and a common responsibility for the authentic passing on of that faith. The final chapter of this book, as it addresses the church's discernment and the ongoing reception of the apostolic faith, will take up the implications for the possibility of change that flow from the fact that the graced dynamism of the church defies any classification of the ecclesial community into an active episcopate and a passive laity.

Janet Soskice offers a helpful image to summarize the conclusions that emerge from the historical survey in this section, including the teaching of Vatican II. Soskice claims that "to stand in a tradition is not to stand still but to stand in the deep, loamy soil that feeds further growth."[91] The recognition that tradition can be the source of potential for "further growth" affirms that the church's foundations, which this book has repeatedly identified with Christ and the Spirit, can be the catalysts of change. Authentic change is neither a rejection of those foundations nor damaging to them, but expressive of their generativity.

In framing the church paradoxically as "bounded openness," Serene Jones captures succinctly the unique identity of the ecclesial community in history.[92] As the work of grace that spans history, the ecclesial community is not free to remake itself on the basis of something other than God and the apostolic faith, but the same grace is the source of the church's freedom to change, to grow into all that grace enables. Through affirming its dependence on Christ and the Spirit at work through the history of the church, the community of faith at each moment in time "experiences itself as a gift . . . it understands itself as inhabited *by* the story."[93] The "story," which is that of God's life-giving love, began in the past, continues today, and will have its denouement

91. Janet Soskice, "Tradition," in *Tradition and Modernity: Christian and Muslim Perspectives*, ed. David Marshall (Washington, DC: Georgetown University Press, 2013), 29.

92. Serene Jones, *Feminist Theory and Christian Theology: Cartographies of Grace* (Minneapolis: Fortress, 2000), 170.

93. Ibid., 158; original emphasis.

in the eschatological future. Along the way, the story "grasps the church by pulling it into its drama and remaking it in its own image."[94]

This "remaking" requires the engagement of the entire ecclesial community, which can apply its Spirit-generated capacity for creativity to the particular circumstances of its moment in history. This community can do so in ways that are compatible with the faithful embodiment of the church's enduring apostolicity, whose orientation is to the ever-new future of God. The grace that tills the church, that promotes conversion and ever-deeper faithfulness, makes possible the creativity that expands rather than diminishes the legacy that today's ecclesial community has received from its forebears. In this depiction, "change" is not opposed to reception of the past, but can be an instrument to convert elements of the past that could obstruct both the church's transparency to grace in the present and the authenticity of its pilgrimage to the future.

The magnitude of the challenge inherent in attaining a faith-formed perspective on history is evident in the two facets of the church's tradition that must be held together, even if in tension with each other. On the one hand, as Yves Congar argues, "What has been thus unanimously 'traditional' for fifteen centuries and is derived manifestly, not only from the apostles but from the Lord himself, cannot cease to be traditional today."[95] On the other hand, it is crucial to establish that what claims a grounding in tradition is in fact consistent with what comes "not only from the apostles but from the Lord himself." The church, in short, cannot preserve as authentic to the living tradition of faith anything that contradicts the gospel.

Feminist theologians in particular have played a major role in identifying areas of ecclesial practice where what is "traditional" is not consistent with the church's proclamation of, for example, the equality of the baptized.[96] Most recently, Black theologians in the United States have confronted the wider ecclesial community with the racism that

---

94. Ibid., 158.

95. Congar, *Meaning of Tradition*, 89.

96. For an overview of the history of women in the Catholic Church, see Mary Doak, *A Prophetic Public Church: Witness to Hope Amid the Global Crises of the 21st Century* (Collegeville, MN: Liturgical Press, 2020), 75–115; see also Elisabeth Schüssler Fiorenza, *In Memory of Her: A Feminist Theological Reconstruction of Christian Origins* (New York: Crossroad, 1983), 42.

was also "traditional," even as it distorted the relationship between the gospel and the church. Shawn Copeland makes this point strongly when she points out that "accommodation to anti-Black logics not only contested Catholic social teaching regarding the *imago dei* . . . not only defied the intention and effect of Baptism, but interrupted the power of Eucharist to collapse barriers of space and relation."[97] In each instance, the status of the prevailing norms of faith and practice is acutely problematic, as is their claim to the endorsement of "tradition."

The recognition that no expression of the church's inherited faith and practice can be sacrosanct if it is a danger to the gospel requires a commitment to redress past distortions. This commitment suggests that an authentic reception of tradition may well be discontinuous with the immediate past. Such a discontinuity, far from being vandalism against all that the tradition properly represents, is for the sake of ensuring the future of the tradition and of faithfulness to grace:

> A reception model of reform highlights the creative involvement with God on the part of the receivers of the revelation, that is, the creative involvement of human beings in the decisions of history and in the creative interpretation of "what God would want" the church of the future to be. [The] human receivers of revelation are to be portrayed as active participants in discerning the way forward, co-deciders with God's Spirit, assuring continuity through creative discontinuity. . . . What has been given as the ultimate criterion, the *regula fidei*, is the life, death, and resurrection of Jesus, which must be received over and over in the power of that Spirit who "will guide you into all truth" (Jn 16:13).[98]

To reflect accurately the complexity inseparable from the church's existence in history, ecclesiologists, along with each member and every community in the church, must resist one-dimensional interpretations

---

97. M. Shawn Copeland, "White Supremacy and Anti-Black Logics in the Making of U.S. Catholicism," in *Anti-Blackness and Christian Ethics*, ed. Vincent Lloyd and Andrew Prevot (Maryknoll, NY: Orbis, 2017), 74.

98. Ormond Rush, *Still Interpreting Vatican II: Some Hermeneutical Principles* (Mahwah, NJ: Paulist, 2004), 76.

of the church's history, be they either laudatory or condemnatory. The key to meeting this requirement is the maintenance of receptivity to the Spirit's voice speaking through Scripture, the liturgy, and the church's history of faith embodied in the lives of holy women and men, as well as through present-day realities. Those latter realities can include the questions through which members of the community of faith interrogate what has been settled practice. The impact of the questions can be disturbing, but just as the history of the church's faith is far from being "merely a beautiful and undisturbed 'unfolding' of the original substance of faith," so the pilgrimage of the contemporary church will differ from a gentle stroll on a well-sealed and sheltered path through pleasant—but not too exciting—countryside.[99]

The pilgrimage to a more faithful, equitable, and inclusive ecclesial community, one that reflects more deeply and transparently the grace that gives it life, requires neither the wholesale rejection of tradition nor the refusal to engage with emerging needs and questions. What it does require is Spirit-filled creativity, which the living tradition of apostolic faith can engender: "Whether we are reflecting on Scripture or some other aspect of the Christian tradition, we are not simply working with texts or analyzing practices, but are being invited into living fellowship with God through the presence of the Holy Spirit in these texts and practices. Spiritual life is thus clearly seen as the root of theology, in all its forms."[100] The *ressourcement* and *aggiornamento* of the Second Vatican Council model this graced possibility.

To engage the world that faced the prospect of nuclear annihilation and to end centuries of division in the one Christian Church, the council sought to revive in the church the dynamism of God's self-gift in Jesus Christ and the Holy Spirit, which was the basis of the ecclesial community's faithfulness from the time of the first Pentecost. Vatican II did so aware that the church of the twenty-first century would need to differ dramatically from the one that bore so deeply the imprint of

99. Karl Rahner, "Yesterday's History of Dogma and Theology for Tomorrow," in *Theological Investigations*, vol. 18, trans. E. Quinn (New York: Crossroad, 1983), 9.

100. Clare Watkins, "Texts and Practices: An Ecclesiology of *traditio* for Pastoral Theology," in *Keeping Faith in Practice: Aspects of Catholic Pastoral Theology*, ed. James Sweeney, Gemma Simmonds, and David Lonsdale (London: SCM, 2010), 172.

the Reformation and reaction against social changes that the French Revolution initiated, even though the diverse effects of those two events continued to mark the Catholic Church into the twentieth century. Addressing that challenge required the bishops to explore how the church might best order its own life, including its worship and the relationships within the ecclesial community, to serve its mission in the emerging world.

Vatican II, of course, is not the end of the story. The reception of the council has taken place in a world that has continued to change at a pace that the bishops at the council could never have anticipated. This fact highlights the ineradicable complexity of the church's existence in history. Nor could the bishops have envisaged all that has occurred in the Catholic Church itself, and in the church's engagement with the world, in the wake of Vatican II.[101] Yet, it is this very unpredictability that is characteristic of the life of a pilgrim. What remains for this book is to consider how the ecclesial community can best give expression to its ongoing, graced pilgrimage of faith amid the oft-dramatic exigencies of the twenty-first century.

101. For an analysis of the influence that the context of the council's reception has exerted on the shape of the church since Vatican II, see Gerald Arbuckle, *Catholic Identity or Identities?: Refounding Ministries in Chaotic Times* (Collegeville, MN: Liturgical Press, 2013), 31–67.

6

The Art of Faithfulness

Art engages with life's breadth and depth. As "a product of that human transcendentality by which, as spiritual and free beings, we strive for the totality of all reality," art gives imaginative expression to what eludes humanity's definitive grasp.[1] Through creativity in music and literature, as well as human movement and various visual media, artists resist resignation to the seeming randomness of the events that punctuate history. The work of artists embodies quintessentially human qualities that include an appreciation of beauty and a sensitivity to suffering. Art also reflects humanity's quest for hope amid all that enchants, baffles, and at times overwhelms everyday life. Whether striving to express joy or protesting against injustice, artists testify to the human project of meaning-making that arises in the present but looks to the future. Interpreted theologically, these characteristics of art identify it as a graced expression of transcendence, and so as a response to humanity's encounter with the mystery of God.[2]

1. Karl Rahner, "Art Against the Horizon of Theology and Piety," in *Theological Investigations*, vol. 23, trans. J. Donceel and H. Riley (New York: Crossroad, 1992), 165.
2. David Tracy argues that if art rejects transcendence, it can become "ersatz religion"; see David Tracy, "A Correlational Model of Practical Theology Revisited," in

F. Scott Fitzgerald depicts the art of the novelist in terms indicative of humanity's capacity for transcendence. Fitzgerald identifies the motive for writing as the effort to gain perspective on experiences that are "so great and moving that it doesn't seem at the time that anyone else has been so caught up and so pounded and dazzled and astonished and beaten and broken and rescued and illuminated and rewarded and humbled in just that way ever before."[3] Since these experiences exceed the existing instruments of meaning-making, they call for a response that is creative enough to match the magnitude of the stimulus. The novelist writes not to reduce what has occurred to something more manageable, but in the hope of gaining insight into extraordinary experiences by sharing them and their effects with readers.

The grappling with experience that Fitzgerald describes contrasts with efforts to "solve" life's complexity, whether through privileging the quantifiable above all else or, more radically, seeking to corral the uncontrollable within the limits of a single worldview. Rather than remove from life all that is unwieldy, art, as David Tracy contends, "encounters me with the surprise, impact, even the shock of reality itself. In experiencing art, I recognize a truth I somehow know but I know that I did not really know except through the recognition of the essential compelled by the work of art."[4] In this way, art challenges the temptation to domesticate or conceal those aspects of life that remain stubbornly resistant to neatness and the familiar.

Nor is art itself one-dimensional. Within any genre of art there are shared elements—all writers, for instance, use words—but each genre is also home to what can seem to be an infinite variety of styles—Charlotte Brontë, Toni Morrison, and F. Scott Fitzgerald himself, are all cherished writers but their works are not interchangeable. This diversity reflects the talent and imagination unique to each artist, but also the individual backgrounds of artists, and the cultural and historical settings that form the context for their artistic undertakings.

Invitation to Practical Theology: Catholic Voices and Visions, ed. Claire Wolfteich (Mahwah, NJ: Paulist, 2014), 84.

3. F. Scott Fitzgerald quoted in *The Short Stories of F. Scott Fitzgerald: A New Collection*, ed. Matthew Bruccoli (New York: Simon and Schuster, 1995), 13.

4. David Tracy, *The Analogical Imagination: Christian Theology and the Culture of Pluralism* (London: SCM, 1981), 111–12.

Art has flourished in hostile environments, but freedom is significant for the flowering of the human imagination. Mandates directing artists to conform to an officially sanctioned ideology usually result in uninspiring products that give little evidence of the beauty revelatory of the human capacity for transcendence.[5] Equally, an assembly line approach to manufacturing art is unlikely to result in stirring works.

Creativity in art owes much to the "stuff" of art itself: the words, music, and other "ingredients" proper to the manifold forms of art are malleable rather than fixed, so they invite and enable imaginative engagement. The meeting of human imagination, historical circumstances, and the raw materials at the disposal of artists does not result in mere repetition of what already exists. As the history of multiple forms of art attests, the whole artistic endeavor is an area rich with possibilities for innovation.

As crucial as is the link between art and creativity, not all innovations find ready acceptance into the artistic canon. The rejection of certain offerings reflects the judgment that a particular work is simply not art. This judgment can be a response to "the shock of the new," the unease that is a common reaction to a confrontation with unorthodox styles and objects, ones that do not tally with the prevailing norms.[6] At a deeper level, denying legitimacy to certain approaches gives voice to the conviction that art has boundaries, boundaries that permit no transgressions. This assessment aligns with the way in which the application of "God-given" to an element of the church's life often identifies it as beyond the possibility of change.

Boundaries can be a mixed blessing. For artists, there is always a danger that the space inside the lines is too narrow or constrained to be compatible with the freedom to experiment that feeds the liveliness of

---

5. Proof for this claim abounds in the variety of art produced at the direction of both fascist and communist dictators in the twentieth century; see, for example, Michael Kater, *The Twisted Muse: Musicians and Their Music in the Third Reich* (New York: Oxford University Press, 1997), and Igor Golomstock, *Totalitarian Art in the Soviet Union, the Third Reich, Fascist Italy and the People's Republic of China* (New York: Icon, 1990).

6. The Australian art critic Robert Hughes uses this term as part of his description of the reception, and non-reception, of modern art; see his *The Shock of the New: The Hundred-Year History of Modern Art—Its Rise, Its Dazzling Achievements, Its Fall*, rev. ed. (New York: Knopf, 1991).

art. This rigidity implies that the best of all art resides in past achievements rather than in possible futures. More fruitful are those boundaries
that are flexible enough to support rather than inhibit creativity. Such
borders are sympathetic to the history of art as a history of variety and
change. Boundaries that help to distinguish good art from its pretenders
embody the wisdom from the past, while being able to accommodate
the present and future. This wisdom is other than the product of either
laws or actuarial calculations: it is the inheritance of an affinity with art,
an affinity that expresses the same imagination and insight at work in
the creation of art.

This chapter applies an appreciation of artistry to the life of the
pilgrim church, especially to its decision-making in matters of faith
and practice. In so doing, this chapter builds on chapter 5's argument
that the Spirit-formed capacity of the church's inherited faith fuels the
eschatological orientation of the ecclesial community. Viewed through
this lens, even "God-given" is not an absolute barrier to movement.
The present chapter explores a particular task that the pilgrim church
confronts regularly: the need to determine the right relationship between the old and the new, the relationship that does justice to both
preservation and innovation by enabling faithful continuity in the
midst of change.

The thesis of this chapter is that the faithfulness of the church, especially in decisions about change, is more a matter of graced creativity
than of adherence to precedent, obedience to authority, or submission
to "popular opinion" within the ecclesial community. At the same time,
faithful artistry in the church differs from a disregard of precedent,
disdain for authority, or rejection of the graced experiences and insights
of members of the church, for which "popular opinion"—or, more accurately, as a later section of the chapter will discuss, *sensus fidei*—can act
as a synonym. This paradox illuminates ecclesial artistry as a response
to the Holy Spirit, who as "life, movement, color, radiance, restorative
stillness in the din" initiates and supports creativity in the church.[7]

7. Elizabeth Johnson, *She Who Is: The Mystery of God in Feminist Theological
Discourse* (New York: Crossroad, 1993), 129.

Tilling as Art

The analogy to art highlights that appropriate tilling of the church differs from the application of a theoretical construct drawn from general principles, including theological ones. Still, the focus on artistry does not negate the important role of theological reflection in the church. Without this reflection, the embrace or rejection of change could only ever be a spontaneous affection, one likely to go in either direction on any given day. By illuminating the relationship between revelation, the dynamics of grace in history, and the possibilities for the authentic transmission of faith, theology contributes to the ecclesial community's determination of how to receive the tradition faithfully, respond to present needs, and support the church's orientation to the future.

If theology cannot prescribe the most appropriate way for the community to respond to a particular challenge, it can clarify a framework for such decisions. The framework that this chapter will present is duly attentive to the church's living tradition of faith, but also to its ongoing need for conversion and its engagement with the graced world. Those elements are a dimension of the unfinished reality of the church, which includes, too, the complex and fluid relationships within the one community of faith, a community whose authenticity is inseparable from remaining open to the fulfillment of God's reign.

Theology can also indicate the criteria that have guided authentic change throughout Christian history. These criteria are not exotic or obscure, but constellate around service to the church's mission and communion, both of which are necessary for the ecclesial community's faithfulness in its relationship to God. Theology and the church's history affirm the legitimacy of change as at least a possibility for the church, the difficulties and anxieties that accompany specific changes notwithstanding. Acknowledgment of this possibility is unlikely to eliminate future arm wrestling over individual proposals for changes, but does suggest that the willingness to grapple with those proposals can itself be an expression of faith in the Holy Spirit's presence to the church.

Without a formula for change that is able to guarantee the rightness of its conclusions, change is inevitably an ill-defined process in the life of ecclesial communities. The life of the ecclesial community, then, is not a series of seamless transitions from one well-ordered state to another. Indeed, the church's history would confirm Ladislas Orsy's opinion that "change has always caused problems in the Church; it still does."[8] Orsy's sobering appraisal, especially its use of "always," makes plain that problems associated with determining the faithfulness of the church are not unique either to any particular period of ecclesiastical history or to any single aspect of ecclesial life. Faithful change, in short, is messy.

Authentic change in the church, consistent with all that "tilling" suggests, preserves rather than fractures the continuity of the church's faith, addresses present deficits in the realization of the church's mission and communion, and maintains the church's orientation to God's ever-new future. The many strands of that task suffice to endorse Karl Rahner's view that maintaining continuity and identity amid change in the church, far from being a matter of calculation, is "an object of believing hope and of that faithfulness which dares to commit itself on the basis of hope."[9] In light of the magnitude of the challenge, it is scarcely surprising that the Christian community experiences a major measure of angst as it makes choices, especially when it is impossible to anticipate every consequence of all decisions.

The lack of precision in matters touching on faithful change in the church reflects the complexity endemic to human interactions with the grace of the Holy Spirit. It reflects, too, the particularity of the historical settings in which the ecclesial community makes its decisions about change. Assessed positively, the lack of precision is less a matter of regret than yet another witness to the freedom that grace confers on the church. The forms of tilling that aid the mission of the church express this graced freedom in ways that have an affinity with all that gives the church its specificity.

The affinity with art that empowers judgments about "good" and "poor" art, no less than the affinity with all that gives the church its specificity, resonates with John Henry Newman's argument for the "il-

---

8. Ladislas Orsy, *The Evolving Church and the Sacrament of Penance* (Denville, NJ: Dimension Books, 1978), 12.

9. Karl Rahner, "Basic Observations on the Subject of the Changeable and Unchangeable Factors in the Church," in *Theological Investigations*, vol. 14, trans. D. Bourke (New York: Seabury, 1976), 7.

lative sense." As Newman explains it, the illative sense enables human beings to have "certitude" about their beliefs. He emphasizes that certitude "is not a passive impression made upon the mind from without, by argumentative compulsion, but in all concrete questions it is an active recognition of propositions as true." [10] Certitude, then, involves the knower, not simply what is known; it is personal without being idiosyncratic.

The illative sense involves a being-at-one-with the particular theme that is the subject of belief. Newman proposes that it is possible for people to be certain about their judgments and the accuracy of their conclusions on the basis of "a sort of instinct or inspiration, not an obedience to external rules of criticism or of science." [11] This instinct takes arguments into account, but is more than the conclusion of a logical process: it "determines what science cannot determine, the limits of converging probabilities and the reasons sufficient for a proof." [12] Consistent with being a human reality, the instinct itself is not static but develops over a lifetime of practice.

The being-at-one-with that is critical for the illative sense applies, Newman suggests, to expertise in enterprises as diverse as ship-building, gymnastics, and singing. [13] It applies, too, to matters of faith. In relation to faith in God, the trustworthiness of the illative sense does not derive from philosophical or theological expertise, but from "due devotion" to God. [14] The latter refines decision-making through the discipline of a life attentive to the movement of grace. Certainty, then, is the product of faith as much as it is a measure of faith. As such, the certainty of faith requires an ongoing conversion to grace, a theme that has been a major emphasis of this volume. This requirement distinguishes faith from self-assertion and from efforts to conform God to the convictions of individuals and groups.

10. John Henry Newman, *An Essay in Aid of a Grammar of Assent* (1870; repr., Notre Dame, IN: University of Notre Dame Press, 1979), 271.

11. Ibid., 280.

12. Ibid., 282.

13. Ibid., 280.

14. Ibid., 276.

Since the trustworthiness of artistic decisions depends on intimacy with the subject matter, it is unsurprising that the God of the biblical narrative exhibits to a high degree the artistic creativity that is innovative and even "rule breaking." In providing guides for Israel, for example, God eschews the obvious candidates, but chooses, in Moses (Exod 4:10-11), Ruth (Ruth 1:15-17), David (1 Sam 16:1-13), Jeremiah (Jer 20:7-9), and Amos (Amos 7:14-15), an individual lacking a healthy measure of self-confidence, a foreigner with little social standing, the youngest sibling in a society where primogeniture was determinative of influence, someone reluctant to fulfill the designated role, and a person deficient in credentials that common sense would endorse as necessary, respectively.

Even more dramatically, the known facts of Jesus's background confirmed for his contemporaries that he was a most unlikely contender to be the bearer of God's word (Mark 6:3). The fact that Jesus seemed to lack any insight into the sort of people acceptable to God (Luke 7:36-50) and that his relationship to God's law, particularly to the keeping of the sabbath (Matt 12:1-8; Mark 2:23-28; Luke 6:1-11, 13:10-17, 14:1-6), was far from being in accord with contemporary norms, all suggested to the religious leaders of his day that Jesus was more renegade than prophet. God's choice of Mary Magdalene as first witness to the risen Christ (John 20:11-18) and God's call of Saul for the work of proclaiming the risen Christ (Acts 9:10-19) are no less contrary to general expectations about God's way of proceeding. Despite these concerns, God's choices furthered God's purposes, identifying God as the paradigmatic creative artist.

As the work of grace, the artistry of faithful living in the church can never be independent of the "due devotion" to God that Newman describes. It requires, too, "kinship" with all that gives the church its specificity, as well as an awareness of the concrete historical and social circumstances that affect the church's self-understanding, organization, and way of being in the world in specific times and places. Consistent with the incarnational tendency of grace, to which this book has referred often, responsiveness to the Spirit is inseparable from due attention to human activities. These activities, such as dialogue and discernment, will be the focus of the final section of the chapter.

The interweaving of grace and humanity at the heart of the church may generate forms of theology, practices in the ecclesial community, and ways of engaging the world that can be faithful to the tradition while being other than facsimiles of earlier forms. The fact that grace and humanity meet amid the particularities of each ecclesial community suggests that theology, practices, and forms of presence in the world might vary between local churches in different places. While this possibility will always raise concerns for the unity of the church, it reinforces that unity in a catholic church is distinguishable from the uniformity of corporations whose "head office" legislates for every subsidiary group.

Artistic creativity at the service of the church's faithfulness is not in competition with the stability that derives from the church's structures and the faith-forming decisions that earlier eras of ecclesiastical history have "traditioned." Yet, the creativity is distinct from repetition of the past, as the exploration of "reception" in the chapter's next section will show. Artistic creativity in decision-making about change gives priority to the church's continuing pilgrimage of faith. This pilgrimage brings together the past, present, and future of the unfinished project that is the one, holy, catholic, and apostolic ecclesial community that never outgrows its need for tilling.

The features of ecclesial life on which the chapter will concentrate—the reception of tradition, dialogue, discernment, the *sensus fidei* and *sensus fidelium*, and the exercise of authority—are all activities, rather than ontological characteristics. They are also communal activities, consistent with the existence of the church as a body of baptized believers. As expressions of the grace that forms the ecclesial community for its mission in the world, these activities are most faithful to their source when they promote the conversion of the church, its members as well as its structures. Engaging in these activities, then, is never less than an event that tills the ecclesial community, orienting it, and reorienting it when necessary, toward God's ever-new future.

One critical qualification about the scope of this chapter is necessary before launching an analysis of reception. The chapter does not aim to produce a "how-to" guide for faithful ecclesial change. As already indicated, the focus on artistry is incompatible with belief in a formula for decision-making that could operate seamlessly in every ecclesial community, regardless of circumstances. What the following pages do offer is an analysis of the ingredients that can facilitate faithful change in the church, ingredients that derive from the church's existence as a graced and human reality.

Clarity about ingredients is useful, but not an end in itself. As is evident in assembling bookcases, and a myriad of other large and small projects across multiple human undertakings, the possession of a list of ingredients is far from sufficient to ensure that such an endeavor reaches its goal by a method other than trial and error. Ingredients benefit greatly from directions for how to proceed to the desired outcome. Directions can guide the steps in the process, while minimizing uncertainty about results. There is undoubtedly a degree of artistry involved in putting together a stable bookcase, but instructions can streamline the task.

The argument here is that decision-making in the church, unlike assembling a bookcase from ready-made components that come in a box, does not have instructions for a step-by-step procedure to reach its goal. It is the artistry of faithful living that can combine grace, history, and the present-day circumstances of the ecclesial community into decisions and actions responsive to the impetus that God's yet-to-be-fulfilled reign provides.

As this book has maintained throughout, the life of the church does not reflect what would be possible for a community with a blueprint or the patterns of an orderly, predictable mechanism. In a programmable church, tilling might never be necessary, or could at least be a process with a set schedule and clear parameters that would render redundant the creativity and imagination emblematic of the church's existence as a graced community. Proposals for change in such a church could avoid the tensions they have usually aroused throughout the church's history. This order and predictability might reduce the uncertainty endemic to life within a complex world, and a complex church, but would be inconsistent with the church's reality as a pilgrim community that lives by faith and engages with the transcendent mystery of God in every time and place.

The focus on artistry, which is appropriate for the human reality of the church, underscores the need for members of the church to be Spirit-centered if they are to develop the affinity with grace that faithfulness requires. The absence of a comprehensive guide to the initiation and conduct of change does not condemn the church to dispirited inactivity or aimless striving. Nor does this absence leave divine intervention, which might miraculously illuminate a pathway for the interweaving of faithful continuity and faithful change, as the sole option for the ecclesial community. In fact, the ingredients that the chapter will identify all have their own, graced dynamism. The church does not possess a recipe for change or a manual to direct its tilling, but it does have resources through which the Holy Spirit is at work. These resources are adequate for developing responses to the circumstances prevailing at particular times and places. The responses, in turn, can embody the faithful appropriation of grace, the grace integral to both preservation and innovation in the life of the church.

The three remaining sections of this chapter will each explore elements that have a role in "the art of faithful change." The first of these is the reception of tradition. Reception is a paradoxical act, one that involves both faithfulness to the tradition and the creativity, evoked by the church's social and historical context, that distinguishes it from an identical reproduction of the past. The artistry inherent in such a combination brings into relief the intimate bond between reception and the presence of the Holy Spirit in the ecclesial community.

Receiving the Past for the Present and Future

The analysis of reception in this section will build on the principal themes of this volume, especially the implications of God's self-revelation in Jesus Christ and the Holy Spirit. This revelation brings the church into being as a community of faith and mission, a community that lives in history but looks for its fulfillment in God's future. The book has stressed that human beings, through their graced freedom, are active participants in the process of revelation. This participation encompasses the myriad activities that give shape to the faith of the ecclesial community. Since the church does not begin anew in each generation, the ecclesial community in every time and place receives from the generations that preceded it all that embodies the living tradition of faith.

Reception is the pivotal aspect of the church's historical existence: it takes place in the present, but connects the past to the future. Unless the present-day community of faith receives the tradition as life-giving, what comes from the past does not have a future. Yves Congar defines reception as "the process by means of which a church (body) truly takes over as its own a resolution that it did not originate in regard to its self, and acknowledges the measure it promulgates as a rule applicable to its own life."[15] In the life of the church, the process of "taking over as its own" applies not simply to "resolutions," a category that can include the church's professions of faith and the teaching of its authoritative offices, but also to other "spiritual goods"—such as liturgical forms, institutional structures, practices of justice and compassion, and techniques for evangelization—that the community of faith transmits through history.[16]

What comes from the past constitutes the raw material for reception, but reception is far from being the imposition of the past on the present. If "resolutions" and "spiritual goods" from the past come to play a role in the present, it is not because of commands from authorities or from deference to age. In fact, reception depends on "a degree of consent and possibly judgment as to whether what is being received serves the common good" of the particular community in which it is to find a home.[17] By definition, then, reception establishes that material from the past remains life-giving.

David Tracy, via his description of a "classic" in literature, offers a helpful way to situate the importance of both the past and present in the process of traditioning. In a framing that resonates with Rahner's theology of symbol that chapter 2 showcased, Tracy associates a classic text with "an excess of meaning," a formula indicative of the text's capacity to sustain more than a single way of reading it, and so to engage readers in more than one era of history.[18] This "excess" enables the text to transcend its particular moment in time, even as it also addresses its

15. Yves Congar, "Reception as an Ecclesiological Reality," in *Election and Consensus in the Church*, ed. Giuseppe Alberigo and Anton Weiler, *Concilium* 77 (New York: Herder and Herder, 1972), 45. See also International Theological Commission, *Sensus Fidei in the Life of the Church* (2014), 78, http://www.vatican.va/roman_curia/congregations /cfaith/cti_documents/rc_cti_20140610_sensus-fidei_en.html.

16. Edward Kilmartin, "Reception in History: An Ecclesiological Phenomenon and Its Significance," *Journal of Ecumenical Studies* 21 (1984): 37.

17. Ibid.

18. Tracy, *Analogical Imagination*, 102.

contemporaries.[19] In the life of the church, the excess applies not simply to written texts on which Tracy concentrates, but also to the other "spiritual goods" that the tradition of faith mediates. Tracy stresses that the potential of the classic to communicate with readers in times and places very different from the setting of its origin is not a quality that operates independently of any human engagement:

> The classical text is not in some timeless moment which needs mere repetition. Rather its kind of timelessness as permanent timeliness is the only one proper to any expression of the finite, temporal, historical beings we are. The classic text's real disclosure is its claim to attention on the ground that an event of understanding proper to finite human beings has here found expression. The classic text's fate is that only its constant reinterpretation by later finite, historical, temporal beings who will risk asking its questions and listening, critically and tactfully, to its responses can actualize the event of understanding beyond its present fixation in a text. Every classic lives as a classic only if it finds readers willing to be provoked by its claim to attention.[20]

Tracy's assessment makes plain that the continued impact of the classic, its liveliness and generativity beyond the period from which it emerged, is neither something that the age of a document secures nor the result of some alchemy in the text itself. Rather, it is "readers willing to be provoked by [the classic's] claim to attention" who play an essential role. So essential are these readers that "a work is dead until it is read."[21]

A classic text, especially one that grapples with core elements of what it means to be human, has breadth and depth that distinguish it from an ephemeral advertising slogan. These qualities imply a capacity to connect with readers beyond a single time and place. Even

---

19. It is important to note that "the classic" does not begin life as such but acquires over a history of reading an acceptance and significance that it might not have had at the time of its origin; on this point, see Francis Schüssler Fiorenza, *Foundational Theology: Jesus and the Church* (New York: Crossroad, 1992), 118–21.

20. Tracy, *Analogical Imagination*, 102.

21. Ormond Rush, "Reception Hermeneutics and the 'Development' of Doctrine: An Alternative Model," *Pacifica* 6 (1993): 127.

more, texts that are classics of a religious tradition can be catalysts for an encounter with God: "To identify a written text as sacred is to claim that the continuous possibility of re-reading, the impossibility of reading for the last time, is a continuous openness to the intention of God to communicate."[22] This quality, too, as Vatican II's *Dei Verbum* attests, reflects the relationship between the Holy Spirit and the human authors—"God speaks through human beings in human fashion" (DV 12)—rather than being the result of a divine action with no human footprints.

Still, the application of even a religious text to the world of its noncontemporary readers involves activities that those receivers alone can practice—"who will risk asking its questions and listening, critically and tactfully, to its responses." The original process of writing was the work of a human author employing imagination and creativity, rather than being the artifact of an algorithm or a composite of ideas that market research generated. The understanding, interpretation, and application of the text to contemporary realities are likewise human activities, ones through which the receivers of a classic text affirm and contribute to its continuing capacity to shape human communities.[23]

The centrality of the receivers as meaning-makers resonates with the incarnational tendency of grace. Applied to the reception of tradition in the church, to the work of recognizing and responding to the movement of the Spirit through all that history transmits, this incarnational tendency underscores that reception is creative, that it is always other than an exercise in "joining the dots" or "painting by numbers." Neither of those approaches would allow any departures from a fixed pattern that leads to only one possible outcome.

Reception, on the other hand, is likely to yield results distinct from the accents that prevailed in the past. This effect is partially a consequence of the "excess of meaning" in the original work, but is equally a

22. Rowan Williams, *Holy Living: The Christian Tradition for Today* (London: Bloomsbury, 2017), 42.

23. For the importance of the triad of understanding, interpretation, and application for the hermeneutics of texts, see Ormond Rush, *The Eyes of Faith: The Sense of the Faithful and the Church's Reception of Revelation* (Washington, DC: Catholic University of America Press, 2009), 72–74; see also *Dei Verbum*, 12.

product of the "translation" that the receivers enact in their particular context. It is this element of reception that highlights it as a creative process, not a "repristination" of the past.[24] The endeavor to "recontextualize" what the tradition hands on, an endeavor that produces a "different" tradition witnesses to the excess that is proper to the living tradition of faith.[25] It witnesses, too, to the responsibility of the receivers to ensure that they communicate God's message in ways that address their own time and place.

Significantly, the crucial role that present-day believers play in the process of reception does not impute to them any superiority over the ecclesial community of the past. Since, as Clare Watkins notes, "It is through gazing at what has been received that we come to glimpse something of what God is," reception underscores that present-day believers do not create *ex nihilo* either the church itself or the central aspects of its faith.[26] Reception, rather, affirms both the importance and limits of the present. It recognizes the present as part of the story of God's movement in human history and in the life of the church, but not the whole story.

This acknowledgment, in turn, requires humility before the wisdom of the past and a sense of communion with believers from the past, who share with those in the present an orientation to the future. For this reason, Rowan Williams cautions receivers against being "dominated by the time we think we occupy, so that anything coming at us through an alien text is likely to be processed into whatever most concerns us now and subjected to the criteria by which we judge something as useful or useless for the time of our plans and projects."[27] When self-absorption and an exclusive interest in "today" block out receptivity to the past, present-day believers might fail to see "what God is already

---

24. William Rusch, "The Landscape of Reception," in *Seeking the Truth of Change in the Church: Reception, Communion and the Ordination of Women*, ed. Paul Avis (New York: T. and T. Clark, 2004), 4.

25. Lieven Boeve, *Interrupting Tradition: An Essay on Christian Faith in a Postmodern Context*, trans. B. Doyle (Louvain: Peeters, 2003), 22–24.

26. Clare Watkins, "Texts and Practices: An Ecclesiology of *traditio* for Pastoral Theology," in *Keeping Faith in Practice: Aspects of Catholic Pastoral Theology*, ed. James Sweeney, Gemma Simmonds, and David Lonsdale (London: SCM, 2010), 170.

27. Williams, *Holy Living*, 33.

working out ahead of us."[28] A more constructive alternative, evident in Blondel's approach that the previous chapter discussed, accepts that the past can illuminate the present or even correct its shortcomings, thereby furthering the church's movement into the future.

The "newness" that the retrieval of the humanity of Jesus generated in Christology, a retrieval that chapter 1 chronicled, and the expanded vision for the church and its mission that emerged from the *ressourcement* that Vatican II embraced, exemplify positive receptions of the church's faith that predates the present. In those instances, the "classics" were not only written texts, but the liturgy, piety, and pastoral practices of prior eras in the history of the ecclesial community. The creative faithfulness of those receptions notwithstanding, their connection to "change" identifies them as a locus of tension in the church.

Reception and "Change"

Edward Kilmartin diagnoses succinctly the causes and symptoms of the tension that accompany even the possibility of "change" in the church:

> When a significant spiritual good is newly introduced into the global perception of the life of faith, and thereby begins to affect the practice of the faith, a new synthesis of understanding and practice of the faith is initiated. Since this threatens the equilibrium of the community's self-understanding, it may cause a serious negative reaction in some quarters. Elsewhere, the good may be immunized by a superficial adaptation.[29]

The experience of the Catholic Church in the wake of Vatican II confirms resoundingly Kilmartin's assessment. Similarly, the views of critics who reject Pope Francis's *Amoris Laetitia,* the document on marriage and the family, as not being in accord with Catholic doctrine on those topics, demonstrate the hostility that creative reception can arouse.[30] In the latter instance, no less than in the post–Vatican II experience,

---

28. Watkins, "Texts and Practices," 170.

29. Kilmartin, "Reception in History," 37.

30. Pope Francis, *Amoris Laetitia,* On Love in the Family (2016), https://www.vatican.va/content/dam/francesco/pdf/apost_exhortations/documents/papa-francesco_esortazione-ap_20160319_amoris-laetitia_en.pdf. For discussion of the critics of

the combination of reception with *aggiornamento*, the responsiveness to contemporary questions, exacerbates opposition to possibilities for change in the church's way of proceeding.

In light of the tensions that reception can initiate, it is vital to examine whether the present-day ecclesial community is free to adapt the bequest of its ancestors in faith. What the church in every age receives from the past has its own integrity, but the eschatological dimension of the church's tradition, which the previous chapter detailed, would suggest the legitimacy of an affirmative answer to the question of the church's freedom for change. On the other hand, the fact that the church in every age depends on the apostolic witness to Christ, as chapter 5 also demonstrated, implies that faithfulness necessarily requires continuity in order to ensure that the church remains "one, holy, catholic, and apostolic." Hence, the dilemma that reception poses to the ecclesial community.

To address this dilemma in ways that provide space for the movement that tills the church—even if not in ways that would dissolve the dilemma absolutely—it will be useful to revisit once again the church's foundations. As this book has maintained, it is the event of God's self-communication in human history that brings the ecclesial community into being and remains its active source of meaning and mission. A principal corollary of this origin is that "all of the massive institutional power of the Church, all of the varied articulation of its life in traditions, dogmas, relations, institutions, roles, liturgies, devotions, movements, etc., exists and functions as preparation, mediation, or explication of the founding event of communication and reception of the word and grace of God."[31] Every aspect of ecclesial life, then, derives its authenticity from the grace that expresses the self-communicating God, manifest historically in Jesus Christ and present sacramentally in the world and the church through the Holy Spirit.

The impact of theological principles, juridical enactments, popular movements, and of all other elements of the ecclesial community can never be independent of their connection to Christ and the Spirit. This

---

the document, see Massimo Faggioli, *The Liminal Papacy of Pope Francis: Moving Towards Global Catholicity* (Maryknoll, NY: Orbis, 2020), 19–21.

31. Joseph Komonchak, "The Epistemology of Reception," *The Jurist* 57 (1997): 193.

relationship is eschatological, not simply historical. "The church," for this reason, "has a nature that precedes its legislation and which stems from the final and irreversible salvific event of Jesus Christ and from faith in Christ which necessarily follows from its definitive nature."[32] As such, the authenticity of all components of the church's life, including its tradition and the reception of that tradition, depends on maintaining and deepening the due devotion to God that Newman associated with the efficacy of the illative sense.

The relationship with the God of Jesus Christ directs the ecclesial community toward the eschaton while simultaneously constituting the heart of the tradition that sustains the church's apostolicity in the present. Jean-Marie Tillard offers a way to envisage the complex interweaving of potentially divisive influences: "Through *paradosis* [handing over] the *eschata* continue to be transmitted as the unchangeable foundation, already grounded in the eternal feast of the kingdom. Through *reception*, this salvific gift of God becomes concretely part of human history and the human condition."[33] The church's eschatological orientation, itself a feature of the ecclesial community's foundation in grace, ensures that the pilgrimage of faith and hope that defines the church remains unfinished. As a pilgrimage to fulfillment, the life of the ecclesial community differs, too, from an endless, unvarying repetition of a single experience.

Apropos of the church's future-oriented status, the Orthodox theologian John Zizioulas contends that "the body of Christ *is* by *becoming* again and again what it is as if it were not at all that which it is. The Spirit brings the charismata from the future, from the *eschata*, as new events; he does not elicit them out of history as out of a deposit of grace."[34] Even in its intricacy, Zizioulas's description is a claim for "becoming" and "the future" to be no less critical for the life of the church than is the preservation of what has come from the past. The

---

32. Karl Rahner, "Open Questions in Dogma Considered by the Institutional Church as Definitively Answered," *Journal of Ecumenical Studies* 15 (1978): 217.

33. Jean-Marie Tillard, "Tradition, Reception," in *The Quadrilog: Tradition and the Future of Ecumenism*, ed. Kenneth Hagen (Collegeville, MN: Michael Glazier, 1994), 342; original emphasis.

34. John Zizioulas, *Communion and Otherness: Further Studies in Personhood and the Church* (New York: T. and T. Clark, 2006), 296; original emphasis.

need to synthesize those elements for the sake of the church's mission and communion establishes that reception will always require the exercise of artistic creativity.

"Becoming" has been integral to the church's pilgrimage in history from its beginnings. This centrality was not because the church's members were always restless for change and hostile to continuity. Movement as an imperative, not simply an option, is unimaginable outside of the eschatological orientation of grace, grace that is irreducibly "part of human history and the human condition," as Tillard referenced. No less pivotally, the incarnational dimension of grace means that movement also arises through the need to respond to new questions and new circumstances in the life of the ecclesial community, including those that interrogate aspects of the church's inherited faith and practice. These questions and circumstances emerge without warning to disrupt settled patterns of profession and action, challenging the disciples of Christ to respond with an artistry reflective of God's creative love in the world.

Earlier chapters have used the advent of gentile converts as the paradigm for unanticipated events that require artistic responses from the ecclesial communities. Such occurrences did not cease in the first century, nor have intra-ecclesial matters alone marked their scope. Incidents as diverse as the eclipse of the Roman Empire, contact with other religions, the rediscovery of Aristotelian thought and the formation of universities, the founding of nation-states, industrialization, and the emergence of feminism all illustrate the range of forces that require the church's inherited faith and practice to respond continually to the inescapable realities of a changing world.

For the present-day ecclesial community throughout the world, the COVID-19 pandemic is emblematic of the unanticipated—and "unanticipatable"—events that call for a response that the past can inform, but not dictate. Matters of race, gender, sexuality, and other areas of justice and equity in a suffering world, including all that "the ecological crisis" summarizes, also require creative responses from the contemporary church. It is certainly not inevitable that these responses will serve the mission of the church by witnessing lavishly to the grace and compassion of God. Rather, the likelihood of generous response depends radically on the willingness of the ecclesial community to be attentive to the Spirit, who "speaks" through the voices of those who suffer, the wisdom that the tradition of faith offers, and the lessons that the church's failures to live out the demands of its faith can teach. All of these actions embody Newman's "due devotion" to God and build a platform for the artistry of faithful decision-making that shapes the church's future.

It is important to acknowledge—although it is hardly "breaking news"—that, at every level of the church's life, the response of the ecclesial community to its challenges is often not commensurate with all that a thoroughgoing appropriation of the tradition would enable. Nor has the response always reflected all that constitutes authentic witness to the Spirit at the heart of the tradition. As Orlando Espin argues, "Christian traditioning, furthermore, is only made credible by compassion that is *constatable* [verifiable], demonstrable, lived, since it is the dawn of a new real world of real compassion that traditioning announces."[35] If the members of the church are to satisfy this standard, they must do more than merely profess orthodox faith; they must incarnate that faith in their words and actions. Doing so, requires creativity and artistry.

Rather than creativity and artistry, it is often defensiveness that presents itself as faithful reception of God's revelation that the church's tradition mediates. The church's hostility to the wider world during the emergence of the "secular age," from the sixteenth to the nineteenth century, is perhaps the archetype of this attitude.[36] Defensiveness in the midst of social upheavals is understandable, as is the hesitancy among members of the church in the face of proposals for changes to policies and practices long unquestioned. Nonetheless, a blanket rejection of movement can signal a failure to appreciate the potential for change consistent with faithful reception of the tradition, and resistance to the Spirit's call from the future. Openness to learn from new questions, from emerging practices, and even from protests against the church's

---

35. Orlando Espin, *Idol and Grace: On Traditioning and Subversive Hope* (Maryknoll, NY: Orbis, 2014), 123–24; translation added.

36. For the most detailed analysis of this period, see Charles Taylor, *A Secular Age* (Cambridge, MA: Belknap, 2007); for an accessible presentation of Taylor's approach, see James Gerard McEvoy, *Leaving Christendom for Good: Church-World Dialogue in a Secular Age* (Lanham, MD: Lexington, 2014), 3–27.

official stance on various issues can be consistent with an appreciation of the tradition's eschatological orientation. This openness is also
consistent with recognizing that faithful decision-making is an art that
necessarily operates in an ill-defined space.

No epoch in the church's history, and no ecclesial community in the
present, has exhausted all that God's once-for-all self-giving in Christ
and the Holy Spirit enables. There remains, then, the potential for
forms of creative reception that illustrate the capacity of the tradition
to address multiple generations and the panoply of human cultures.[37]
For this reason, the process of inculturating faith, of expressing it in
"categories of thought, symbols, liturgical practices, and ethical models
which are newly formulated by a local people with fidelity both to the
cultural heritage and to Christian revelation," is essential to the reception of tradition.[38]

The inculturation of faith takes into account the fundamental human
need to bring new experiences into relationship with existing knowledge and understanding—"The human mind is not like a photographic
plate, which without preference or alteration simply registers anything
which falls upon it at a particular isolated moment."[39] Rahner, writing
as early as 1954, contends that expressing faith in new ways can be
consistent with the church's movement toward God's absolute future,
and without implying rejection of God's revelation or the superiority
of the present over the past:

> The decisive feature of such change is not "progress" in the sense
> of acquiring a sort of plus-quality of knowledge (as though the
> Church were somehow to become "cleverer"), but (in principle,
> at least) the change, the new look, of the same reality and truth,
> appropriate to just this age of the Church: it is change in, not of,
> identity (*der Wandel im selben*). . . . If we fail either to preserve
> or to change we should betray the truth, either by falling into error
> or by failing to make the truth our own in a really existential way.[40]

---

37. Tillard, "Tradition, Reception," 337–38.

38. Kilmartin, "Reception in History," 46.

39. Karl Rahner, "The Development of Dogma," in *Theological Investigations*, vol.
1, trans. C. Ernst (New York: Crossroad, 1982), 44.

40. Ibid., 45. See also Rahner's "Considerations on the Development of Dogma,"
in *Theological Investigations*, vol. 4, trans. K. Smyth (New York: Crossroad, 1982), 5.

A helpful way to envisage the possibilities for the "change in, not of, identity" that Rahner champions is through the notion of "congruence" that John Thiel develops. Thiel defines congruence as "an interpretative relationship characterized by meaningful continuity between the authoritative past and the contemporary theological claims, a continuity that believers understand as the unity of tradition and the basis of Christian faithfulness through the ages."[41] Establishing congruence between the past and the present eschews the rejection of either period.

Affirmation of the congruence between the old and the new is a creative act. Through it, "the entire community of faith comes to affirm a developing continuity that, in any present moment, may look quite like the faith of times long past in some respects, and quite different from the claims of earlier believers in other respects."[42] Thiel, echoing Congar's "analogy of faith" that chapter 5 profiled, argues that there can be an "analogy of tradition." Through it, the community of faith, in response to the Holy Spirit, identifies "similarity-in-difference" between the present and the past, "marking the truthful presence of the Holy Spirit through time, place, circumstance, and culture."[43] No less significantly, Thiel contends that the ecclesial community can come to regard even "long-standing" aspects of faith and practice as "questionable or even rejectable," and so as being "disanalogous" to authentic continuity of the church's tradition.[44]

Both possibilities—analogy and disanalogy—underscore that the church's faithfulness is always an unfinished project, one dependent on authentic responses to the Holy Spirit. Faithfulness is not a constant of the church's constitution, not an attribute that the ecclesial community can take for granted as a "given" that is present always and everywhere, requiring no engagement of the community itself. Likewise, faithful reception is inseparable from the church's due devotion to God, which locates it as a dimension of the church's pilgrim existence.

As an expression of faith, reception is integral to the lived hope of the ecclesial community. This hope, of course, differs from mathe-

41. John Thiel, "The Analogy of Tradition: Method and Theological Judgment," *Theological Studies* 66 (2005): 359.

42. Ibid., 370.

43. Ibid., 374.

44. Ibid., 376.

matical certainty, underscoring that faithful reception is art rather than mechanics. The emphasis on hope aligns reception with the movement of the Spirit that is the source of both the dynamism integral to the church's faith and the vibrancy of the ecclesial community's life. As the following section of the chapter will demonstrate, dynamism and vibrancy can be compatible with structures, authorities, and instruments for teaching and decision-making in the church, but not with efforts to stifle the freedom of the Holy Spirit.

The Holy Spirit and the Ordering of Ecclesial Faith and Life

There is an intimate relationship between the ordering of the church's faith and life and the "resolutions" and "spiritual goods" that the preceding section identified as integral to the process of reception. All that the ecclesial community in every age is to receive from the past exists because the Christian community has fashioned over time teachings, laws, forms of worship, and an array of spiritual practices to support faithfulness to Christ and the activities that flow from the urgings of the Spirit. The community has also developed structures and authorities to regulate multiple aspects of its life for the sake of faithfulness to God's self-communication and the service of the church's mission. Further, as Vatican II's *Lumen Gentium* presents the church's structures, the tradition of faith has framed such developments as responses to the Spirit and the explicit direction of Jesus Christ: "In order to ensure that the people of God would have pastors and would enjoy continual growth, Christ the Lord set up in his church a variety of offices whose aim is the good of the whole body" (LG 18).

These various instruments emerged and evolved through history in response to the needs of the church's mission and communal life. The questions and debates about faith at particular times and places were catalysts for ordering the church's faith and developing the various disciplines intrinsic to Christian living. Since the church, through "its life, its confession and its celebration of divine worship, is to bear witness to its faith before the world," clarity about that faith is a necessity, an integral part of the church's due devotion to God.[45] Faith in

45. International Theological Commission, "On the Interpretation of Dogmas" *Origins* 20 (1990): 5.

Christ, while it always exceeds its articulated content, is far from being amorphous, ineffable, or individualistic. Statements of faith center the Christian community on the self-communicating God, rather than on "the transactions of mythological subjects."[46]

The church's teachings are more than a catalog of the church's faith. From their earliest formulations, these teachings have intended "to elicit faith commitment, not affirm factual data; they had a *performative* function."[47] As it "performs" its faith in ever-changing historical settings, the ecclesial community seeks to align itself with all that the Holy Spirit enables. This alignment includes faithful reception of what has guided the ecclesial community through its history of faith, but also a commitment to God's ever-new future. The latter reminds the church that the self-communicating God remains the transcendent, incomprehensible mystery.

The relationship of the church's faith to the mystery of God has implications for the comprehensiveness of the church's statements of faith, and also for the processes and structures that play a critical role in formulating those statements. More specifically, an enduring focus on the mystery of God can preserve the church from turning its own statements of faith into an idol:

> A dogmatic definition is doubly relative: it is historically dated and thus includes a limitation. It calls for a new unveiling, not by deduction, but by integration. It is also relative in the sense that it is not enough on its own. Its meaning can never be deduced by simply analyzing its content. It is not "the deposit" of faith per se, which is something else. It is thus relative to the whole way in which the Church receives the revelation of Scripture and Tradition and lives from this. It is in this ecclesial context, which is its milieu for life having been its matrix, that the definition takes on

46. Rowan Williams, "Theological Integrity," *Cross Currents* 45 (1995): 323. See also Richard Lennan, "Making Sense of Doctrine," in *The Possibility of Belief: The Challenges and Prospects of Catholic Faith*, ed. Richard Lennan (Strathfield, NSW: St Pauls, 2004), 159–74.

47. Richard Gaillardetz, *By What Authority?: Foundations for Understanding Authority in the Church*, rev. ed. (Collegeville, MN: Liturgical Press, 2018), 156; original emphasis.

its whole meaning, a meaning which remains open to the future to the very extent that the formula remains inadequate to the mystery it signifies.[48]

The mystery of God is beyond the articulations of the ecclesial community that seeks to illuminate that very mystery. These articulations proceed from and respond to encounters with the mystery itself, which remains inexhaustible while it also "beckons believers to inexhaustible interpretation."[49] The fact that no doctrine can exhaust God underlines, to return to a principle from Karl Rahner that has been central to this book, that the core of Christian faith is "the state of radical openness to the question of the mystery of the absolute future that is God."[50]

This openness highlights that statements articulating the church's faith are "a modality of this radical commitment to refuse to call a halt at any point and to seek the fulfillment of its life, its 'salvation' in something to which no further name can be assigned."[51] At their best, then, statements of faith are not efforts to "capture" God, but stimuli for a deeper encounter with God. Consequently, Rahner claims, the goal for the development of the church's faith is not the production of as many statements as possible, but movement "in the line of simplification, towards an ever clearer view of what is really intended, towards the single mystery."[52] In other words, neither the articulation of myriad doctrines nor the existence of an expansive structure for their ongoing production and defense is sufficient to indicate a church responsive to the Spirit. A community that lives the faith that the doctrines express is a more reliable criterion.

Rahner's analysis resonates with the Second Vatican Council's recognition in *Unitatis Redintegratio* (UR), its text that reshaped the Catholic Church's approach to ecumenism, that there is "an order

48. Bernard Sesboüé, *Gospel and Tradition*, trans. P. Kelly (Miami, FL: Convivium, 2012), 90.

49. John Thiel, *Senses of Tradition: Continuity and Development in Catholic Faith* (New York: Oxford University Press, 2000), 4.

50. Karl Rahner, "The Question of the Future," in *Theological Investigations*, vol. 12, trans. D. Bourke (New York: Crossroad, 1974), 189.

51. Ibid., 189.

52. Rahner, "Considerations on the Development of Dogma," 26.

or 'hierarchy' of truths since they vary in relation to the foundation of Christian faith" (UR 11).[53] The council's emphasis supported the possibility that those Christian churches that were in "some, though imperfect communion" (UR 3) with the Catholic Church might move toward broader and deeper communion on the basis of shared faith in what constituted the heart of Christian faith and action.

Neither the emphasis on God's mystery nor the reference to the hierarchy of truths functions to discount the value of the church's teaching for the life of the ecclesial community. This teaching can be an aid to faith, rather than the equivalent of merely talking about God. As an indicator of the importance of objective statements of faith, it is noteworthy that the ancient classification of the creed, the profession of faith that continues to be a feature of the church's liturgy, names it as the "symbol" of the church's faith.[54] As such, the profession of faith is a unique means of deepening awareness of the ecclesial community's particularity. These symbols of faith likewise accentuate the communal reality of the church. The inclusion of the profession of faith within the church's liturgy supports this communal dimension, uniting and directing the church's worship and action toward God, while also amplifying the faith that unites the church.

As chapter 2 highlighted, symbols are a means of encounter with what they symbolize, but not its substitute. The many categories of the church's teaching, then, do not replace faith in God or reduce faith to assent to authority. In addition, to draw again on Rahner, since the doctrines themselves are not "chemically pure" but dependent on the authors, language, and culture from which they emerge, they are not an unmediated word of revelation.[55] Even the church's dogmas, so Rahner argues, contain "amalgams" that reflect the influences inseparable from

---

53. The Second Vatican Council, *Unitatis Redintegratio*, Decree on Ecumenism (1964).

54. See Robert Krieg, "Creeds," in *Encyclopedia of Catholicism*, ed. Richard McBrien (San Francisco: HarperCollins, 1995), 378.

55. For discussion of doctrine as other than "chemically pure," see Karl Rahner, "Basic Observations on the Subject of the Changeable and Unchangeable Factors in the Church," in *Theological Investigations*, vol. 14, trans. D. Bourke (New York: Seabury, 1976), 10–11.

the time and place of their formation, influences that are inevitable given the incarnational reality of grace.[56]

The cultural factors inseparable from ecclesial doctrines, both in their formation and reception, do not disqualify them from being "sacramental," from being agents for a deepening discipleship. Nonetheless, the existence of such factors does heighten the importance of historical study and interpretation to appraise the doctrines' applicability to the life of the contemporary church. The impossibility of chemical purity highlights, too, the importance of avoiding any depictions of the church's teaching as equivalent to the unalloyed word of God.

Challenges in the Articulation of the Church's Faith

A positive reception of the church's teaching becomes more likely when the link between a specific teaching and faithful discipleship is clear, the existence of cultural amalgams notwithstanding. What can also enhance or impede the likelihood of positive reception is the process by which the church's authorities arrive at decisions. When that process is not transparent—and even more when "process" is not evident—the possibilities for reception suffer.

Well-documented instances of excessive centralization and authoritarianism have rendered the church's official teaching, and the institutions that do this teaching, subject to a great deal of suspicion among present-day Catholics. Official teaching that shows little evidence of engagement with theologians, the wider community of faith, and an appreciation for the Spirit's presence in current cultural circumstances does not stimulate a positive reception. As is most often evident in official pronouncements relevant to human relationships and sexuality, the perception that the church's teaching is insufficiently attentive to and respectful of, for example, the efforts of gay people to live by the gospel, results in the non-reception of such teaching.

The church's authorities, through the grace of the Spirit, "are authentic teachers, that is, teachers endowed with the authority of Christ, who preach to the people assigned to them the faith which is to be believed

---

56. Karl Rahner, "Yesterday's History of Dogma and Theology for Tomorrow," in *Theological Investigations*, vol. 18, trans. E. Quinn (New York: Crossroad, 1983); the discussion of "amalgams" is at 11–22.

and applied in practice" (LG 25). As such, the church's bishops are not mere echoes of the majority opinion in the church and society. At the same time, the bishops are part of the communion of faith, not the sole arbiters of faith. This means that bishops are most likely to teach well when they also listen well, listen for the presence of the Spirit in all the faithful and in the wider world. For this reason, Newman, who was unequivocal in affirming the authority of the church's bishops, stressed that *pastorum et fidelium conspiratio*, the "breathing together" of all the baptized, was more conducive to authentic expression of the church's faith than was any separation between those in authority and other members of the church.[57] This communal dynamic is integral to contemporary theologies of "synodality," the theme for the final section of this chapter.

A hermeneutic of generosity and trust toward the church's teachings, and the structures that articulate them, includes both as part of the endeavor to express the church's faith in specific situations. At the same time, this hermeneutic is compatible with the historical study that uncovers whether "some aspects of the question were overlooked or simply omitted, what theological opinions were left open (neither rejected nor approved), what presuppositions, not recognized at the time, may have exercised a hidden (but decisive) influence on the way the church's doctrine was formulated."[58] In pursuit of these questions, historical study provides yet more confirmation that the church's doctrine is always other than the product of divine dictation. This recognition supports the need for the ecclesial community in every age to sift what is central from what is less crucial for the life of faith.

Equally, historical study makes clear that the formation and definition of the church's faith has never been a seamless movement from certainty to certainty; in fact, it was often a bitter struggle between sharply divided camps. Even after the church's authorities promulgated formal statements of faith, "difficulties, obscurities and frictions" remained, not because of "stupid and malicious heretics," but because all forms of human knowledge, including in matters of faith, never

---

57. John Henry Newman, *On Consulting the Faithful in Matters of Doctrine*, ed. John Coulson (1859; repr., London: Collins, 1986), 104.

58. Francis Sullivan, *Creative Fidelity: Weighing and Interpreting Documents of the Magisterium* (Mahwah, NJ: Paulist, 1996), 111.

outgrow the possibility of questions and the need for clarifications, all of which have a place in the processes of reception.[59]

It is far from surprising, then, that questions about the church's faith, and so the need for further clarity, continue to arise. The eschatological nature of the church's faith as faith in the ungraspable and mysterious trinitarian God suggests that "as new questions emerge in a way that cannot be blamed simply on the malice or human presumption and pride of theologians, it cannot be maintained that everything is actually clear from the outset or that an answer is immediately available for every question."[60] This perspective offers an alternative to the critique, one that often aims at Pope Francis, that "confusion"—itself a vague term—is the inevitable result when the ecclesial community is willing to acknowledge questions, hear the voices of its own marginalized members, and consider its faith in the light of each new moment of history.

Consistent with both the insights of historical study of the church's doctrine and the emphasis on the transcendent reality of God, Orlando Espin warns of the danger of "doctrinification," the "turning of doctrine into the definitive measure or object of faith," an outcome that he identifies as destructive of hope.[61] Similarly, Pope Francis, in *Gaudete et Exsultate* (GE), stresses that

> doctrine or better, our understanding and expression of it, "is not a closed system, devoid of the dynamic capacity to pose questions, doubts, inquiries. . . . The questions of our people, their suffering, their struggles, their dreams, their trials and their worries, all possess an interpretational value that we cannot ignore if we want to take the principle of the incarnation seriously. Their wondering helps us to wonder, their questions question us." (GE 44)[62]

The possibility of "doctrinification" and its failure to "take the principle of the incarnation seriously," as well as the recognition of "amalgams" in the church's teachings, indicates that creative reception is

---

59. Rahner, "History of Dogma," 7.

60. Ibid., 8.

61. Espin, *Idol and Grace*, 113.

62. Pope Francis, *Gaudete et Exsultate*, Rejoice and Be Glad: On the Call to Holiness in Today's World (2018), http://w2.vatican.va/content/francesco/en/apost_exhortations /documents/papa-francesco_esortazione-ap_20180319_gaudete-et-exsultate.html.

distinct from unquestioning repetition of inherited forms of faith and practices. Creative reception reflects the church's unfinished reality and is faithful to the eschatological dynamics of tradition. The same principles suggest, too, that reception itself is an activity that can occur in different ways in different times and places.[63]

In his opening address at Vatican II, Pope John XXIII gave an impetus to creative reception of the church's articulated faith when he endorsed the need to study the church's doctrine "through the methods of research and through the literary forms of modern thought."[64] The pope's expectation was that such study would make the church's tradition of faith more accessible to contemporary Catholics, and so enliven the church's mission. The fact that "modern thought" has not always been welcome in official circles of the Catholic Church, as earlier sections of this book have indicated in surveying aspects of the history of theology, brings to the fore a key aspect of reception that is often problematic: the role of ecclesial authority in relation to other participants in the process of reception.

Congar is adamant that reception requires more than obedience to a superior. Reception must embody, he stresses, "a degree of consent, and possibly of judgment, in which the life of a body is expressed which brings into play its own original spiritual resources."[65] This assessment reinforces the "ecclesial" dimension of reception without excluding the church's authorities from any role in the process. At the same time, Congar acknowledges that throughout much of the church's history, reception involved "a wholly pyramidal conception of the Church as a mass totally determined by its summit, in which there is hardly any mention of the Holy Spirit other than as the guarantor of an infallibility of hierarchical courts."[66]

The pyramidal theology privileged the church's ordained ministry, especially that of the episcopate, above any possible contribution that

63. For a detailed overview of approaches to the reception of doctrine, see Richard Gaillardetz, "Reception of Doctrine: New Perspectives," in *Authority in the Roman Catholic Church*, ed. Bernard Hoose (Burlington, VT: Ashgate, 2002), 95–114.

64. Pope John XXIII, "Pope John's Opening Speech to the Council," in *The Documents of Vatican II*, ed. Walter Abbott (London: Geoffrey Chapman, 1966), 715.

65. Congar, "Reception as an Ecclesiological Reality," 45.

66. Ibid., 60.

might come from the rest of the community. The "primacy of an authority," then, replaced the "primacy of truthful content" in the church's understanding of reception.[67] Consequently, reception came to be coterminous with obedience to legitimate ecclesial authority. This approach meant that "non-reception" automatically bore the stigma of disobedience, to both ecclesial authority and, by extension, to God.

As an alternative to this narrow vision, Congar emphasizes that the body of the faithful, including local churches, are "not inert and wholly passive in regard to the structures of belief and ethical and cultic rules."[68] From the perspective of the church as a community, reception "affirms, acknowledges and attests that this matter is good for the church," just as non-reception "means that this decision does not call forth any living power and therefore does not contribute to edification."[69] Paradoxically, then, even non-reception has an authentically ecclesial dimension. As such, it is not an unequivocal rejection of ecclesial authority, and still less is it tantamount to a rejection of God's self-offer in Jesus Christ through the Holy Spirit. The nuances inseparable from reception affirm still further that the ecclesial community must remain alert to the need for tilling all that exists to symbolize the Spirit.

To Congar's analysis of the ways in which the emphasis on authority, specifically clerical control, can narrow the expansiveness proper to the processes of reception, Rahner's theology adds the reminder that no doctrinal definition is the final statement in the church's history of faith. The recognition that "the Church's magisterium can err and often has erred in its authentic declarations, and that this is obviously possible also in future," is an aspect of this reminder.[70] It is a recognition that reinforces both the pilgrim identity of the church and the need for ongoing discernment of the church's faith, a discernment that remains the responsibility, and gift, of the entire community of the faithful, as the next section of the chapter will discuss.

67. Ibid., 61.
68. Ibid., 62.
69. Ibid., 66; see also Kilmartin, "Reception in History," 40.
70. Rahner, "History of Dogma," 10.

In an evocative image, Francis Schüssler Fiorenza expresses a preference for depictions of the relationship between the past and the present that resemble a "crumpled handkerchief," where the material often folds over itself to obscure any clear shape and obvious beginnings and endings, rather than "mountain peaks," which are clear-cut and definitely distinct from each other.[71] Fiorenza's option for blurry connections over unambiguous differences fits well with an appreciation of the Spirit's involvement in the articulation of the church's faith and the ordering of its life. The reception of the past in the present, a healthy relationship between ecclesial authorities and the wider community of faith, and the embrace of change within continuity all have more in common with fuzzy rather than sharp edges.

A mechanism allowing the ecclesial community to make precise demarcations between what expresses and what hinders the Spirit would remove manifold complexities and sources of tension from the life of the church. Were such a mechanism available for the articulation of the church's authentic faith and the determination of legitimate ecclesial practices, a streamlining of ecclesial life would follow. Ironically, this benefit would come at a heavy cost. The cost would include the removal of the ecclesial community from participation in the everyday human reality of "unknowing," making ecclesial life less of a pilgrimage. Decisions about change in the ecclesial community, no less than those about preservation, require the faith-formed instinct of artists; they are not the product of a mathematical calculus. The final section of this chapter will elaborate on the formation and practice of those instincts, and so on their artistry.

Discernment, Dialogue, and Decision-Making

The faithfulness of the church, and so its forms of unity that are genuinely holy, catholic, and apostolic, is always the project of the whole Body of Christ. Determining faithfulness, including in the context of negotiating change, is not the accomplishment of any single commu-

---

71. Francis Schüssler Fiorenza, "Beyond Mountain Peaks and a Crumpled Handkerchief: Hermeneutics and Critical Theory," in *Beyond Dogmatism and Innocence*, ed. Anthony Godzieba and Bradford Hinze (Collegeville, MN: Michael Glazier, 2017), 36.

nity, and still less of individual virtuosi or private contractors. There is certainly a role for prophetic figures in the church, but genuine prophets are solicitous of the community's faith, rather than acting in isolation from the community or with a sense of superiority over it. In the church, prophets are "people who creatively shape the intractable here and now out of an affinity with the soul of a common tradition."[72] In this regard, it is worth remembering that the church's reverence for the saints—"those friends and coheirs of Jesus Christ who are also our sisters and brothers and outstanding benefactors" (LG 50)—recognizes them as God's gift for the inspiration of the whole community, not as heroes separated from the rest of the baptized.

The well-being of the church requires a commitment to build genuinely catholic unity within the whole body of faith. Critical to doing so is holding together the church's past and present, but with an eye to its future. Also urgent is acknowledgment that the thriving of the whole church, as well as the thriving of its mission, is impossible without the holy living of all the baptized. This thriving depends on the work of theologians, the responsibilities of officeholders, and the insights and experiences of particular communities and their members, all of which can cast light on what the Holy Spirit enables for the church. Accordingly, the greater the effort to involve the whole community of faith in discernment of major decisions and directions, the more likely it will be that the voice of the Spirit will find a hearing.

Discernment, the basis of which is faith in the constancy of God's life-giving presence to God's people, seeks to be attentive to the movement of the Spirit and to what the Spirit is asking of Christ's disciples at each time and place. The willingness to undertake and follow this discernment is especially crucial when the summons of the Spirit differs from what individuals and groups might prefer the summons of the Spirit to be. Pope Francis describes discernment as being "not a solipsistic self-analysis or a form of egotistical introspection, but an authentic process of leaving ourselves behind in order to approach the mystery of God" for the sake of faithfulness to the church's mission in the world (GE 175). Discernment, then, is demanding; its results do

---

72. Frans Jozef van Beeck, "Divine Revelation: Intervention or Self-Communication?," *Theological Studies* 52 (1991): 221.

not necessarily coincide with anyone's favored outcome.[73] At the same time, authentic discernment enables "the newness of the Gospel to emerge in another light" (GE 173).

The dominance of episcopal power, and clerical authority in general, has often eclipsed the practice of discernment at every level of the church's life. Congar's notion of "a wholly pyramidal conception of the Church," which the analysis of reception discussed, describes a body in which structure and authority displaced discernment. Beyond this obstacle, discernment, like much to do with the life of the Spirit in the church, has suffered by acquiring overtones of "mysticism" that link it to exotic practices.

The link to mysticism can imply that discernment is only for a spiritual elite, one separated from the everyday world of the community of the baptized. Integral to reclaiming discernment as a discipline appropriate for decision-making throughout the church is not the rejection of mysticism, but framing it to recognize that "what the mystics talk about is an experience which any Christian (and indeed any human being) can have and can seek, but which is easily overlooked or suppressed."[74] This affirmation is consistent with St. Paul's insistence that the Spirit "dwells" in all the followers of Christ (Rom 8:9). Since the Spirit "intercedes for the saints according to the will of God" (Rom 8:27), those same "saints" have a connection to the Spirit, a connection that enables individual and communal discernment.

Sensus Fidei and Sensus Fidei Fidelium

In the context of discerning the church's faith, *sensus fidei*, "the sense of faith," plays a pivotal role. Like Newman's illative sense, *sensus fidei*

---

73. In the context of discussing reform in the church, Yves Congar identifies four "conditions"—the primacy of charity and pastoral concern; remaining in communion with the whole church; having patience with delays; and respect for authentic tradition over "novelty"—indicative of faithful discernment; see Yves Congar, *True and False Reform in the Church*, trans. P. Philibert (1950; revised in 1968; repr. Collegeville, MN: Michael Glazier, 2011), 215–307.

74. Karl Rahner, "Experience of the Holy Spirit," in *Theological Investigations*, vol. 18, trans. E. Quinn (New York: Crossroad, 1983), 193. For the context of Rahner's famous claim that "the devout Christian of the future will either be a 'mystic,' one who has 'experienced' something or he will cease to be anything at all," see his "Christian Living Formerly and Today," in *Theological Investigations*, vol. 7, trans. D. Bourke (New York: Crossroad, 1977), 15.

names an "instinct" that is a gift of the Holy Spirit. For all people seeking to respond to the Spirit, this instinct "enables them to recognize and endorse authentic Christian doctrine and practice, and to reject what is false."[75] While *sensus* is "elusive and evocative," John Burkhard insists that it is "not simple 'feeling,' 'intuition,' or 'blind-groping,' but is grounded in a true grasp of the faith and its contents."[76] In a related way, Ormond Rush defines *sensus fidei* as "an imaginative capacity which, within their daily reception of God's self-communication, Christians, in some relatively adequate way (at least adequate in terms of salvation), 'make sense' of their lives and 'make sense of' the God reaching out to them in their lives through Christ in the Spirit."[77] *Sensus fidei*, then, is constructive, a trait reflective of its source in the Holy Spirit.

Rush speaks of *sensus fidei* as an "interpretative instrument" and a "spiritual sixth sense," terms resonant with artistic endeavors.[78] Rather than being a source of knowledge, *sensus fidei* is "a faculty or organon for interpreting the past, giving shape to Christian identity in the present, and envisaging future possibilities."[79] These features bring *sensus fidei* into relief as a force in the discernment that is integral to the tilling of the church. As such, it contributes to realizing the unfinished project that is the church.

The most consequential aspect of *sensus fidei* for the faithful determination of the church's faith and practice is its universal application in the ecclesial community. Rush details the unique ways in which *sensus fidei* applies to specific groups in the church: to bishops, theologians, and the laity in the ecclesial community, respectively.[80] While the three groups interweave, and multiple belonging is possible—except as "lay bishops"—Rush's identification of the distinct categories of *sensus* point to the diversity of the Spirit's presence within the one community of faith.

75. International Theological Commission, *Sensus Fidei*, 2.

76. John Burkhard, "The *Sensus Fidelium*: Old Questions, New Challenges," *CTSA Proceedings* 70 (2015): 37.

77. Rush, *Eyes of Faith*, 66.

78. Ibid., 68.

79. Ibid., 68.

80. For Rush's description of the various forms of *sensus fidei*, see *Eyes of Faith*, 251–74.

The proclamation of the church's unity in faith has always recognized that "to each is given the manifestation of the Spirit for the common good" (1 Cor 12:7). Accordingly, the various expressions of *sensus fidei* are to function together for the well-being of the church's communion and mission. Together, the three forms express *sensus fidei fidelium*, "the sense of faith of the faithful," that is indicative of the unity of the church in believing, worship, and discipleship in the world. As Burkhard defines it, *sensus fidei fidelium* "is a living, dynamic deepening of the understanding of divine truth that proceeds throughout history as humankind (and the cosmos) moves towards its eschatological goal."[81] A corollary of this description is that *sensus fidei fidelium* serves the mission of the church: it is not a timeless, static designation, but a means to support the church's faithfulness in response to specific needs and circumstances.

Sensus fidei fidelium, if it is to express the faith of the whole church, is not reducible to control by any single group in the church. Rather, it depends on respect for and sensitivity toward the contribution of every group within the church. When episcopal authority dominates, as has long been true in the Catholic Church, the emphasis on obedience usurps the proper role of communal discernment in determining *sensus fidei fidelium*, as indicated above. Correcting this imbalance does not imply wresting authority from the bishops to hand it to theological experts or an assembly of the lay faithful. What is necessary is the more challenging task of developing and continually refining mechanisms that enable the interweaving of the various "voices" and the collective effort to be attentive to "listen to what the Spirit is saying to the churches" (Rev 2:7).

By definition, *sensus fidei fidelium* requires the interweaving of all parts of the church. Within the present-day Catholic Church, the achievement of this interweaving requires particular attention to what has been historically the most neglected of the three forms of *sensus fidei*: the laity's. While theologians have often been on the margins and subject to official suspicion, they have had various "moments in the sun"—the most momentous one being Vatican II—and retain multiple platforms for the articulation and dissemination of their insights. Beyond those who are academic theologians, the faith of lay members

---

81. Burkhard, "*Sensus Fidelium*," 36.

of the church has rarely received the hearing proper to those who live by the gospel in the complexities of daily life. Daily life is, as Gemma Tulud Cruz stresses, "the context of all other contexts and hence the one existential space and ever-present moment in which God reveals God's self and humans respond in faith (or not)."[82] Neglect of this context can only impoverish efforts to articulate the church's faith and to promote faithfulness to the gospel.

An appreciation of the insights into faith of lay members of the church, whose "world" extends beyond the rarefied environment of ecclesiastical structures and the academy, recognizes the everyday as a locus for the activity of the Spirit. This recognition opens the church's discernment to the faith that expresses itself in the joys and hopes of families, and often in the midst of suffering and poverty, all of which are venues for the Spirit, even if not always prominent in the interests of both ecclesiastical structures and the academy. Taking account of the laity's *sensus fidei* is not a concession, but, as Rahner argues, acknowledges the following:

> It is the faith in the Church that actually exists in heads and hearts, and not properly official Church doctrine, that immediately and in itself is *the faith* that constitutes the Church. . . . The faith of the average Christian is not just a pitiable sketch of the official faith. It is a salutary faith borne by God's self-communication. It is really the faith that God's grace wishes to bring forth and keep alive in the Church. . . . Even when its objectification in words and concepts is very poor and deficient, it is still God's action in us, constituted by the self-communication of God in the Holy Spirit.[83]

In advocating for the importance of attentiveness to the faith of the whole church, Newman affirms that one virtue of "the Consent of the

82. Gemma Tulud Cruz, "Theology as Conversation: *Sensus Fidelium* and Doing Theology on/from the Margins," in *Learning from* All *the Faithful: A Contemporary Theology of the* Sensus Fidei, ed. Bradford Hinze and Peter Phan (Eugene, OR: Pickwick, 2016), 350; original parentheses.

83. Karl Rahner, "What the Church Officially Teaches and What the People Actually Believe," in *Theological Investigations*, vol. 22, trans. J. Donceel (New York: Crossroad, 1991), 169; original emphasis.

faithful" was its "jealousy of error."[84] Newman, in other words, regards the lived faith of the church as trustworthy since believers want to be faithful, want to be open to the Spirit. Even more, as Shawn Copeland illustrates with the example of Black Catholics in the nineteenth century protesting their exclusion from many aspects of the church's life in North America, the *sensus fidei* of lay Catholics can call the church's structures to conversion, to faithfulness that can never be taken for granted. Copeland stresses that "in their loving indignation at the failures of the Church and its ministers to live boldly the message of justice and equality . . . these Black Catholic laypeople demonstrated a critical understanding and appropriation of the faith that created the conditions for the possibility not only of transmission of Tradition, but of traditioning."[85] This example illustrates powerfully that faithfulness in the church is not coterminous with conformity to social norms or the maintenance of an undisturbed ecclesiastical apparatus.

Today, it remains urgent that the often-intersecting voices of Black Catholics, women, migrants, gay people, and other groups whose faith has clung to the peripheries of the church's life find a hearing. These voices can call the whole church, including in the exercise of its structures, to greater authenticity and responsiveness to the Spirit. For this to happen, an enhanced environment of dialogue in the church is a necessity. Rather than the mutuality that dialogue requires, the contemporary church is often the site of an unhelpful division between those who prioritize a commitment to evangelical living and those affirming the importance of clear statements of communal faith. When one or other side of that divide is "too quick to recover the language of anathema" for those on the opposite bank, the witness and the profession of the church suffer.[86]

Chapter 4 discussed dialogue in the context of the church's relationship with the world, but the theme is applicable to the inner life of the church as well. Vatican II affirmed the importance of dialogue in the church, recognizing that the church's mission in the world "requires

84. Newman, *On Consulting the Faithful*, 73.

85. M. Shawn Copeland, "Tradition and the Traditions of African American Catholicism," *Theological Studies* 61 (2000): 646.

86. Sesboüé, *Gospel and Tradition*, 181.

us first of all to create in the church itself mutual esteem, reverence and harmony, and to acknowledge all legitimate diversity; in this way, all who constitute the one people of God will be able to engage in ever more fruitful dialogue" (GS 92). Paralleling the link between *sensus fidei* and discernment, the basis for intra-church dialogue is the fact that all the baptized "have a divinely bestowed interest through the gift of faith in guarding the saving truth of the gospel that is mediated through tradition."[87] This shared life in the Spirit indicates that dialogue contains within it the potential for an outcome that exceeds the pre-existing views of every participant. The outcomes of dialogue can also be an alternative to making absolute the experience of either the past or the present.

Through dialogue, "deeper dimensions of the topic can be revealed and new courses of action and mission opened, and the very transfiguration of self, community, and God can occur."[88] Authentic dialogue does not remake the church according to the current preferences of any single participant, but it does attest to the conviction that the church's faith has not yet reached its final form, in either articulation or practice. Even in relation to matters that touch on revelation, "the Church can and must also be she who learns as well, she who is capable of being led into still deeper levels of her own truth and her understanding of that truth. In such a dialogue she can be purified from misunderstandings and distorted interpretations . . . and she can herself become more believing."[89] In this way, dialogue accords with the church's eschatological pilgrimage, and so its unfinished state.

Equally, the broadest possible practice of dialogue in the church bears witness to the fact that the presence of the Holy Spirit is not subject to any limitations, including those that might arise within the ecclesial community. This expansive approach means that dialogue will engage not only bishops, theologians, and lay members of the

87. Bradford Hinze, *Practices of Dialogue in the Roman Catholic Church: Aim and Obstacles, Lessons and Laments* (New York: Continuum, 2006), 264.

88. Ibid. See also, Michele Dillon, *Postsecular Catholicism: Relevance and Renewal* (New York: Oxford University Press, 2018), 40.

89. Karl Rahner, "Dialogue in the Church," in *Theological Investigations*, vol. 10, trans. D Bourke (New York: Crossroad, 1977), 105.

church who are "practicing Catholics," but, crucially in the age of the "nones," those whose relationship to the ecclesial community might be more distant and even strained. Along this line, Rush notes that "Catholics who are inactive, lapsed, disaffected, or marginalized in the church can provide voices through whom the Holy Spirit is genuinely challenging the church."[90] Ecumenical dialogue with other Christians, who are themselves striving to be faithful to the gospel, and the larger ecumenism with other forms of faith, work to the same effect. Taken together, the range of sources speaks to the universality of grace.

Effective dialogue within the Catholic Church requires all the members of the ecclesial community to recognize and accept that no individual or "party" can legitimately claim a monopoly of the Spirit's gifts. No single group in the church represents the sum total of graced insights into what might contribute to the thriving of the church and its mission. Just as dialogue between the churches can "liberate the specific gifts and concerns of the individual church from the self-inhibiting cocoon of egotistic isolation and contraposition, by reintegrating them into the whole and reconciling them with one another," so dialogue within the Catholic Church can build communion and invigorate mission.[91]

The fact that dialogue within the church can be productive only when all the church's members abandon "egotistic isolation" identifies it as no less demanding than the dialogue with the world and other religions. As a result of the freedom to accept or reject God's reconciling grace, the freedom that this volume has accentuated throughout, harmony in the church is an ongoing project. Reflecting other forms of dialogue between those with divergent attitudes and priorities, dialogue in the church obliges members of the ecclesial community "to display towards others within, just as to those outside, that very Christian love that is meant to characterize the Christian life."[92] Positive relationships

90. Rush, *Eyes of Faith*, 280.

91. Walter Kasper, "*Credo Unam Sanctam Ecclesiam*—The Relationship between the Catholic and the Protestant Principles in Fundamental Ecclesiology," in *Receptive Ecumenism and the Call to Catholic Learning: Exploring a Way for Contemporary Ecumenism*, ed. Paul Murray (Oxford: Oxford University Press, 2008), 86.

92. Gerard Mannion, *Ecclesiology and Postmodernity: Questions for the Church in Our Time* (Collegeville, MN: Michael Glazier, 2007), 150.

between local churches and the church as a whole, between the pope and the bishops, between the bishops and the rest of the faithful, and among all the baptized requires, like a pearl "of great value" (Matt 13:46), self-sacrifice and diligent commitment. Building these relationships is not an effortless accomplishment or an obligation applicable solely to one group rather than to all members of the church.

Dialogue, especially when it benefits from processes of discernment that can enhance its fruitfulness, is characteristic of the church as a communion of faith and life. It is a step toward the embodiment of the belief that "the whole body of the faithful who have received an anointing which comes from the holy one cannot be mistaken in belief" (LG 12). This graced body, and the discernment and dialogue intrinsic to it, takes a structural dimension in the process of synodality. Synodality is a means by which the ecclesial community can clarify its faith and set its pastoral priorities in light of prevailing social needs and in response to the movement of the Spirit in the questions and challenges of contemporary culture.

Synodality is "the specific *modus vivendi et operandi* of the Church, the People of God, which reveals and gives substance to her being as communion when all her members journey together, gather in assembly and take an active part in her evangelizing mission."[93] In *Evangelii Gaudium*, Pope Francis claims that "the whole is greater than the part, but it is also greater than the sum of its parts" (EG 235). Consistent with this principle, synodality attests that no single group or individual is alone determinative of the church's faith and faithfulness. The burgeoning of synodality at every level of the church's life is, like dialogue, a means to align the church on the Holy Spirit by giving institutional expression to the Spirit's presence in all of God's people: "The Spirit is the conduit; and the Spirit's instrument of communication is the *sensus fidei* in each believer and in the church as a whole. But the church listens to the Spirit when all listen to one another."[94]

---

93. International Theological Commission, *Synodality in the Life and Mission of the Church* (2018), 6, http://www.vatican.va/roman_curia/congregations/cfaith/cti _documents/rc_cti_20180302_sinodalita_en.html.

94. Ormond Rush, "Inverting the Pyramid: The *Sensus Fidelium* in a Synodal Church," *Theological Studies* 78 (2017): 321. See also Bradford Hinze, "Can We Find

In assemblies that give expression to synodality, in the coming to-gether of the one communion of faith, what becomes evident is the diversity and richness of the church. As chapter 4 noted, Pope Francis describes the church that embodies this richness as a "polyhedron, which reflects the convergence of all its parts, each of which retains its distinctiveness" (EG 236). This diversity and richness of cultures, peoples, attitudes, and roles within the one community of faith is an irreplaceable asset for decision-making in the church, for the effort to determine and respond to the summons of grace.

Synodality, and the communal discernment and dialogue it pre-sumes and requires, is not antithetical to the church's structures and its institutional authorities. What synodality does offer the church is a way to contextualize the role of the episcopate in terms of encourag-ing and promoting the gifts of all members of the church, rather than asserting power over the rest of the ecclesial community:

> If there is a crisis of authority in the Church today, it is crucial that in order to resolve it, we do not indulge the view that au-thority exists in order to relieve people of the burden of personal authenticity in the exercise of their own intelligence, reason, and freedom. . . . To resolve any crisis that may exist will have to entail the restoration of the full context of the existence and good functioning of authority, and that is the community of intersub-jective relations that authority must presuppose but cannot by itself guarantee.[95]

Resonant with the emphasis on relationships as the setting for epis-copal authority, Pope Francis refers to a variegated ministry for bishops. Episcopal ministry, then, is one requiring that a bishop at times will "go before his people, pointing the way and keeping their hope vibrant. At other times, he will simply be in their midst with his unassuming and merciful presence. At yet other times, he will have to walk after them, helping those who lag behind and—above all—allowing the flock to strike out on new paths" (EG 236). While bishops have a particular

---

a Way Together? The Challenge of Synodality in a Wounded and Wounding Church," *Irish Theological Quarterly* 85 (2020): 215–29.

95. Komonchak, "Epistemology of Reception," 197.

responsibility for "the *ministry of memory*, which constantly renews the Church in hope," this ministry, too, flourishes as part of the "symphony" of the whole people of God.[96]

In economic terms, synodality adds value to the life of the church. Rather than synodality turning the church into a debating society or "democratizing" it in ways that generate the caricature that the community might vote to increase or decrease the number of persons in the Trinity, synodality reveals the church as a co-responsible body of pilgrims. In this body, everyone has the opportunity "to open up points of view which might surprise them, sometimes shock them, and to verify them in the light of the Gospel, which remains unique."[97] Synodality, then, gives space to the striving of the community of faith to determine what "has seemed good to the Holy Spirit and to us" (Acts 15:28).

The experience of synodality in other Christian churches confirms that it can be a messy process, one inseparable from conflict, clashes of opinions, and struggles over decision-making. Such circumstances, far from damning synodality, highlight the necessity of conversion in the church—"Whenever such frictions arise, we must first of all call for an examination of consciences and not for an examination by the jurists."[98] By its oft-exclusive reliance on authority, the Catholic Church for much of its history avoided this messiness, even though it is certainly evident throughout the Acts of the Apostles and so is part of the church's DNA.[99]

The reduction of ecclesial life to matters that authorities alone can address has the virtue of "neatness." That virtue—itself not one that carries the gospel's explicit endorsement—has the considerable deficit of offering little opportunity to learn from the *sensus fidei* of most members of the church. The absence of this opportunity makes the achievement of *sensus fidei fidelium* less likely. Once upon a time, the

96. Anglican-Roman Catholic International Commission, *The Gift of Authority* (1999), 30, in *Origins* 29 (1999): 17–29; original emphasis.

97. Sesboüé, *Gospel and Tradition*, 178.

98. Karl Rahner, "Peaceful Reflections on the Parochial Principle," in *Theological Investigations*, vol. 2, trans. K-H. Kruger (New York: Crossroad, 1990), 315.

99. For an argument in praise of conflict as a possible context for the action of the Holy Spirit, see Bradford Hinze, "The Grace of Conflict," *Theological Studies* 81 (2020): 40–64.

imposition of various sanctions on those who advocated for alternative possibilities to decisions of ecclesial authorities provided a veneer of calm to the church, as if it were untroubled by any issues with a disruptive potential. Real unity, however, relies on the awareness of shared faith with breadth and depth.

Ultimately, the faithfulness of the church is inseparable from artistry. This artistry is necessary for interweaving within the one, yet manifold, ecclesial community, the tradition, its reception in multiple settings, discernment, dialogue, and decision-making. The only artist capable of such an accomplishment is the Holy Spirit. The artistry of the Spirit, as this book has stressed as an integrating theme, expresses itself in and through the community of faith. Through the willingness of the church's members to recognize themselves as pilgrims on a shared journey, to open themselves to the questions and needs of the world, and to respond in ways that draw from their lived memory of faith, the Spirit both tills the church and furthers its mission.

Conclusion

Y2K stalked the final months of 1999. Its specter raised a single, anxiety-inducing question: Would the appearance of "2000," a string of figures foreign to twentieth-century coding, initiate a collapse of the world's computers, thereby throwing into disarray myriad industrial processes and commercial enterprises? When the first day of January dawned free of digital mayhem, Y2K vanished from society's collective consciousness. If Y2K has a legacy, it is simply as a reminder that visions of the future are vulnerable to the non-appearance of what they claim will certainly occur. Like every discredited prediction, then, Y2K witnesses to the unpredictable nature of what is to come. This inescapable truth, however, does little to discourage fascination with "the future."

Thinking about the future may be fertile soil for escapism or romanticism—"tomorrow we will run faster, stretch our arms further . . . And one fine morning –"[1]—but it can also be an alternative to "a mere apathetic sinking into the obviousness of the present."[2] Viewed positively, contemplating what might lie beyond the horizon of contemporary experience displays an appreciation of the links between periods of history. This awareness subverts the assumption that "the future" is what appears when "the present" becomes "the past," an assumption that artificially divides history into a series of discrete units. In fact, as this volume has emphasized often, and as "tradition" and "reception" illustrate, historical eras interweave. Yesterday's decisions

---

1. F. Scott Fitzgerald, *The Great Gatsby* (1926; repr., London: Penguin, 1972), 188.
2. Karl Rahner, "Perspectives for the Future of the Church," in *Theological Investigations*, vol. 12, trans. D. Bourke (New York: Crossroad, 1974), 203.

regularly have an impact on what happens today, just as present-day actions and inactions affect the shape of tomorrow.

Many dystopian novels and films use this interweaving of the past, present, and future as their backdrop. While the future is the usual setting for works of this genre, their frequent subtext is that today's dysfunctions, which may themselves represent the harvest of long-standing attitudes and behaviors, are blighting tomorrow's prospects, casting a pall over the well-being of coming generations. Whether located in a post-apocalyptic wasteland or a soulless high-tech city, the fictional "worlds" of tomorrow attest to the conviction that the ills of the past and the present will surely contaminate the future.

Beyond fiction, a swath of environmental campaigns seeks to shape the future by redressing the deficits of the past, whose footprints continue into the present. These campaigns, which include efforts to reduce global carbon emissions, clear the world's oceans of plastic waste, preserve rain forests, and ensure racial justice in both the development of energy resources and the location of industrial infrastructure, acknowledge the inextricable links between the past, present, and future. The overarching goal of climate activists is to steward the vigor of the earth's resources for the benefit of future generations, especially for the communities that experience disproportionately the deleterious effects of practices common yesterday and today.

The struggle to repair, even reverse, human-driven climate change embodies the belief that human beings are agents in their own future, not passive victims of circumstance. As this book has contended throughout, human beings may not control every variable that affects the future, but the present-day exercise of human freedom can affect what is to come, for better or worse. For this reason, actions in the present are answerable to the future. *Laudato Si'* establishes Pope Francis as a clear voice advocating not only for an appreciation of the links between history's various eras, but for actions that reflect what it means to be part of humanity's interwoven history: "We can no longer speak of sustainable development apart from intergenerational solidarity. Once we start to think about the kind of world we are leaving to future generations, we look at things differently" (LS 59). For Pope Francis, this perspective is essential for the "integral ecology" (LS 159) that the introduction profiled.

The efforts to address environmental degradation confirm not only the continuing impact that human beings have on the planet, but that life on earth is itself an unfinished project. When "unfinished project" applies to buildings or books, it usually indicates that all is not well, that finance or inspiration, respectively, has collapsed. In relation to life on earth, "unfinished project" can have a positive overtone, suggesting opportunities for change and for the construction of a hopeful future, one that may redress past failings. Those same positive overtones apply when "unfinished project" refers to the ecclesial community.

The church's incompleteness, so this book has argued, is a dimension of its eschatological orientation. The fact that the only "home" of the church is the fulfilled reign of God, frees today's members of the church from a misplaced adulation of any past "golden age." Short of fulfillment in the God "who is above all and through all and in all" (Eph 4:6), the church remains a pilgrim people. As such, not only does the ecclesial community live in a world that is unpredictable and beyond every attempt at regimentation and regulation, it manifests those same features within its own life. "The future of the church," consequently, is a topic that defies exact analysis. While it might well be prudent, therefore, to eschew Y2K-type predictions for the church's future, this does not imply that the ecclesial community is exempt from any need to consider its future.

Indeed, taking the future into account is necessary if the church, in all of its manifestations, is to do justice to its own identity as both a human reality and the work of grace. As a human community, the church is a body in history, one whose "story" does not belong exclusively to the past or present. Like all such communities, the church, in its multiple expressions and instruments, can plan, evaluate its efforts to fulfill its mission, and set priorities that accord with this mission, rather than allowing every random event to determine its direction. As a community of faith, the church pays attention to the future in a way that is compatible with its relationship to the God of Jesus Christ, the God whose Holy Spirit draws the church toward God's fullness that transcends the past and present.

The Holy Spirit of God endlessly invites the disciples of Christ to deeper faithfulness and more generous service of their mission to symbolize the hope and mercy of God. In this way, the summons of the Holy Spirit draws the ecclesial community into the future, just as it empowers the ecclesial community to be a locus of hope in the present. While grace enables this possibility, the efficacy of grace, as this book has maintained, is not independent of human freedom.

God neither limits the freedom of the ecclesial community nor programs the church to ensure compliance with divine directives. The community of faith, then, as it confronts the uncertainty, fear, and sinfulness inseparable from its movement through history, must discern the most appropriate responses to all that shapes its moment in history. As it does so in the present, the church is forming its future. Lacking a detailed guide to the future, the church's discernment must judge whether the circumstances of a specific time and place represent "the void of absurdity and death that engulfs us or the blessed holy night already shining within us is the promise of eternal day."[3] Such is the irreducible reality of a pilgrim people.

How the church addresses its present-day challenges will demonstrate whether, to echo Karl Rahner's charge to the church at the conclusion of the Second Vatican Council, "it has the courage to undertake an apostolic offensive into [the] future and consequently the necessary courage to show itself to the world sincerely, in such a form that no one can have the impression that the Church only exists as a mere survival from earlier times because it has not yet had time to die."[4] This task continues and renews across the multiple contexts of the church's life. It challenges the church to enact its faith in God as the "absolute future." A church that attunes itself to grace at work in the world, one that is open to the conversion that tills the many facets of its own life, will be unafraid of the future. Such a church will meet its challenges constructively, with expressions of faith, hope, and love. In so doing, the ecclesial community witnesses to the reign of God that encompasses all people and the physical universe.

There is, of course, always the possibility for members of the church to resist conversion, succumb to fear, choose stasis over pilgrimage, and even to rebel against following the pathways that the light of the Spirit

---

3. Karl Rahner, "Experience of the Holy Spirit," in *Theological Investigations*, vol. 18, trans. E. Quinn (New York: Crossroad, 1983), 200.

4. Karl Rahner, *The Christian of the Future*, trans. W. J. O'Hara (London: Burns and Oates, 1967), 36.

illumines. Yet, the living foundations of the church in Christ and the Spirit continue to prompt alternatives to sinfulness and complacency, to spur the church to faithful creativity, no matter what the obstacles that the present offers:

> Complacency is seductive; it tells us that there is no point in try-
> ing to change things, that there is nothing we can do, because this
> is the way things have always been and yet we always manage to
> survive. . . . Yet let us allow the Lord to rouse us from our torpor,
> to free us from our inertia. Let us rethink our usual way of doing
> things; let us open our eyes and ears, and above all our hearts, so
> as not to be complacent about things as they are, but unsettled by
> the living and effective word of the risen Lord.[5]

The grace that draws the church to imaginative engagement with the world is the same grace that encourages the ecclesial community to self-criticism, to accept that its own life can never be beyond the need for review. Faithfulness to the church's foundations is likewise fully consistent with the discernment that aims at creative reception of the tradition for the sake of the future, rather than an uncritical repetition of the past. Writing in the mid-1970s, Rahner affirmed both the possibility of faithfulness and the need for creativity:

> What the Church will look like in the year 2000 or 2500; whether
> the pope will then be in Rome, or somewhere else; whether there
> will still be all the bureaucratic machinery that we see and ac-
> cept today in Rome and under which we perhaps groan; whether
> perhaps many other things of which we have no idea today will
> then be taken for granted; whether the Church will perhaps learn
> suddenly or slowly that women, too, can be holders of the priestly
> office . . . to all these, and to many other perhaps more important
> questions which we can regard as open, we cannot expect to find
> an answer purely deductively from theological principles or solely
> from ancient tradition.[6]

5. Pope Francis, *Gaudete et Exsultate*, 137.
6. Karl Rahner, "The Church's Redemptive Historical Provenance from the Death and Resurrection of Jesus," in *Theological Investigations*, vol. 19, trans. E. Quinn (New York: Crossroad, 1983), 36–37.

Just as neither "theological principles" nor "ancient tradition" inoculates the church against the vicissitudes of life in history, they do not offer the church a blueprint for the future or an unequivocal answer to "open questions." Theology and tradition might not pave the path into the future, thereby sparing the ecclesial community from the need for discernment, dialogue, and decision-making, but both theology and tradition are assets for constructive discernment, dialogue, and decision-making. Each of the two resources teaches the church across generations that "unfinished" is not a designation to fear or regret, but an opportunity for an encounter with the grace that permeates the life of the world. This same grace also draws the church more deeply into the life of the ungraspable mystery of God.

Both theology and tradition underscore the link between "tilling" and "unfinished." They reinforce that the church is a project, one that is more compatible with nuance than one-dimensional approaches. Theology and tradition bring into relief the potential for movement in a church that is one, holy, catholic, and apostolic, the church that grace constitutes and sustains. Indeed, movement in response to grace is a central means for the church to proclaim its faith in the mystery of the God at the heart of ecclesial life. In the movement that embodies the church's faithfulness, the ecclesial community affirms that the mystery of God resists domestication, whether by individuals or structures.

At its best, the ecclesial community realizes that God's resistance to domestication is a gift to the church. It is a source of hope that reminds the church that the power of God's grace "at work within us is able to accomplish abundantly far more than all we can ask or imagine" (Eph 3:20). Trust in this grace propels the tilling of the church. Critically faithful reception of the past, constructive engagement with the present, and abiding openness to the ever-new future of God are all possible for the ecclesial community because of grace. The specifics of the church's future remain unknown and unknowable, but the ecclesial community's commitment to conversion, its embrace of tilling as a gift of grace, can generate both hope for the future of the church and a church whose presence in the world can be a source of hope.

Index

Abraham, 98, 119
abuse, sexual, 5, 83–84
actualism, existential, 168–69
Ad Gentes, 128, 136, 138–39
Adam Bede (Eliot), 63
aggiornamento, 34, 223
alienation, 83–84, 92
ambiguity, 70, 77–80
Amoris Laetitia, 222
analogy of faith, 199
analogy of tradition, 228
anamnesis, 185–88
apostolic era, 178–79, 181–82, 190
apostolic succession, 189–90
apostolicity, 178–80; and
    discipleship, 189–91; and Holy
    Spirit, 191; and permanence,
    180–85
art, 207–10, 250; and tilling of
    church, 211–17
ascension, the, 115–16
assembly lines, 1–2, 43
Augustine, St, 46
authenticity, 20–21, 40, 78, 150–51,
    175–76
authoritarianism, 233
authority, 2, 236–37, 248, 249–50

Badcock, Gary, 18
Barchester series (Trollope), 81–82
becoming, 224–25
beliefs, 213
Benedict XVI, Pope, 118
Bevans, Stephen, 140
Bible. *See* Scripture
bishops, 201–2, 234, 248–49
Blondel, Maurice, 33, 169–70,
    196–97
blueprint (ecclesiology), 14–15
Burkhard, John, 241

Camino de Santiago, 100–101
Catholic Church: depictions of,
    2–4; Eurocentrism in, 8–9;
    and global insights, 11–12; as
    perfect society, 26–29; self-
    understanding in, 8; and state,
    26–27. *See also* church
catholicity, 37; and church as
    communion, 153–62; and Holy
    Spirit, 153–55
causality, 43–44; quasi-formal,
    44–45
centralization, 173, 233
certainty, 213

change, 81–82, 93, 135–36, 163–65,
    173–74; and faithfulness, 194–96,
    197, 210, 212; freedom for, 223;
    and Holy Spirit, 165, 176–77;
    ingredients for, 215–16; and
    pilgrimage, 104–5; and reception,
    222–29; tension in, 222–23;
    and theology, 211; and tradition,
    200–203
Chaucer, 100
Chauvet, Louis-Marie, 76–77, 158,
    159–61, 186
Christology: Catholic, 32–34; tasks
    of, 66–67
Christus Vivit, 145
church: attractiveness of, 92;
    and churches, 12; as datum of
    experience, 4–10; dynamism of,
    108–9; early, 131–33; equilibrium
    in, xvii; as event, 3; foundations
    of, xxi, 41, 223–24; as gift, 172;
    health of, xv–xvi; instituting of,
    123, 126, 181; metaphors for, xiv,
    15–16, 35–36, 72; as museum,
    175–76; as open system, 150–53;
    orientation of, 20, 121, 174, 224–
    25; as project, 4; as unfinished,
    19, 24. *See also* Catholic Church
churches, 6–7, 12
clericalism, 30
common good, 90–91
communion, 157–59
community, Christian. *See* church
community, ecclesial. *See* church
compassion, 226
complacency, 4, 83–84, 152, 255
conflict, xx
confusion, 235
Congar, Yves: on catholicity, 37,
    154; on church as human and
divine, 18, 106; on Holy Spirit,
    198; on reception, 218, 236–37;
    on reform, 165; on tradition and
    gospel, 203
congruence, 228
constitutions, civil, 179–80
continuity, 228
control, 87–88
conversion, 97; and church, xiv–xv,
    3, 24, 47, 86, 147; and grace, xii,
    106–7; and hope, 116–17; and
    self-limitation, 50–51. *See also*
    self-criticism
Copeland, M. Shawn, 204, 244
Council, Second Vatican. *See*
    Vatican II
Council of Trent, 192–93
covenants, 64–66, 91
creation: and God, 42–46,
    53–61; history of, 42–43; and
    incarnation, 69; and love, 46;
    and Trinity, 53–54
creativity, 207, 209, 214; and
    church, xxi, 45–46, 175, 184, 215;
    and human freedom, 48–49; and
    reception, 220–22, 235–36; of
    reign of God, 144
Cruz, Gemma Tulud, 243
culture, 5–10, 15, 92–94
culture wars, 164
customs, 150

death, 59–60, 111–13
decision-making, 16, 103, 211–17
deconversion, 83–84
defensiveness, 226
Dei Verbum, 64, 67, 126, 172, 191,
    201–2, 220
dialogue, 7, 139–41, 244–47
disaffiliation, 83–84

discernment, xxii–xxiii, 93–94, 127–28, 132–33, 177; and dialogue, 247; and faithfulness, 238–40; and grace, 122; and mysticism, 240

discipleship, 129, 144, 189–91

diversity, xxiii–xxiv, 12–14, 105, 148–49, 154–56, 215, 248

division, xviii, 6–7

doctrines, 229–33

doctrinification, 235–36

dogma, 197, 199

Drey, Johann Sebastian, 194, 197

Dulles, Avery, 190

ecclesiality, 78

Ecclesiam Suam, 139

ecclesiologies: and abstraction, 9–10, 11–12; as aspirational, 13; New Testament, 35–36; notions governing, 9–10; sacramental, 74; tasks of, 22–23, 85; tradition-specific, 6–7; trends in, 10–17; Tridentine, 26–31; Vatican II, 31–32, 34–35, 37–38

ecology, integral, xi–xii, 89, 90

ecumenism, 8, 231–32

Eliot, George, 63

enclaves, 156

encounter, 149

Espin, Orlando, 226, 235

Eucharist, 105, 158, 161, 186–87

Eurocentrism, 8–9

Evangelii Gaudium: on complacency, 152, 255; and descriptions of church, 11, 13; on diversity, 248; on God's love, 142; on grace, xxi–xxii, 138, 147; on Holy Spirit, 102, 130; and ignored questions, 4; on memory in church, 171; and mission, 150; on newness, 175; and peripheries, 149; on the poor, 12; on whole greater than part, 247

evangelization, 12, 80, 137–38

extrinsicism, 33

failure, 118–19, 120, 243–44

faith: as act, 230; analogy of, 199; articulation of, 238; and certainty, 213; and church, 91–92; as communal, 89–94, 183–84; and control, 87–88; and dogma, 197, 199; dynamics of, 86–97; elements of, 86; and grace, 22; as a grammar for life, 88–89; and hope, 87, 110–11; inculturation of, 227; as a journey, 96–97; and knowledge, 87; as a lens, 88–89; as listening, 88; and love, 87–88; orientation of, 94–96; and pilgrimage, 100–109; and purpose of life, 86–89; questions about, 235–36; and reason, 86–88; and re-ordering, 86–87; statements of, 229–33; symbols of, 232; and tradition, 201; transmission of, 199. *See also sensus fidei*

faithful, the, 201–2. *See also* people of God

faithfulness, xiv–xv, 85, 152, 170, 214; and change, 194–96, 197, 210, 212, 228; and discernment, 238–40; and diversity, 215; and tradition, 197, 205. *See also sensus fidei*

fides qua: and *fides quae*, 85n8

Fiorenza, Francis Schüssler, 144, 238

Fitzgerald, F. Scott, 208
Ford, Henry, 1-2, 16
forgiveness, 182
Francis, Pope. *See Amoris Laetitia*;
   Christus Vivit; *Evangelii
   Gaudium*; *Fratelli Tutti*;
   Gaudete et Exsultate; *Laudato
   Si'*; *Lumen Fidei*
Fratelli Tutti, 40, 49, 50, 110-11,
   140, 148
freedom, human, 24, 209-10;
   and creativity, 48-49; and
   creatureliness, 45-46; and
   grace, 40-49; and hope, 118;
   orientation of, 46-47; and self-
   disposal, 47-48; and sinfulness,
   49-51; and societal health, 39-
   40. *See also* liberation
Fuellenbach, John, 147, 149
future, the: and church, 26, 94-96,
   136, 251-56; and God, 65; and
   hope, 119-20, 121-22; and
   memory, 187-88; and past
   and present, 166-71, 188; and
   theology, 21-22

Gaudete et Exsultate, 235, 239, 240
Gaudium et Spes, xix, xxii, 93, 101-
   2, 103, 149, 245
God: as artist, 214; and church,
   25-26, 34-38, 82; and creation,
   42-46, 54-61; experience of,
   90, 92-93; and future, 65; and
   humanity, 55-59, 64-70, 114-15;
   love of, 58-59; mystery of,
   23-24, 57-59, 60-61; people of,
   37, 64-66, 91, 94-95, 97, 152;
   presence of, 59, 93; purposes
   of, 93; reign of, xvi, 21, 41, 103,
   112, 141-50; responses to, 90;

self-communication of, 61-66,
   76, 170
good, common, 90-91
gospel, 203-4
grace, xiii, xv, xxi-xxii, 52, 147;
   and church, xvi-xxii, 17-24, 41,
   83-86, 125-31, 138, 150-53,
   159-60; and complexity, 85;
   and conversion, xii, 106-7;
   created and uncreated, 54-62,
   146; and creation, 42-43; and
   discernment, 122; and faith,
   22; and history, 18-19, 125-31;
   of hope, 117-22; and human
   freedom, 40-49; and humanity,
   xiii, xix, 64; incarnational
   tendency of, xiii, xix; and past,
   present, and future, 188; as
   unconditional, 40; and world,
   xix
Graesslé, Isabelle, 108
Grantly, Theophilus, 81-82
Grenz, Stanley, 156
Gutiérrez, Gustavo, 142, 151, 161

Healy, Nicholas, 18-19, 79
hierarchology, 27-28, 30
Himes, Michael, 146
history, 5-10, 15, 92-94, 166-71;
   and church, 38, 103, 125-36,
   168-71; and God's self-
   revelation, 170; good or bad, 169;
   and grace, 18-19, 125-31
holiness, 30, 79
Holy Spirit, xx; and apostolicity,
   191; and catholicity, 153-55; and
   change, 165, 176-77; and Christ,
   126-27; and church, 31, 75-80,
   100-102, 105, 108-9, 123-27,
   131-33, 152-53; in history,

125–26; and journeying, 99–100; listening to, 177; *modus operandi* of, 75; and paradox, 108; response to, 130; and Scripture, 201; and tradition, 198; and Trinity, 102–3

hope, 147, 212, 228–29; and the ascension, 115–16; and church, 110, 116–17; and conversion, 116–17; and failure, 118–19, 120; and faith, 87, 110–11; and future, 119–20, 121–22; grace of, 117–22; and human freedom, 118; and justice, 121; and mission, 117; and paschal mystery, 111–17; and receptivity, 117–18; and reign of God, 142; and self-criticism, 116–17; and sinfulness, 118–19; and tilling, 119; and waiting, 120–21

humanity: and God, 55–59, 64–70, 114–15; and grace, xiii, xix, 64; materiality of, 61

ideologies, 164
idolatry, 66
illative sense, 212–13, 224, 240
images, 35–36
imagination, xxi
incarnation, 69
inculturation, 149, 227
individualism, 49–50
innovations, 81, 93, 163–64, 168. *See also* change
institutions, 134, 158–60
integral ecology, xi–xii, 89, 90
Israel, 64–66, 91, 94–95

Jeanrond, Werner, 175
Jesus Christ: ascension of, 115–16; and church, 25, 74, 75; death

of, 111–13; expectations about, 214; in gospels, 67–68; and Holy Spirit, 126–27; as human and divine, 114–15; journeying of, 98–99; perspectives on, 33–34; and reign of God, 112, 141–44; resurrection of, 113–15; as self-expression of God, 66–70

John XXIII, Pope, 236
John Paul II, Pope: on communion, 157; on faith and reason, 86; on Holy Spirit, 34–35, 102, 123, 134; on inculturation, 149; on reign of God and church, 146; on sin, 161
Johnson, Elizabeth, 33, 67, 111–12
Jones, Serene, 202
journeying, 97–100
justice, 97–98, 121

kairos, 186
Kasper, Walter, 95, 112, 114, 139, 152
Kelly, Anthony, 115–16
Kilmartin, Edward, 222
kingdom of God. *See* reign of God
knowledge, 87
Komonchak, Joseph, 74, 109

laity, the, 30–31, 242–43
Lakeland, Paul, 78
Lash, Nicholas, 60
Laudato Si': on creation, 46; on destiny in God, xvi; on development, 252; and faith, 89; and physical environment, xvii, 44; on solidarity and spirituality, xii; on technology and economy, 167; on tilling, xi
liberation, 151–52. *See also* freedom, human
Linden, Ian, 140

listening, 88, 177
literature, 208, 218–20
liturgy, 185–88
Lohfink, Gerhard, 117, 144, 157, 188
love: and church, 71; and creation, 46; and faith, 87–88; of neighbor, 58–59; and reign of God, 142–43; symbols of, 63
Lumen Fidei, 87, 88, 91, 94, 96–97
Lumen Gentium: on church as pilgrim, 101; on church order, 229, 233–34; on communion, 183; on faith and responsibility, 202; on holiness, 79; on Holy Spirit, 102, 105; and metaphors, xiv, 37; on mission, xix, 137; and reign of God, 25; on renewal, 160; on sacramentality, 72, 76; on saints, 106, 239; and *sensus fidei*, 247

marginalization, 7, 19–20
Mary, 98, 106, 123, 126
materiality, 61
meaning: excess of, 218–19; making of, 207–8
memory (church's): and *anamnesis*, 186; and future, 187–88; and mission, 189
Metz, Johann Baptist, 60, 151
ministries, 172
miracles, 141
mission, 16–17, 136–41, 150; and hope, 117; and memory, 189; and reception, 148
Möhler, Johann Adam, 194–95, 197
movement, 224–25. *See also* change
Murray, Paul, 155
mysticism, 240

nature, 44
Newman, John Henry: on assent, 89; on authenticity, 234; on continuity and change, 176, 195–97; on faith, 87; on illative sense, 212–13; and *sensus fidei*, 243–44
newness, 175, 188. *See also* creativity
nones, 83–84
non-reception, 237
nostalgia, 168

O'Collins, Gerald, 53
O'Malley, John, 173
Orsy, Ladislas, 212

parables, 141
paradox, 46, 49, 57, 68, 76, 104, 108, 210
parishes, 156
paschal mystery, 111–17
past, the: and present and future, 166–71, 188; reverence for, 170–71; value of, 168, 171–72
Paul VI, Pope, 139
Pentecost, 123–24
people of God, 37, 64–66, 91, 94–95, 97, 152
perichoresis, xv
peripheries, 149, 244
permanence, 180–85
pilgrimage: and change, 104–5; and church, 97–109, 122; elements of, 104–5; and faith, 100–109
Pius IX, Pope, 137
potential, obediential, 56, 64
Power, David, 186–87
progress, 166–67, 168
prophets, 95, 239

questioning, 235–36

Rahner, Karl, 151, 188, 212; on apostolicity, 181–82; on church's future, 254, 255; on church's identity, 227; on church's institutions, 158–59; on church's self-understanding, 162; on coming to faith, 77; on death, 113; on doctrine, 231, 237; on evangelization, 80; on faith, 87–88, 243; on future, 96, 115, 254, 255; on God and humanity, 55–59; on God's self-communication, 115; on grace, 52, 54–61; on grace and human freedom, 42–45; on historical revelation, 54; on individualism, 50; on Jesus, 68–69; on love of God and love of neighbor, 58–59; on mystery of God, 57–59; on presence of God, 59; on the resurrection, 114; on sacraments, 73; on self-criticism, 162; on self-disposal, 47; on sin, 49; on symbols, 61–62, 70

reason, 86–88

reception (from the past), 135–36, 184–85, 217–18; and *aggiornamento*, 223; and authority, 236–37; and change, 222–29; and creativity, 184, 220–22, 235–36; and defensiveness, 226; facilitators of, 233–38; and mission, 148; obstacles to, 221–22, 233–38; positive, 222; potential for, 227; and reform, 204; and tension, 222–23

receptivity (to grace), 117–18

reconciliation, 7

reform, 204

reign of God, 21; and Christ, 112, 141–44; and church, xvi, 41, 103, 144–50; creativity of, 144; as gift, 141–42; and hope, 142; images for, 141; and love, 142–43

ressourcement, 31–32

resurrection, the, 113–15

revelation, 22, 51–54, 170; historical, 52, 54; and Scripture, 192; special, 62; theology of, 32

Rush, Ormond, 75, 102, 241, 246

sacramentality, 41; of church, 71–72, 73–74, 76–77, 145, 159–61; and structures, 159

sacraments, 70–74

Sacrosanctum Concilium, 105

saints, 106, 239

salvation, 96

Schillebeeckx, Edward, 34

Schneiders, Sandra, 126–27, 191

Schner, George, 60

Schroeder, Roger, 140

Scripture: and Holy Spirit, 201; interpretation of, 192–93, 220; and tradition, 192–93, 199, 201

Second Vatican Council. *See* Vatican II

Segundo, Juan Luis, 71

self-criticism, xvii, 20–21, 29, 116–17, 146, 161–62, 176. *See also* conversion

self-disposal, 47–48

selflessness, 90–91

self-limitation, 50–51

self-protection, 84–85

sensus fidei, 240–44

sensus fidei fidelium, 242

sexual abuse crisis, 5, 83–84

sinfulness: of church, 79; and hope, 118–19; and human freedom, 49–51; structural, 50

Sobrino, Jon, 117, 142
societal health, 39–40, 128–29
sociology, 10–11, 14–15
sociopolitical order, 179–80
Soskice, Janet, 202
Spe Salvi, 118
Spirit, Holy. *See* Holy Spirit
spirituality, 129
state, 26–27
structures, 158–60; of church, 76;
    and creativity, 215
symbols, 61–63, 65, 68–69;
    ambiguity of, 70; of faith, 232
synodality, 247–49

technology, 163–64, 167, 168
theology, 9–10, 17–24, 173–74;
    Black, 203–4; and change, 211;
    and church, 17–24; feminist,
    203; and future, 21–22; purpose
    of, 21; of revelation, 32;
    sacramental, 41, 72–74; tasks of,
    22, 211; and tradition, 256
Thiel, John, 228
Thiessen, Gesa Elsbeth, 154
Tillard, Jean-Marie, 185, 186, 224,
    225
tilling: of church, xiv–xvi, xxii, 122,
    211–17; of earth, xi; and hope,
    119; and keeping, xiii. *See also*
    change
Tracy, David, 60, 208, 218–19
tradition, xxi, 191; 19th-century
    views on, 193–96; 20th-century
    views on, 196–205; analogy of,

228; and change, 200–203; and
    compassion, 226; and faith, 201;
    and faithfulness, 197, 205; and
    gospel, 203–4; and Holy Spirit,
    198; as process, 200; reception
    of, 217–18, 220–22; and
    Scripture, 192–93, 199, 201; and
    theology, 256; and unity, 199
Trent, Council of, 192–93
Trinity, xv, 53–54; and Holy Spirit,
    102–3
Trollope, Anthony, 81
Tübingen school, 194

Unitatis Redintegratio, 108, 231–32
unity, xx, 9, 106, 154–55, 199

Vatican II, 100, 156–57, 205–6. *See
    also Ad Gentes*; *Dei Verbum*;
    Gaudium et Spes; *Lumen
    Gentium*; *Sacrosanctum
    Concilium*; *Unitatis
    Redintegratio*
Vorgrimler, Herbert, 72

waiting, 120–21
Watkins, Clare, 155, 221
Westhelle, Vitor, 18, 189
Williams, Rowan, 169, 221
world, xix, 145–50, 225–26. *See also*
    history
World Council of Churches, 179,
    200

Zizioulas, John, 148, 224